BARBARA VICTOR worked for CBS television for fifteen years, where she covered the Middle East. Her books include *Terrorism*, an account of the Lebanon War from 1975 to 1982; *A Voice of Reason: Hanan Ashrawi and Peace in the Middle East*, a biography of Hanan Ashrawi, which was nominated for the 1995 Pulitzer Prize; *Getting Away With Murder*, a study of domestic violence in the United States; *The Lady*, a biography of Aung San Suu Kyi, the Burmese Nobel Peace Prize Laureate; *Le Matignon de Jospin*, an inside look at the workings of the French government; and *Army of Roses*, a study of Palestinian female suicide bombers. A documentary on that same subject, written and directed by Barbara has aired on television stations throughout Europe. A frequent lecturer on women's issues and the Middle East, Barbara divides her time between New York and Paris.

ALSO BY BARBARA VICTOR

Non-fiction

A Voice of Reason:
Hanan Ashrawi and Peace in the Middle East

Getting Away with Murder:
Weapons for the War against Domestic Violence

The Lady: Aung San Suu Kyi

Goddess: Inside Madonna

Army of Roses

Fiction

Absence of Pain

Misplaced Lives

Friends, Lovers, Enemies

Coriander

THE LAST CRUSADE

RELIGION AND THE
POLITICS OF MISDIRECTION

Barbara Victor

For Billie
With best regards
Barbara Victor

CONSTABLE • LONDON

Constable & Robinson Ltd
3 The Lanchesters
162 Fulham Palace Road
London W6 9ER
www.constablerobinson.com

First published in the UK by Constable,
an imprint of Constable & Robinson Ltd, 2005

A copy of the British Library Cataloguing in
Publication Data is available from the British Library.

ISBN 1-84119-955-9

Printed and bound in the EU

1 3 5 7 9 10 8 6 4 2

For Gérard

Contents

CONTENTS

Introduction

Rescue me, O Lord, from evil men; protect me from men of violence, who devise evil plans in their hearts and stir up war every day.

(Psalm 140:1-2)

THE United States, in many respects the birthplace of the feminist movement, was also one of the last countries to end slavery and segregation; the country known as the great bridgehead and laboratory of hedonism remains the bastion of Puritanism; citizens who are resistant to laws which control their individual liberties are nonetheless frenzied in their overuse of the legal system to exact payment for real or imagined wrongs inflicted upon their person, property, or reputation. Not surprisingly, the paradoxical mixture of a love of freedom and a desire to control extends to the nation's attitude towards religion. Founded on a formal separation of church and state, America's public life is saturated by religion to an extent unique in the developed world.

Some thirty years ago, Alvin Toffler pointed out, in *Future Shock*,[1] that the 'pace and deracination of modern society left people not only disoriented but alienated, seeking new structures such as religion and participation in church activities to restore a loss of sense of identity.'

1

Despite periods when they have been more vocal and visible than others, Evangelical or born-again Christians were always considered a fringe group throughout the country, with little political power. However, religion has never occupied as important a place in government and in the military as it does today. Though America has always been a Christian nation in spirit, it is only in the past twenty-five years that it has become a country where a certain very special brand of Christianity has garnered enormous power by its sheer numbers and financial privilege. During that time, the symptoms that Alvin Toffler described have been magnified to include a fear of the unknown, and a destabilizing force that permeates society because of the threat of random terrorist attacks. As a result, Americans are seeking different assurances, which make them increasingly predisposed to elect politicians or embrace religious leaders who offer faith in the Bible and belief in God's word to protect them from harm. Since not all Americans believe in God, the next best substitute are those political leaders who claim to have been touched by 'divine intervention', or who offer their faith in the Bible and their belief in the Lord to guide them so they are able to protect their constituents from harm, even those constituents who are not 'believers'.

According to a poll taken in April 2004, around 60 per cent of the American population believes that 'religion plays a very important part' in their lives,[2] far exceeding the numbers for any other industrialized country. Religion in the US overwhelmingly means Christianity. Around 50 per cent of Americans describe themselves as Protestant, 25 per cent as Catholic and another 11 per cent call themselves Christian without specifying a denomination. Only 7 per cent of Americans say they have no religion. Of those born-again Christians polled, all believe that Jesus Christ died for their sins, while 58.7 per cent say they believe the world will end in the battle of Armageddon between Jesus and Satan, and 40.9 per cent favour passage of a constitutional amendment declaring the United States to be a 'Christian nation'. (In April 2004, the Texas Republican Party approved a platform that called the United States a 'Christian nation'. During that same political conference, Texas also denounced the 'myth' of any supposed separation of church and state as written in the United States Constitution.)

While this religiosity has always rested uneasily with America's constitutional separation of church and state, passionate commitment to a secular republic has somehow co-existed with a widespread sense that America is God's own country. Religion has lent strength to America's moral mission abroad. The Cold War was in part seen by Americans as a struggle between godless Communism and the Christian West. To some, moral principles, by definition, functioned as the basis of any rational pursuit of national interests. To others, including some of the nation's foreign policy elite, it was imperative to separate religion and politics at all costs. As Henry Kissinger once remarked, 'Covert action should not be confused with missionary work.'

Those who comprise what is known as born-again Christians or the Christian Right in America all believe in several theories which, as we will see, were invented at various times during the nineteenth century by several preachers who took passages from the Bible and combined them to form so-called irrevocable beliefs that have enthralled and mesmerized a large portion of the American public. Bill Moyers, writing in *Zmag*, recently dissected those distorted ideas, which include the belief that 'once Israel has occupied the rest of its "biblical lands", legions of the Antichrist will attack, triggering a final showdown in the valley of Armageddon.'[3]

3

Those Jews who have not yet converted to Christianity will be slaughtered while those true believers will be transported to heaven to reside for eternity with Jesus Christ.

Not only do Evangelical Christians believe in the special place the Jewish people and Israel have in God's ultimate plan, but they also believe that President Bush's invasion of Iraq is only the beginning of a war against Islam that is predicted in the Bible and that is a pivotal step on the road to redemption. In other words, as American soldiers fall in Iraq and hundreds of thousands of Iraqis are killed, those who embrace these religious teachings consider that the war is not something to be reviled or feared but a positive step before the second coming of the Messiah.

In 2003, Franklin Graham, son and heir apparent of the Reverend Billy Graham, was the honoured speaker at the Pentagon's Good Friday service. His message was very clear. 'There is one God and one faith,' he told an audience of soldiers in camouflage, civilian staffers, and his own son, a West Point cadet. 'There's no other way to God except through Christ . . . Jesus Christ is alive because He is risen, and friends, He's coming back, and I believe He's coming back soon.'

In March 2003, shortly before the United States invasion of Iraq, the Reverend Franklin Graham left for Iraq, ostensibly to supply food, warm clothing, and medical supplies for the Iraqi people under the aegis of his charity, Samaritan's Purse. During an interview shortly before he left, Mr Graham explained to me the purpose of his trip in the following way. 'Operation Iraqi Freedom is a lucky break for Jesus,' he said. 'We are going there to reach out to love the Iraqi people and to save them, and as a Christian I do this in the name of Jesus Christ.'

After Graham arrived in Iraq, Iraqis recounted several incidents concerning his staff and their efforts to spread the 'word of Christ'. One American soldier, who spoke to me on condition of anonymity, substantiated those stories; he had witnessed one of Graham's Evangelical pilgrims, offering fresh water to a group of Iraqis, but only if they would agree to be baptized into the Christian faith.

On 13 December 2003, the day that Saddam Hussein was finally apprehended in Tikrit, the first five phone calls that George W. Bush made after his closest political advisors had been informed, were to his father George H.W. Bush, to the Reverend Billy Graham and the Reverend Franklin Graham, to the then Attorney General John Ashcroft, and to his preacher from the United Methodist Church in Dallas. Twenty minutes later, with John Ashcroft at his side and the three preachers on a conference call, he again called his father and mother. When everyone was joined by telephone, President George W. Bush asked Reverend Franklin Graham to lead them in prayer. On their knees in the Oval Office, the President and the Attorney General bowed their heads as Graham prayed: 'Jesus, your fingerprints are on this mission, and it is because of you, O Lord, that the Evil that is Saddam Hussein has been brought to justice. In the name of Jesus Christ, we thank you for bearing this great gift to the good people of the blessed United States of America.'[4]

The power of faith and the miracle of prayer are everywhere. During the months that I did research for this book, and interviewed Evangelicals in America and in Israel, and members of the Jewish American community as well as Orthodox and secular Jews in Israel, most people, regardless of their religious beliefs or political tendencies, were willing to make concessions which often sacrificed the rights of some to guarantee the safety of all. In Washington, where I interviewed congressmen, senators and members of the administration, it became apparent that George W. Bush has surrounded himself with people who are determined to intervene militarily wherever Islam threatens western values. Some were even quick to justify any military invasion on the basis of God and religion. One example of that mentality is a man who holds the position of Deputy Undersecretary of Defense for Intelligence, one of the most sensitive jobs in the government, given America's current involvement in Iraq.

Dressed in his military uniform, which meant that he was on active duty representing his country and his position, Lieutenant General William Boykin made several public speeches in which he derided the Muslim belief in Allah as God. Boykin cited his battle experiences in Somalia in 1993. 'I knew that my God was bigger than [my Islamic foe's], and I knew that my God was a real God and his was an idol.' Following that pronouncement, Boykin called the United States a 'Christian nation'. Referring to the current conflict in Iraq, he said, 'We are in an army of God for such a time as this.'[5]

The general's uncensored anti-Islamic sentiments, and his linking of America's war on terrorism with Jesus and Christianity, illustrate that there is no reluctance on the part of certain members of the military to view the war in Iraq as a Crusade or a Holy War waged between Judeo-Christian values and Islam. While not all of President Bush's advisors or entourage are Evangelical Christians, nor are other politicians from other parties, their perception of the world and of the threat of Islam is the same, separated only by priority as to which comes first, military might or religious right, in order to vanquish this new global enemy. Since 11 September 2001, if God is on the battlefield, He is also very much present in the White House, Senate and House of

Representatives, and guiding the hand that pulls the voting lever on every election day.

Evangelical notions about God's special covenant with the American people have contributed to a quasi-religious nationalism that has permeated other faiths in America, including Roman Catholicism and Judaism. As Joseph Lieberman, a Democratic senator from Connecticut and an Orthodox Jew as well as one of the contenders for the Democratic nomination for the 2004 American presidential election, said, 'We are all Evangelicals now.'[6]

Recently, developments in American Christianity have exacerbated this longstanding tension between the secular and religious portion of America. Around half of America's Protestants – some 80 million people – describe themselves as having been 'born-again'. This indicates a specific kind of religious identity, albeit one that expresses itself across a range of denominations, and indeed outside of the established churches. Born-again Christians tend to be found in, and indeed have their historical roots in, the Methodist and Baptist denominations. They are also variously known as 'Evangelicals' and 'Fundamentalists'. Unlike other religious groups or cults or political extremists who are visibly different – because they wear robes or shave their heads or brandish symbols – Evangelical Christians are unremarkable members of society. As they come from a cross-section of America, they are as diverse in their physical and emotional make-up as other citizens, whether they live in a rural or urban area of the country.

Today, the majority of those at the forefront of the Evangelical movement are sophisticated, serious, self-confident, educated, charming, assertive and highly motivated, and all have their own personal story of salvation that they are proud to share. Some own and operate Christian broadcasting networks while others are simply devout believers who are in unrelated businesses: doctors, lawyers, accountants, actors, singers, painters, teachers, politicians. Whether they are among the politically powerful, like George W. Bush, or simply average citizens, they are comfortable enough within any group to practise their faith regardless of how extreme it might appear. Because Evangelical Christians have become the most powerful religious entity in the United States, they have no compunction about describing their personal religious experiences in meticulous detail in the presence of those who do not share their profound beliefs. They are convinced that those who do not hold the conviction that Jesus Christ is available for conversation and advice, and is guiding their personal lives and professional responsibilities, are to be forgiven for their ignorance and their eventual fate until they choose to be saved. It is often difficult for someone who has not been 'touched by the Lord' to understand how completely self-confident Evangelicals are when they practise their faith in public.

One of the more interesting characteristics of born-again Christians is that many of them consider they have been less than upstanding citizens, while some even admit that they have lived a life of 'sin and deprivation' before 'finding the Lord'. Not surprisingly, every born-again Christian that I met during the course of working on this book volunteered, without prompting, to describe the moment when he or she accepted Jesus Christ into his or her life.

During a visit to a Baptist Church in a small town in Texas, the born-again parishioners welcomed a 'potential new soul' with fervour. The three people charged with my 'care' during the four days I spent in their homes and in their church were motivated and impassioned by an inner joy that was difficult to explain or define. Clearly, all of them and, in

fact, the several hundred members of their Baptist congregation, literally glowed with what they described as the 'glow
of Jesus who inhabits my soul'.

One of my hosts was a former exotic dancer named Minna
Blue who still had the glamorous and overly made-up allure
of a faded showgirl. In a bizarre contradiction with her
appearance, her tidy home was adorned with religious
symbols, christian souvenirs, paintings and posters of Jesus
Christ. Warm, friendly and completely uninhibited about
her special relationship with Jesus, she claimed her greatest
joy in life was to tell her 'sordid story' to potential converts in
order to prove that if she could find God, 'then anyone could
find his way into His heart'. Whenever Minna talked about
her past, she did it with a tinge of humour.

Another host, a refined and intelligent young woman
named Kara who had been a lesbian and who had 'hung
out in gay bars, done drugs and drink, and broke every
commandment that God put down, and even some He
probably hadn't even thought of', was less flamboyant than
Minna but just as steadfast in her commitment to God.
According to Kara, the turning point in her life happened
after she woke up in a motel one morning with a two-inch
slash across one arm and all her clothes missing. Forced to call
the police because she was naked, wounded, and without any
identification or money, she claims that it was the moment
when 'God was right there, forcing me to make a choice
between a life of sin or a free ticket into heaven.' Today, she
doesn't touch drugs, drink, or women, and holds down a
respectable secretarial job. Her only leisure activities are
church, prayer and Bible study. Her constant companion,
and another of my hosts, is a convicted child molester named
John Jack. John Jack and Kara held hands constantly during
the entire time we were all together. When one spoke, the

other nodded in agreement and occasionally emitted a subdued 'Amen'. Dressed impeccably in khaki pants and a blue and white checked shirt, with his white hair plastered against his head, John Jack wore an electronic ankle bracelet to monitor his movements as part of his conditional release from prison. There was also a sign on his front lawn which read, 'Convicted Child Rapist Lives Here – Beware'. When I asked him how he felt about the fact that his neighbours insisted upon putting up the sign in return for allowing him to live in their community, he replied, 'It is my cross to bear, just as Jesus bore His cross to Golgotha.'

According to my three hosts, they had all sinned and had all repented, which allowed them to live in unabashed bliss with Jesus as their best friend and constant mentor. These are the Evangelicals of the heartland of America, the typical born-again Christian population that currently boasts being 80 million strong and rising in the United States. They are not sophisticated politicians who claim God has chosen them for political office; they are not fast-talking preachers who do sleight-of-hand miracles or make sweeping statements promising to heal the sick or raise the dead; nor are they rich celebrities who relinquish drugs and drink at posh detoxification centres and embrace religion as the latest Hollywood trend. Minna, Kara and John Jack are average, well-meaning Evangelicals with unquestioning faith in Jesus who they believe has saved them from the clutches of the devil. They are also intelligent people who will vote for any politician who upholds their religious beliefs and promises to protect America from becoming a country without a moral core. And while these three people who are touched by God might not know the capital of Germany, France or Italy, and may not be able to locate Israel on the map, they firmly believe that President Bush, under the guidance of Jesus Christ, is leading a war against terror to protect the Christian democratic values of the United States. They are also convinced that the Jewish people are God's 'chosen people' and that the land of Israel belongs to the Jews for eternity, until Jesus Christ reappears as the Messiah.

The point of my visit to Texas was to accompany my three hosts to church, which I did, twice in the evening and once on Sunday. Not only did I meet their preacher, I also met more than two hundred other men and women who, while diverse in their personal histories of sin and redemption, were identical to Minna, Kara and John Jack in their fervent religious and moral beliefs.

Pastor Ron is in his late thirties, plump, pasty-skinned, with a full head of dark brown hair and a thick moustache. Dressed in a shiny grey silk suit, white tie and white-on-white shirt, with black patent pumps, he is articulate, talented, able to conjure tears on demand, and delighted to be part of a book that will feature him as a 'man of God who knows Jesus intimately and was put on this planet to save as many souls as the Lord sends him'. And I was one of those potential souls.

Was I open to receive Jesus? Why not?
Had I ever thought about turning over my life to Him? No.
Did I read the Bible? Some.
Was I a sinner? Depends.
Was I a believer? Yes.
Was I aware that it was no coincidence that God had sent me here to witness? Possibly.

To *witness*, not to proselytize. There is a crucial difference between the two. To witness is to attest to the fact that Jesus is present and entering the souls of his congregation. To proselytize is to convert an individual into a specific religion by words, persuasion or other enticements that do not come directly from God.

Before his performance began at the church, Pastor Ron was in his large office, making last-minute adjustments to his hair and his tie, pacing back and forth, sipping water from a small paper cup, clearing his throat, vocalizing like an opera singer, checking the mirror to see if his nervous assistant had successfully mopped the perspiration from his brow. Minutes before the service would begin, five of us – Pastor Ron, his assistant (a muscular man with a crew cut and a broad smile), the woman who applied his make-up (his services are televised live on the local channel), another woman who identified herself as the pastor's personal assistant or 'gal Friday', and I – at pastor Ron's behest joined hands in a small circle for a brief prayer. 'Welcome this woman into our midst,' Pastor Ron began, 'so that she may receive the word and blessing of our Lord, Jesus Christ. Make her see the light, O Lord, and be open and willing to turn her life over to you, Jesus, so she can live in peaceful harmony and be there to meet you in heaven in the final days.'

Dropping hands, Pastor Ron gave me a brief smile before saying, 'Show-time, friends, let's do it! Let's save some souls tonight,' to which those in the room answered in unison, 'Amen!'

I sat between Minna and Kara on the folding chairs in a large room adorned with plastic flowers and cables for the television camera, with fluorescent lighting flickering from ceiling fixtures, and a large statue of Jesus, arms stretched over the congregation in a permanent blessing. Pastor Ron, holding a microphone, whipped the cord as he moved swiftly from one end of the podium to the other. He began quietly before building to a deafening crescendo, talking about the miracle of God, the sacrifice of Jesus, the evil of Islam, the joy of faith, the responsibility of 'our great nation' to lead the world into the light of Christianity, while the two hundred or so people before him swayed, rocked, shook, rattled, nodded, cried, jumped up and down, raised their arms, waved their hands and shouted, 'Praise the Lord!'

Every few minutes, Minna would nudge me and ask, 'Do you feel Jesus yet?' When I shook my head, she would nudge me again and tell me she was praying that 'He would inhabit my soul quicker'.

At the end of the two-hour service, Pastor Ron informed the group that there was a visitor among them, a woman who had 'not yet found the Lord', but who had been 'led into our midst to write a book about Jesus'. He asked me to stand, and after several shocked seconds I complied. I was not prepared for the cheers and applause that broke out. As agreed, Pastor Ron asked the congregation two questions on my behalf. 'Who is the devil?' The response was unanimous: 'Muslims, Arabs, the terrorists who kill Americans.' 'Is George W. Bush a good president?' Again, a unanimous response: 'Blessed by God!'

Finally, Pastor Ron concluded the service by inviting those who wanted to be 'blessed' to raise their hands and 'move forward in an orderly fashion.' Two strong men, one of them Pastor Ron's muscular assistant, got up and walked systematically from one person to the next. Pastor Ron approached each man and women anxious to be blessed and 'receive Jesus'. He pushed each backwards, shouting, 'Find the Lord,' causing them to fall into the strong waiting arms of the two men. This went on for another forty minutes or so before the service was over. The effects of this emotional event lingered long after Pastor Ron left the podium. Kara, holding onto the side of her chair, was squatting and jumping, crying and laughing, while another woman was shaking uncontrollably, emitting unrecognizable sounds. A man, his face flushed bright red, was gasping for breath as he swayed back and forth, muttering, 'Praise the Lord.' By then, John Jack was administering to Kara, who had fainted from excitement. As we walked through the large room, Minna assured me that all the people who were in a 'state of ecstasy' were not in need of medical attention. As Minna and I made our way back to Pastor Ron's private quarters to say goodbye and to thank him for allowing me to witness and participate in this most interesting moment, she asked me yet again: 'Do you feel Jesus yet?'

'Not yet,' I replied, to which she smiled and said, 'Well, I know He's with you, and I know you have been singled out by Him because He loves you and has a special plan for your life.'

More than a year later, when I open my e-mail, I always find messages from Minna, Kara, John Jack and countless other born-again Christians I met in the course of researching this book. These messages say, albeit in different ways, 'Yes, Jesus loves you and has a plan for your life.'

PART ONE

HIS WONDER-WORKING POWER:
THE BIRTH OF EVANGELICAL
CHRISTIANITY

CHAPTER ONE

Being Right with God

*Save me, O God, by Your Name; vindicate me by Your might.
Hear my prayers, O God; listen to the words of my mouth.
Strangers are attacking me; ruthless men seek my life – men
without regard for God. Surely God is my help; the Lord is the
One who sustains me.*

(Psalm 54:1-4)

CHRISTIANITY, while the predominant religion in
America, is not all-inclusive. Evangelical Christians are part
of an exclusionary club that has strict rules for entry. The
Fundamentalist view is that everything happens for a reason.
The notion that each event produces a reaction means that
there is a cause and effect for everything. There are no
coincidences in life; everything is the result of divine intervention, of God's will. Fundamentalism holds the Bible to be
infallible, and Evangelical preachers consider personal faith
the answer to all ethical and moral problems in society. The
most basic belief that Evangelical or Fundamental Christians
hold is that no one is born a Christian. Even if people have
been baptized and schooled in the teachings of their church,
they are no more Christians than Jews, Muslims, Hindus,
Buddhists, or any members of any other religion practised in
the world today. Though the rules for entry are strict, anyone

17

can become a born-again Christian if he commits his life to Jesus Christ and acknowledges that He suffered and died for man's sins on the cross. To be born again or to profess to having committed one's life to Jesus must include an acknowledgment of having fallen short of the truth and moral precepts found in the Bible. Having a personal encounter with the Lord is part of that process and, in fact, having a 'born-again' experience means having a visitation from Jesus Christ during which the person visited makes the decision to live according to His word as written in Scripture. Along with accepting Jesus into one's heart and soul comes the admission that His way is the only way for the individual to live without punishment until the End Times, or final days, when Jesus as the Messiah and the Redeemer will make a reappearance on earth.

For those Christians who have a personal relationship with God, their belief is not merely passive. They are prepared to lead the misguided into accepting the Lord. They are convinced it is their God-given responsibility to spread His word throughout the world. As Marilyn Lake Griffins, an Evangelical preacher whom I met in Kansas City, told me, 'Not spreading the word of the Lord is like having the cure for cancer and not sharing it with the world.'

All born-again Christians consider baptism as a conscious and life-changing decision by adults to accept Christ as their saviour. In addition, the overwhelming majority of born-again Christians believe in the literal truth of the Bible. They tend to place a greater emphasis on faith in Jesus than on good deeds in the world and they usually see missionary activity as central to their duties as a Christian. Born-again Christians are often called 'Evangelical' because of this passion for sharing the good news and winning converts to their cause.[1] Evangelical born-again Christians often worship in the Pentecostal or Charismatic style, which centres on the ecstatic experience of Christ's presence and is characterized by faith healing, speaking in tongues and religious ecstasy. This experience of transformation, both in the context of being born again and in regular religious observance, the doctrinal certainty afforded by fundamentalist readings of the Bible, and the determination to bring to others the good news of Christ's love for the world, combine to make Evangelicals highly effective at building institutions and winning converts.

In important respects, Evangelical Christianity closely parallels the growth of Alcoholics Anonymous and other programmes that seek to help people cope with destructive addictions. In the context of America's highly mobile and often socially atomised culture, Evangelical faith provides its adherents with a narrative of loss, redemption and salvation in the face of personal disintegration. Evangelicals recruit very successfully in prisons where they offer inmates a credible story of rebirth and a fresh start in Jesus. This is only the most extreme form of a conversion effort that appeals strongly to those who find the high pressures of modernity difficult to cope with. And just as Alcoholics Anonymous place great emphasis on rehearsing and refining a story of spiralling addiction that climaxes in a recognition of the addict's helplessness and the need to turn one's life over to a higher power, so Evangelical Christians emphasize the descent into despair and rebirth in Jesus. While it is not by any means true of all Evangelicals, the faith has saved millions of people from personal disaster. For all the demands it makes on its adherents, it does work wonders, and from this blunt fact it derives much of its power.

Evangelical churches are the fastest growing Christian groups in the United States and since the early 1970s their numbers and organizational power have played an increasingly important part in the country's political life.

During the 2004 American presidential election, they accounted for more than 42 per cent of the Republican Party – three quarters of those white Evangelical Christians who voted supported George W. Bush.[2] In the crucial swing state of Ohio, white Evangelical support reached 79 per cent.[3] Of the 120 million voters in 2004, one in five described themselves as having been born again.[4] Further, in this last presidential election, Evangelical voters overwhelmingly identified the country's moral fibre as their most pressing political concern. By definition, that translated into fierce opposition to abortion, stem-cell research, the teaching of evolution in public schools, and violent and sexually explicit lyrics and images in music, film and television. Evangelical leaders have not only been influential in the general media, they have also garnered an increasing presence in other media outlets, such as cable television and radio networks, that attract millions of viewers and listeners.

Before 1960, US broadcasters were required to devote a certain amount of airtime to religious broadcasting. After 1960, the Federal Communications Commission made it possible for the networks to sell this time to programme makers, where once they had given it away free to religious groups. This new market in religious airtime favoured the energetic fund-raising methods of Evangelical preachers, and programming by non-Evangelical groups was gradually pushed aside. Free from the regulations that limit advertising in secular programming, 'paid-time religious programs were allowed to become, essentially, program-length fund-raisers.'[5] Evangelical media have been highly successful in converting public indignation into contributions. Indeed, the prominence of moral values in the recent elections is in part a tribute to their broadcasting skills. Hidden messages in rock albums, controversies over flag-burning, Clinton's sexual escapades in the White House, have all featured heavily in their output. Above all, the Evangelical broadcasters have emphasized the rising tide of obscenity and the ever-greater danger of sexual anarchy in America.

Towards the end of the first Bush mandate in 2003, the Christian Booksellers Association of America put total sales of Evangelical books at $1.77 billion a year, out of an estimated $11 billion in general consumer book sales. Major media corporations in the United States have recognized the significance of this market, and have acted to get a share of this 'Evangelical money'. Zondervan, publisher of the bestselling Evangelical title of the 1970s, *The Late Great Planet Earth*, is now part of the HarperCollins group, while Bantam Dell, part of the Random House group, recently paid $45 million for a series of books by Tim LaHaye.

An Evangelical preacher, LaHaye is one of the most popular authors in America. His 'Left Behind' series has sold more than 55 million copies. LaHaye's books and those of other Christian writers have popularized the notion of Rapture – the moment of truth when the End Times arrive, causing the stock market to plummet and governments to fall, the moment when aircraft, cars and trains crash as born-again pilots and drivers are caught up into the air or 'raptured' up to heaven, while their vehicles careen out of control. A popular picture found in the homes of many Evangelicals shows a man cutting the grass outside his house gazing in astonishment as his born-again wife is 'raptured' out of an upstairs window.

Those 'left behind' will realize they are doomed and that the true believers have been right all along. Those who finally accept Jesus as their saviour will be allowed to accompany Him to heaven, while those who have not will be forced to remain to be slaughtered in the final battle on earth.

In his twelfth and final book in the 'Left Behind' series, *Glorious Appearing*, published in March 2004, Tim LaHaye writes about the return of Jesus Christ. The book opens as the armies of the Antichrist are on the brink of invading Jerusalem and ends with the appearance of Jesus that saves the world. The plot is straightforward: Jesus returns to earth in His second appearance as the Messiah and obliterates all non-Christians from the planet. In a scene that takes the idea of ethnic cleansing to a new level, 'Jesus merely speaks and the bodies of the enemy are ripped open. Christians have to drive carefully to avoid hitting the splayed and filleted bodies of men and women and horses.'

For the American President, it is a familiar theme.

In 1993, George W. Bush told a Jewish reporter from the *Austin American-Statesman* that, according to his faith, 'non-believers in Christ, including Jews, go to hell.' Unfortunately for him, his statement was picked up by the Jewish press, and when he first ran for Governor of Texas in 1994, his opponent, the incumbent Democratic Governor Ann Richards, took out ads in Jewish newspapers quoting that remark. The political spin that resulted was conceived by Marvin Olasky, the born-again Christian advisor to Bush on his 'compassionate conservatism' position, which purports to combine religion (or compassion) with economic, social and political conservatism. Olasky, a Christian scholar, wrote *The Tragedy of American Compassion*, after reading which Bush asked his political strategist Karl Rove to invite Olasky to meet him. That meeting prompted Governor Bush's vision of compassionate conservatism. Shortly after the polemic about who gets into heaven, Olasky defended Bush. 'On the face of it,' Olasky said, 'you have to believe in Christ to go to heaven; Jews don't believe in Christ; therefore, Jews don't go to heaven . . . and the opposite of heaven is hell. I don't think Governor Bush meant anything personal against the Jews. He was simply quoting the common belief about who gets into heaven.'

The often-complicated relationship between Jews and Evangelical Christians was seen even more pointedly with the global success of Mel Gibson's *The Passion of the Christ,*[6] which caused an angry polemic within the two camps concerning Jewish culpability for the betrayal and death of Jesus Christ. Historically, the Jewish-American community in the United States has always been to the left politically and has consistently voted for Democrat candidates. They have also, as a total entity, gone against all the moral imperatives that the Evangelical Christians have tried so hard to impose on American society. And yet, despite Gibson's movie, which only added to a history of ambiguity and enmity, the majority of the Jewish community in America and a majority of Israelis have put their domestic agenda and feelings aside, and formed an unofficial alliance with the Evangelical community in return for their unwavering Christian support for Israel at a time when the Jewish State has a failing economy and few friends in the international community. For the Evangelicals, the alliance remains steeped in biblical history. For the Jewish population, it was for reasons of survival, given the American President's stand on his war against Islam, his condemnation of suicide bombings in Israel and his continued support for the Jewish State. Some say this Jewish-Christian alliance is a match made in heaven. Others say it is a match made in hell. Either way, the Jewish vote in America contributed to a Bush victory in 2004, albeit for vastly different reasons than the Evangelicals' support for the incumbent President.

In the months leading up to the 2004 presidential election, Karl Rove, Bush's chief political advisor, had no doubts about the potential importance in securing a Bush victory of moral values as held dear by the Evangelical community. In fact, it was no coincidence that during those months Rove went around the White House, humming 'Onward, Christian Soldiers'. Speaking about the high levels of support for bans on gay marriage, Rove said, 'I do think it was part and parcel of a broader fabric where this year moral values ranked higher than they traditionally do.'[7]

According to an NBC poll, 22 per cent of voters said that moral values were the most important issue for them in the election. Clearly, the Evangelical community claimed George W. Bush as 'one of their own', which all but ensured him a second term in the White House. During the year since President Bush's re-election in November 2004, there has even been a global transformation of the media infrastructure which has a great and growing influence over the wider culture, especially as it concerns American military action in Iraq. It is a tragic irony that the Christian media that campaign so tirelessly against pornography in records and films have done so much to convince Americans that they are caught up in a crusade against Satanic terror. While Bush was talking of God's 'gift of freedom to every human being in the world'[8], US soldiers in Iraq were generating vast quantities of sadistic pornography as part of America's crusade for democracy.

As we shall see, the media, when covering the war, have taken to marching in sync with the Bush doctrine that combines state and church. For the international community, this trend towards religiosity in America today has become both a danger and a mystery. For Americans, George W. Bush's born-again credentials often seem linked to his political aspirations.

If any one thing sets Evangelical or born-again Christians apart, or makes them easily recognizable to each other, it is their willingness to proclaim their special relationship with Jesus by certain language and inflections of tone that make those beliefs instantly known. For instance, for an Evangelical, 'being among friends' means being with those who share their religious convictions and who, like them, are destined to be spared the tribulations of the End of Times, when those who have not embraced Jesus Christ will be slaughtered in the final battle at Armageddon. Not to be fooled by politicians who are only anxious to further their own careers by capturing the Christian vote, Evangelical religious leaders have certain questions which they ask 'to separate the true believers from the canny pretenders'.

One of George W. Bush's most practised talents has always been his ability to reach the entire Evangelical community with very few words, but words that carry crucial symbolic meaning. Although President Bush has been accused of being inarticulate, of being unable to put together an English sentence that makes any sense, or of using words that either have the wrong meaning or simply don't exist, he is extremely gifted in the language of Evangelical Christians. When Bush meets a group of born-again Christians, he has all the correct answers to their questions, and all the right questions to ask them, to bolster their estimation of him. The Reverend Jerry Falwell, a well-known Evangelical preacher with impressive political clout, says of the President, 'We know instantly that he is one of ours by the way he speaks.'[9]

According to Jerry Falwell, the most common question he asks any presidential candidate is how he would convince the Lord to allow him to get into heaven. When George Bush Senior, an Episcopalian, was asked that question by a group of Evangelical Christians during his 1988 campaign for President of the United States, he replied, 'I would simply tell the Lord that I have been good throughout my life on earth and have done my best to uphold His teachings.' For Evangelicals, that is the wrong answer.

When George W. Bush was asked that same question by a similar group of Evangelical Christians during his campaign for re-election in 2004, his response drew whistles, hallelujahs, amens, cheers and a standing ovation. 'I know we're all sinners,' the President said, 'but I've accepted Jesus Christ as my personal saviour. I know what it means to be right with God.'

What exactly does it mean to be 'right with God'? Who are these true-believing Christians – whether they live in the White House in Washington, D.C., or in a split-level ranch in America's heartland – who have become so visible and vocal throughout America? Perhaps even more important than learning who these Evangelicals are, even when it comes to their sheer strength of numbers, is understanding what they believe. To define Evangelical Christians by their beliefs is to be aware of how different they are from the mainstream Protestant or Catholic population of the United States, how absolute they are in their beliefs, and how determined they are to implement those beliefs throughout the United States and the world.

CHAPTER TWO

God's Chosen Nation

The enemy has got a face. He's called Satan. He lives in Fallujah.
(Marine Lieutenant-Colonel Gareth Brandl,
speaking to the BBC, 7 November 2004)

WHEN I embarked upon this project to write a book about Evangelical Christians in the United States, my initial goal was to understand how they had managed in a little less than three decades to become a force on the American domestic scene. Eventually, it became clear that the Christian Right not only provides crucial support to politicians who appear to share their preoccupation with the nation's moral well-being, but they have also become increasingly powerful in foreign policy, especially in Israel/Palestine, the biblical Holy Land.

One month after Theodore Herzl, the founder of modern Zionism, published *The Jewish State* in 1896, the Reverend William H. Hechler, chaplain to the British Embassy in Vienna, visited him. Herzl's plan for a Jewish homeland in Palestine represented to the Christian minister tangible proof that the Bible prophecy of restoring the Jews to the Holy Land would lead to the Second Coming of Christ. In the beginning of their relationship, Herzl was wary of Hechler since he tried repeatedly to convert Herzl or at least infuse God into his conception of the Jewish State. Herzl remained devoted to his Zionist cause, which was based in socialist politics. In the end, the men developed a deep friendship. When Herzl was dying, at the untimely age of forty-four, he summoned Hechler to his bedside and whispered, 'Carry the torch of Zionism to the Christian world.' As it turned out, Hechler and his fellow Christians not only carried the torch of Zionism, but they continue to infuse biblical meaning into the political destiny of the Jewish State.

The USA and Israel have long enjoyed a close strategic alliance. During the Cold War Israel was, like Turkey, a useful counterweight to Arab nationalist regimes in Egypt and Syria, and to the Fundamentalist movement that gained in strength after the Iranian revolution in 1979. Israeli victories in 1967 and 1973 were widely welcomed in the United States and led to a close strategic alliance. But for the Christian Right, support for Israel was more than a matter of Cold War politics and power calculations. From the very beginning, American Evangelicals had identified strongly with the nation of Israel.

On 29 November 1947, when the nations of the world voted to give the Jews their own state, the relationship between the destiny of the Jews and the church had to be redefined. The late L. Nelson Bell, a former missionary doctor active in Evangelical leadership at the time, whose daughter married the Reverend Billy Graham, wrote in his periodical *Christianity Today*, 'For the first time in more than 2,000 years Jerusalem is now completely in the hands of the Jews. It gives the student of the Bible a thrill and a renewed faith in the accuracy and validity of the Bible.'[1] But even in that glorious moment there was mistrust and dissension within the Evangelical community. Evangelical theologian

Billy Graham, despite his enormous admiration for his father-in-law, expressed disappointment that the founding leaders of the Zionist State had chosen to ignore God's biblical promises to the Jewish people. For the Evangelicals, the return of the Jews was all about God – specifically, the Second Coming. Just weeks after Israel was created, Billy Graham was quoted in the *New York Times* as saying, '. . . the new nation Israel is an immoral miracle since there is no God of Israel present in its political creation.'[2] Gary Burge, another prominent Evangelical Christian, traces the beginnings of his anti-Zionism to the moment in 1948 when Israel officially attained statehood. 'If indeed this was a nation claiming some continuity with its biblical heritage, surely a reference to God would be acceptable.'[3] In his book *Israel in Prophecy* (1962), John Walvoord wrote: '. . . the nation of Israel has been formed, they have all the likeness of one of the nations of the earth; they have their government, their postal, coinage and banking system, but there is no God. They have come together as a nation of Israelites, without the God of Israel.'

Gradually, the Evangelical Christian world became aware that, despite the original concept of Zionism that seemed to exclude God and religion, every subsequent Israeli government was formed by making concessions to the religious parties. The result was that religious laws began to govern daily life in Israel. Not surprisingly, an increasing number of American Evangelicals became intrigued by Israeli leaders who managed to make religion a prominent part of the society. While Israeli secularists opposed the inclusion of religion in everyday life, religious authorities in Israel prevailed, for example, when it came to forbidding movie theatres to carry films judged to be offensive to the religious sensibilities of Christians. The born-again Christian community was even more pleased to see that Judaism was not the only religion to play a prominent role in society, but that a Ministry of Religion was established in the government with separate departments for dealing with the Muslim, Christian and Druze religious communities.

Many American Evangelical leaders studied Israeli politics more carefully, intent on using the model to effect religious influence in the United States. Religious programmes in Israel had an influence not only on religious issues but also in areas of finance, education, settlement policies and immigration. The right-wing Orthodox Jews even managed to get state subsidies for religious schools, or *yeshivas*, as well as for religious instruction in the secular school system.

After the 1967 war, when Israel captured Jerusalem and other territories of the 'Biblical Land of Israel', Evangelicals considered it to be a prophetic sign or the 'super sign' that the End of Days was drawing near when Jesus would reappear on earth.

In explaining this passionate interest in Israel, Evangelicals cite God's Covenant with Abraham as described in Genesis, in which God deeded all the land of Israel to the Jewish people. Evangelicals insist that not only the Book of Genesis, but all Scripture, are scientifically sound in every detail and should be taken literally without interpretation.

The doctrine of the Abrahamic Covenant is a compilation of all the promises that God made to Abraham and, while it has three different sections with several sub-sections, the original promise, as found in Genesis 12:1 and 2, is essentially a real estate contract between God and the Jewish people. 'Get thee . . . unto a land which I will show thee: And I will make of thee a great nation.' In Genesis 13:15, God promised Abraham 'all the land which thou seest, to thee will I give it and to thy seed forever.' The full dimensions of this promise were defined in Genesis 15:18: 'To your descendants I have given this land, from the river of Egypt [Nile] unto the great river, the river Euphrates.'

Ed McAteer died in 2004 at the age of seventy-six. Up until his death, he continued to be held in great esteem by the Evangelical community. A former executive with Proctor and Gamble, he is considered to have been the 'godfather' of the Christian Right. Not only was he one of the founders of the Moral Majority, along with Jerry Falwell, but another of his political achievements was that he organized the Evangelical movement into the most powerful grassroots component of the Republican party. As well, until he died, he directed the Religious Roundtable (which he also founded), a non-profit organization that continues to set the tone and agenda for Evangelical issues, both domestic and foreign.

With his jovial good humour and gregarious personality, his fund of anecdotes, and his infallible memory for people's names and personal stories, McAteer was instantly likeable. Although he admitted during one of his last interviews with me[4] that he had 'never been accused of being modest', he was quick to say that he had profound humility when it came to the belief in Scripture which was his motivating force. During a conversation in November 2003, he described himself to me as 'an unashamed born-again Bible-believing Christian who was taken into a Methodist church when he was only fourteen years old, to hear the gospel preached by a man who died a drunkard'.

'I had an experience,' McAteer said, 'like Apostle Paul on the road to Damascus and I was only a teenager but I was saved by Jesus who became the Lord and master of my life.'

During the Second World War, McAteer was saved again when he was one of the sole survivors on the USS *St Louis*, the first ship sunk by kamikaze fighter pilots in the Pacific Ocean near the Philippines. 'Jesus said the children of this world will all have a born-again experience,' McAteer continued, 'although sometimes the people of the world think they are wiser than those of the kingdoms. After I survived the war, I went to law school for a while and then went right into sales where I was honored year after year as the number one salesman for Proctor and Gamble. Eventually I trained the staff and often opened their eyes and hearts to the Lord.'

During another interview, Ed McAteer explained that the genealogical heritage of the Arab people can be traced back to Ishmael, Abraham's son by his servant Hagar, whom he loved less than Isaac, his son with Sarah. 'It is obvious,' he said, 'that when God made the Covenant with Abraham, He knew exactly what He was doing. He knew that Abraham was predisposed towards the Jewish people long before that.'

Included in the sub-sections of the Covenant are certain blessings concerning the status of the land and protection from anti-Semitism as found in Genesis 15:13–16. One of the most crucial sub-sections, however, concerns the Messiah, for this part of the Covenant explains the Evangelicals' unconditional support when it comes to Israel and the basis for their bond with the Jewish people.

Evangelicals believe that Jesus as the Messiah will not return until all the land of Israel is under Jewish control. The condition for the coming of the Messiah was that Abraham would sacrifice his first-born son, which he agreed to do and which was not accepted by God, as seen in Genesis 22:16: '. . . because you have manufactured this thing, and have not withheld your son, your only son . . . And in your seed all the nations of the earth shall be blessed, because you have obeyed My voice.'

What the Covenant means in religious terms to Christian Fundamentalists, as well as to Orthodox Jews who also take the Bible literally, is that no one, not an Israeli politician, *a fortiori* not a European, nor American, nor Arab leader, has the right to negotiate the borders of Israel which have been set down in that inerrant biblical text. 'A human "no" can never cancel out a divine "yes",' remains one of the Evangelicals' favourite slogans. What the Covenant means in geo-political terms to Evangelicals is that there can never be a Palestinian state on the land that God gave to the Jewish people.

And yet, once again there is ambiguity since, according to Evangelical doctrine, only being born-again or having a 'new birth' through a personal encounter with Christ can bring personal redemption. Since the Jewish people have not accepted Jesus Christ, Evangelical Christians, despite their professed love for Judaism, the land, and the Old Testament, consider the religion to be 'incomplete'. Since Jesus will only return to earth after all mankind has accepted Him as their Saviour, and those who have not will be slaughtered in the final battle between God and Satan in an area in the north of Israel called Megiddo, those slaughtered will also include the Jewish people. The importance of the Jewish people, there-fore, could be construed as nothing more than a means to a glorious end when Jesus reappears on earth. At best, it underscores a philosophical debate about whether or not the Evangelicals' belief in the Abrahamic Covenant and their devotion to the Jewish people is self-serving or altruistic.

The reality today in America is that strong Evangelical support for Israel has become part of a much wider political programme. From the social and sexual controversies of 'the culture wars' to the War on Terror, the Arab–Israeli conflict and the global response to the AIDS epidemic, Evangelical politicians and the communities that support them are increasingly using a faith-based language to describe the world and are seeking faith-based solutions to its problems. As we shall see, much of this use of religion in political life is sincere. Some of it, however, is a matter of conscious manipulation of the public by elite groups.

Immediately following the events of 11 September, the sentiment throughout America was shock, outrage and mourning, before it quickly turned to biblical patriotism which the Religious Right harnessed as adeptly as they had once done when 'godless' Communism was the enemy of Christian civilization. Their message was simple and consistent: love of country goes hand in hand with God, and all the evil that has come to confront mankind on earth is the natural outcome of predictions that have been written in the Bible. Once again, Israel was high on the Evangelical agenda. The Christian Right maintained that the situation in the Middle East, with suicide bombings targeting Israelis and other terror attacks against American installations and citizens abroad, demanded that many biblical references be rethought with fresh interpretation and new resolution. For the Christian Right, the time had come to make God's Covenant with Abraham a reality. For them, the Covenant could not have been written for any better time than after radical Islam declared war on the United States. And it could have been written for no group of people more deserving of His grace than the born-again Christians, who believed it was their calling and their personal mission to act on behalf of the Judeo-Christian world.

In the days immediately after the terrorist attacks on New York and Washington in September 2001, prominent

American politicians began to use a highly religious language to describe the new dangers facing America. On 20 September 2001, the then Attorney General John Ashcroft, a devout Pentecostal Christian, spoke before the National Association of Religious Broadcasters and stated that the 'attacks against America only prove that the United States was God's chosen nation, engaged in a righteous struggle with Evil.

'It says so right in the Book of Revelation,' Ashcroft said, 'that the agony we endure is part of the birth pains of the coming of Messiah.'[5]

The notion that America was engaged in a millennial struggle with 'evil-doers' resonated with millions of American Evangelicals, who have long tended to understand politics in terms of good and evil. Disagreement over public policy became a matter of confrontation with the forces of darkness and America itself, as the home of much of the world's Evangelical population, became a citadel under threat from Satan himself. Bin Laden became a demonic figure in the eyes of many Americans and Islam a direct challenge to God's plan for the earth. The War on Terror was integrated into an older war with the ungodly, fought for the souls of the American people.

During a previous interview, Ed McAteer's words took on a more ominous tone. 'No matter how much good fortune Arabs receive,' he told me, 'they will never know spiritual peace. Suppose you have an Arab who is tall and good looking and rich, with every opportunity for a good life for himself and his family. Suppose he has every chance to be happy and successful; there is always something that stops him from achieving that perfect bliss. And that something is because that Arab is a Moslem, who has something ingrained in his heart and mind against the Jewish people and the

Christian world. So, the result is that man, who has every-thing in the world, only craves that little piece of land that belongs to the Jewish people which makes him dissatisfied about everything in his life. His obsession with the Jewish State is so great that if he sees a Jew walk by, despite all his good fortune, all his happiness diminishes. He's got fever in his soul to kill and destroy Jews and Christians alike.'[6]

In the days and weeks following the 11 September attacks, whenever George W. Bush addressed the international press, he consistently alluded to God, religion and the fight be-tween Good and Evil. 'Either you are with us or against us in our war of Good versus Evil,'[7] the President announced in a speech meant for America's European allies. In another address to the nation after 9/11, he told the American people that finding solace in religion would mitigate the fear and paranoia that was so rampant throughout the country. In other speeches, the American President repeatedly stated that the United States 'can never be safe from terrorists unless we see that our blessed country must extend God's will of liberty for other countries, by force, if necessary'.[8]

In a speech in which he uttered the most memorable phrase of his first four years in the White House, President Bush called Iraq, North Korea and Iran an 'axis of evil'. He then embarked upon an uncompromising foreign policy, stated in stark terms, which changed the behaviour of hostile leaders throughout the world, rendering them more aggressive like North Korea, or more compliant like Libya. Condoleezza Rice, who served as President Bush's national security advisor during his first administration, said, 'Mr Bush . . . changed the landscape when he talked about the axis of evil.'[9]

With the American President setting the religious tone throughout the country, it often became nearly impossible to tell the difference between the politicians who addressed the nation and certain religious leaders who also took to the airwaves to explain the violence that had stunned the country. Faith was no longer a private matter between a political candidate and his God, since every political aspirant shared his or her spiritual awakening with the American people. For Evangelicals it was a response based on their fear that a lack of spirituality and family values would result in the decline of democracy, and the appearance of the devil himself. For the secular portion of America, religion and politics somehow assured the average citizen that the country would be safe, not only because of its inherent wealth and power but also because God was on its side.

Evangelical preacher Franklin Graham, heir apparent to his father, the renowned Billy Graham, maintained that the attacks on 11 September 2001 were 'a warning'.

'This was a wake-up call,' he said, 'because materialism has become the God of America. God allowed it to happen, just as when he took Judah and the Israelites captive and sent the Babylonians against them, just as when He allowed the Holocaust so that Israel, out of the ashes, exists today. The things that concern the Lord the most often cost human beings their lives.'[10]

Jerry Falwell and Pat Robertson, two other prominent members of the Christian Right, also blamed the attacks on the 'evils of mankind', and on mankind's 'refusal to embrace Jesus as their saviour'.[11] They even compared the four separate acts of terrorism and the AIDS epidemic with the plagues that ravaged Europe in the Middle Ages. It wasn't until 10 November 2002, however, that Ed McAteer finally put a name to the 'evil' that had attacked America, when he referred to Mohammed, the founder of Islam, as a 'terrorist'.[12] Not only had evil been defined, but conquering Islam and the terror committed in its name would become the justification for all subsequent military actions. Taking his cue from his Evangelical friends, on 16 December 2002 President Bush made a speech on the site of what had been the World Trade Center. Since Ed McAteer had already described Mohammed as a 'terrorist', President Bush gave himself permission to give a name to the war America was fighting. 'This is a new kind of evil,' the American President said, 'and the American people are beginning to understand that this *crusade,* this war on terrorism, is going to take a while.'

President Bush's use of the word 'crusade' carried a very specific message to his friends and supporters. For the Arab world, however, it was a reminder of the bloodthirsty medieval crusades, when the Christian West invaded the heart of Islam.

After the attack on Afghanistan to dismantle the Taliban regime and bring to justice those who organized the attack on America, and after the subsequent invasion of Iraq, President Bush and high-ranking members of his cabinet, as well as Evangelical leaders, were united in stating that the divine will of God had mobilized the American military to root out the enemies of Christianity and democracy. During a speech before the Religious Broadcasters in Nashville, Tennessee in February 2004, President Bush said, 'The sacrifice we would make for the liberty of strangers was not America's gift to the world but God's gift to humanity. It is God's gift to every human being in the world and America has been called to lead the world to peace.'[13]

As it turned out, George W. Bush was being naïve when he announced to America's allies, 'Either you are with us or against us in our fight against terror.'[14] On 11 March 2004, three years after the attacks on America, Al Qaeda attacked the main rail station in Madrid. Immediately afterwards, in what was the ultimate polarity statement, the terrorists sent a message to the international media: 'You love life and we love death.'

The Islamic terrorists' bombing of Madrid several days before general elections precipitated a Socialist win, resulting in the withdrawal of Spanish troops from Iraq, which was the terrorists' goal.

The events of 2001 not only changed the mentality of the American people, they also resulted in a fracture throughout the country that has not been seen for decades, one that transcends political parties, between those who believe that the struggle between Good and Evil is a last crusade to uphold the moral and religious values of Christianity, and those who maintain that God and religion have no place in domestic and foreign policy. While the justification for violence is always subjective, the idea of the United States of America marching to war on the orders of Jesus Christ or any other God would seem contrary to the premise on which the country was founded – a separation of church and state.

Ultimately it became clear to the rest of the world that a religious majority in America presented a potential global threat to those who did not share the same ideas. As with Islamic Fundamentalism, when the extreme becomes the norm, the assumed rights of all citizens of the world to disagree are threatened under the banner of God, morality and religion.

CHAPTER THREE

An Engine of Civil Policy

Arise, O Lord, let not man triumph; let the nations be judged in Your presence.

(Psalm 9:19)

THE very public religiosity of much of America's ruling elite in the twentieth century is at startling odds with the free-thinking and downright atheism that characterised many leaders during the revolutionary War of Independence. Throughout the 229 years since America has existed, its citizens have always prided themselves on their determination and ability to uphold a separation of church and state. Based on the concepts of the founding fathers of the United States, who – influenced by the Enlightenment – added an Amendment to the Constitution to entrench that separation in 1791, Americans have tried to be vigilant about any religious influence on their country's politics. At the same time, the majority of Americans have also always considered their principles rooted in their divinely given right to life, liberty and the pursuit of happiness, and have believed that God plays a pivotal role in their lives.

By and large, Americans are a spiritual people and belief in God and the influence of religion in government can be traced back to George Washington, Thomas Jefferson, Abraham Lincoln and many other American presidents. The conflict of ideas concerning the relationship between church and state is woven into the fibre of American life.

In 1776, at the birth of the nation, Thomas Jefferson spoke of a wall of separation between religion and the American government: 'every man's soul belongs to himself . . . the evil occurs when man is forced to abandon care of his salvation to another. No man has the power to let another prescribe his faith.'[1]

On 20 January 1804, when Jefferson was President of the United States, he ordered two copies of the King James Version of the New Testament. Jefferson, although not religious, nonetheless admired Jesus as a philosopher and wise man while rejecting any mysticism that surrounded His life. Jefferson went through the entire text of the Bible, and cut out all those passages that referred to the virgin birth, the resurrection, the incarnation, and anything else that touched on the supernatural. The verses that survived Jefferson's editing were eventually published as *The Philosophy of Jesus of Nazareth*, which portrayed Jesus as the philosopher Jefferson had always envisaged. By doing this, Jefferson created Jesus to fit his own needs, as a man whose lessons to others while He was alive were far more important than the story of His death in order to atone for the sins of mankind.

In the nineteenth century, Jefferson's belief in Jesus the man attracted religious leaders. Among those who embraced Jefferson's views were Baptist and Methodist travelling preachers, who went from town to town spreading the gospel and making Jesus into someone human, approachable and capable of offering comfort in life to those who accepted Him.

Another founding father, James Madison, wrote about the

relationship of church to state in his *Memorial and Remonstrance* of 1785, in which he condemned the use of 'religion as an engine of civil policy'. Disestablishing religion, he argued, does not demote religion but rather protects it from exploitation by political authority, from 'an unhallowed perversion of the means of salvation'.

Jefferson, Madison and their colleagues could easily have designated Christianity as the official religion of the United States but they consciously chose not to do so. The founders of the American Republic meant to separate the institutions of church and state and to prohibit the establishment of a state religion. By providing the Constitution as the basis for religious pluralism, they also endorsed the notion of religious tolerance. Under the law, no religion can become the favoured or established church, and all faiths throughout America are free to try to win the hearts and minds of the people. The only time in history when there was public debate on that particular point was when Patrick Henry and Thomas Jefferson, both strong supporters of American independence, sharply differed on whether the Anglican Church should be the established religion in their home state of Virginia. Henry wanted the church to receive preferential standing in the Old Dominion, while Jefferson opposed any form of 'state religion'. Jefferson won, and he considered his authorship of the 1786 Virginia Statute of Religious Freedom one of his greatest achievements.

Despite Thomas Jefferson's determination to redefine Jesus, religion has dominated almost all major political debates in the United States. In fact, religion and faith in God have always been a comfort to the American people during times of extreme political and military tension. In 1847, for example, the New York *Globe*, a mainstream newspaper, urged the annexation of Mexico because 'it

42

would almost seem' that its citizens 'had brought upon themselves the vengeance of the Almighty, and we ourselves had been raised up to overthrow and utterly destroy them as a separate and distinct nation'. During the First World War, President Woodrow Wilson claimed that the war 'showed America marching to heights upon which there rests nothing but the pure light of the justice of God, reflecting the glimmer of light which came at Calvary, that first dawn which came with the Christian era'.[2] During the Cold War, President Harry S. Truman called Communism 'godless' so many times that 'godless Communism' became a catch-phrase.

In 1832, Abraham Lincoln began his political career by running for a seat in the Illinois legislature against Peter Cartwright, an Evangelical circus performer who spread the word that Lincoln was an infidel. It was far from the truth. Lincoln, while campaigning for the presidency in 1860 in Trenton, New Jersey, made the following statement: 'Americans are the chosen people, and I hope that I might become the humble servant of the Almighty and of his chosen people.'

Abraham Lincoln was not only a religious man, but the son of a Baptist minister who had insisted that his son read the Bible every day of his life. As a result, Lincoln quoted extensively from the Holy Book. In his Second Inaugural Address, in March 1865, he said, 'Both North and South read the same Bible, pray to the same God, and each invokes His aid against the other. It may seem strange that any men should dare to ask a just God's assistance in wringing their bread from the sweat of other men's faces, but let us not judge that we be not judged. The prayers of both could not be answered, that of neither has been answered fully. The Almighty has His own purposes.'

For Lincoln, not only were Americans the 'chosen people', but America was 'God's country'. Never was that more visible than during a conversation that Lincoln had with an Evangelical minister, Angus Lephardt, who came from a large city in the North. Lephardt told Lincoln that he 'hoped the Lord is on our side', to which Lincoln replied, 'I am not at all concerned about that . . . but it is my constant anxiety and prayer that I and this nation should be on the Lord's side.'[3] (During John Kerry's acceptance speech before the Democratic Convention in July 2004, he quoted that line from Lincoln's conversation with Lephardt.) During the Civil War, when Abraham Lincoln was in the White House, the Battle Hymn of the Republic was composed, with its echoes of Isaiah 63:3 and Revelation 14:20: 'He is trampling out the vineyard where the grapes of wrath are stored.'

After the Civil War, the task of humanizing Jesus fell to liberal Protestant ministers, who, seeking to better society, cast Jesus as 'more a moralist than a miracle worker', a figure who walked the earth not to pay a debt owed to an angry Father 'but to reveal to human beings the loving character of God, and to prompt them to develop the same character in themselves'. In more recent times, the Jesus People of the 1960s – hippies and drop-outs from Haight-Ashbury and Hollywood – began to see Jesus as a better way to get high than on hashish or LSD. Preaching on street corners, selling buttons with slogans like 'The Messiah is the Message', inspiring such rock musicals as *Jesus Christ Superstar*, they sought to convert the counter-culture into one that embraced God rather than drugs.

Evangelical elements have always been important in the Christian churches in the West. The early church was above all concerned to spread the 'good news' of Christ's birth, death and resurrection. The concern to establish a personal relationship with Christ and first-hand understanding of God's will through the study of the Bible is at the heart of the Lutheran rejection of the Catholic Church's right to mediate between man and God. The modern Evangelical movement in the United States and its sister churches in Africa and Latin America itself marks the confluence of several strands of religious development.

At the beginning of the nineteenth century, American Christians, concerned by the spread of secular ideas associated with the Enlightenment and the recent successful revolution against Britain, embarked on a grand project of religious revival. This movement focused on missionary work in the cities and on the frontier of the States and developed a new form of religious congregation to reach the scattered populations of the plains – the camp meeting. Here settlers would meet for several days of often-fervent religious services. Baptist and Methodist churches benefited most from this religious activity. In the eastern United States, revivalist sentiment found expression in the creation of the Society for the Promotion of Temperance in 1816.

While modern Evangelical Christianity owes a great deal in formal terms to the Methodist and Baptist churches, it derives much of its fierce renunciation of the world and its evils from John Nelson Darby (1800-82), the British preacher who founded the Plymouth Brethren and who toured the USA on six occasions between 1859 and 1877. Darby, unsuccessful as a preacher in his native England, settled in America where he found parishioners far more receptive than in his own country.

In the nineteenth century, among the radical Christians who embraced Darby the United States was referred to as the 'great whore of Babylon', taken straight from the New Testament Book of Revelation. People used biblical or apocalyptic language to describe what they believed were society's evils: sexual immorality, hedonism, atheism or generally rebellious behaviour.

Those Evangelicals who believe what is written in Revelation 9, that 'the four angels who are bound at the great river Euphrates . . . kept ready for this very hour and day and month and year, will be released to kill a third of mankind,' are the theological descendants of John Nelson Darby who popularized the belief that Christ would soon return to earth, defeat the Antichrist in the battle of Armageddon, and establish God's promised thousand-year reign.

During the eighteenth century, many Christians had come to believe that human beings were responsible for their own actions and for the existence of God's Kingdom, and that Christ would return to earth only after the millennium was established – an idea called 'Post-millennialism'. Darby preached a new theory that he called 'Pre-millennialism'. According to his beliefs, humanity had become so evil that God was prepared to intervene and punish the entire human race. Darby's followers were comforted by the belief that Christ would return to earth *before* He established His thousand-year reign, which made the waiting more bearable. Since most of his followers were poverty-stricken and miserable, it was a welcome scenario that promised them their just rewards based not on monetary wealth or success but on something else – a steadfast and unquestioning belief in Jesus Christ and His revealed word.

Darby, also known as the 'father of dispensational theology', believed that history unfolds in a series of distinct preordained periods or dispensations. He promised his followers that out of the fiery destruction of the world, only those Christians who took Scripture literally would be exempt from the suffering and pain that the unfaithful would endure during Armageddon. Darby appealed to the masses because he rejected any interpretation of biblical text, which for them was complicated and time-consuming. Instead, he preached that the prophets and the authors of the Book of Revelation were making very precise predictions which would come to pass exactly as they were recounted within the biblical text which divided history into seven separate dispensations. These two different schools – dispensationalists and mainstream Christians – became the two sides of a definitive rupture within the Christian churches which would forever separate mainstream Protestants from Evangelicals or born-again Christians.

According to Darby, the world had already endured six of the seven Dispensations, which included the Fall, the Flood and the crucifixion of Jesus Christ. As he told it, the Seventh Dispensation was now upon humanity and would be the most horrific and terrifying of all. He told his followers to be prepared for Satan to descend upon earth and fool humanity into believing that he was God, leading them astray to commit unspeakable immoral acts. After seven years of total evil, Christ would finally appear and engage in battle with Satan on the plain of Armageddon outside Jerusalem. Only after He defeated evil and inaugurated the Seventh Dispensation would peace and harmony prevail for the next thousand years until the Last Judgment brought all history to an end. Written in Revelation 16 is a confirmation of how this battle will occur: 'the drying up of the Euphrates River which will clear the way for the armies of the Antichrist to reach Israel where in Megiddo, the final battle or Armageddon will be fought'.

This apocalyptic belief that we are living in the End Times provides the modern Evangelical movement with much of its energy and sense of urgency. It echoes the enthusiasm of the very early church, and the anxieties provoked by the passing of the first millennium, the Black Death and the Thirty Years' War. Why it should have gained so many adherents in the last part of the nineteenth century is not hard to imagine. Rapid and unregulated industrialization had led to huge social and political upheaval. Just as socialism and anarchism offered salvation in this life from the ills of capitalist exploitation, dispensationalist preachers promised an escape from the immorality that characterized urban living. Christ's return to earth was imminent, as was fiery and much-deserved punishment for all manner of sinners.

While John Nelson Darby is to be credited with introducing the term 'Pre-millennialism' as a new Christian theory, the brothers Lyman and Milton Stewart, oil barons who founded the Bible College in Los Angeles, should be credited with coining the word 'fundamentalism'. In 1910, they published a twelve-volume series of books entitled *The Fundamentals*, which contained ninety articles written by several Protestant theologians. The message in these books, which were given out to three million pastors and preachers in the United States, was not only to spread the gospel but also to encourage Christians to go back to the basics or the fundamentals when it came to reading and interpreting Scripture. The response to these works from religious leaders and their flocks was extremely positive, especially since the Stewart brothers also discouraged any recognition of modernism which was, at the time, part of the intellectual wave which included Darwin's theory of evolution and Sigmund Freud's focus on the subconscious mind.

To the outside observer, the religious beliefs of Evangelicals may often seem excessive, and their claims of having met and talked to the Lord difficult to fathom. Although enthusiastic religious observance was a feature of revivalism and is prominent in the history of both the Catholic and Protestant faiths, its most powerful modern example, the Pentecostal or Charismatic movement, dates to the early part of the twentieth century.

The Pentecostal movement first began in 1901 in Topeka, Kansas, at a Bible school run by Charles Fox Parham. Five years later, the movement reached national prominence at a now-famous revival meeting led by the black evangelist William J. Seymour at the Azusa Street mission in Los Angeles. Seymour, a former slave freed after the Civil War, was searching for an alternative faith that was separate from the classic White Protestant establishment. On 9 April 1906, a Mr Edward Lee became convinced that he was receiving the Holy Spirit at a prayer meeting at his house in Los Angeles. Others followed, and by 18 April the story had reached the front page of the *Los Angeles Times*. Pentecostalism had been born.

Although the movement was at first marked by its racially integrated services, the spectacle of black and white combining in ecstasy eventually proved too much, and in 1924 the movement split, only reuniting in 1998. White Americans were initially attracted to the Azusa Street mission because of a joyful style of worship found among Africans who had been converted by Christian missionaries. Yet when integration became an issue in the South, those same white Pentecostal Christians who had no compunction about worshipping with blacks nonetheless opposed integrating schools, hotels, restaurants and bathrooms throughout the South.

Many of the white population who joined the movement did so because they believed it was the best way to have a direct relationship with God and because it gave them a certain status. The most sensational aspect of the Pentecostals is their physical transformation, during which, they believe, the Holy Ghost enters their spirit, enabling them to 'speak in tongues'. Once called Holy Rollers, their religious services are filled with raw emotion, bodily contortions, and gibberish. As for being able to 'speak or pray in tongues', first-hand reports by Pentecostals attest that it was rare for any person 'possessed by the spirit' to break out in tongues. Many of the early adherents, to their great dismay, were unable to do so. For example, according to the Christian historian Barton W. Stone, 'the physical anguish that led up to actually speaking in tongues included piercing screams, shrieks of distress and lying in a lifeless state for often more than an hour. Often the head would jerk back and forth while the person possessed fell to the floor, his facial features indistinguishable.' Then again, people would 'bark or laugh raucously, or run out of fear or sing in a state of joy'.[4] Though their initial belief was that 'speaking in tongues' would hasten the second coming of Jesus on earth, when that did not happen, Pentecostals changed doctrine. 'Speaking in tongues' became a more direct way to reach God through prayer.

In the beginning, the early Pentecostal membership was largely destitute and alienated from the rest of society, poorly educated and socially marginal outcasts who looked for escape from their own miseries. The leaders, however, were of the upwardly mobile segment of the middle class. When the Pentecostal movement began, it tended to embrace Evangelical doctrine, although in recent years, Pentecostal worshippers have increasingly remained within their churches rather than leaving to form their own, and this has greatly strengthened the links between Evangelical theology and the Charismatic style of worship.

Currently, Pentecostals worship in suburban megachurches as well as city storefronts. Bolstered by indigenous Christian movements in Africa, Asia and Latin America,

Pentecostal and Charismatic Christians have more than two hundred and fifty million members worldwide, making it the largest form of Christianity after Roman Catholicism, and the fastest growing. Membership includes some of the most powerful, rich and educated people throughout the world. One devout Pentecostal Christian is John Ashcroft, who served as Attorney General during George W. Bush's first four years as President of the United States. Ashcroft is only one of four million Pentecostal believers among the eighty million Evangelical Christians in the United States today, according to a study undertaken by Aris (the most comprehensive religious survey organization) in January 2004. More than any other member of Bush's administration, John Ashcroft, when he was head of the United States Department of Justice, managed to change the judicial climate as well as the civic and cultural atmosphere of the United States. Though Ashcroft was not the first Assembly of God member to serve in a presidential administration – James Watt served as Secretary of Interior in the Reagan administration – he had far more influence on domestic policy than Secretary Watt had. James Watt, however, is remembered for getting up on the floor of the United States Congress to announce that protecting natural resources was unimportant in the light of the imminent return of Jesus Christ. In public testimony, he said: '. . . after the last tree is felled, Christ will come back.'[5] As for Ashcroft, on numerous occasions he used the power of God to justify his actions when he repeatedly tried to supersede civil law on the grounds that he was exercising the Lord's will. In December 2003, a United States district judge had to reprimand him for his repeated efforts to criminalize doctors in the state of Oregon who were merely obeying the law that allowed physician–assisted suicide, a law that had twice been approved by voters in that state.

The former Attorney General, throughout his entire time in the Bush administration, believed that government should legislate morality, although he conceded that it cannot legislate spirituality. Ashcroft, along with a large number of senators, congressmen and high-ranking military officers, participated in weekly prayer breakfasts, which still continue today. As well, Ashcroft held daily prayer sessions in his office at the Department of Justice. According to a source in his office, three quarters of Ashcroft's staff were also Pentecostal Christians, who under his guidance took part in a prayer session every morning before the start of the business day. Ashcroft, throughout his tenure as Attorney General, did not relinquish his belief that 'speaking in tongues' meant his prayers would go directly to God, thus avoiding the devil who lingers in the second level of heaven, intent on hijacking the prayers of good Christians so they will never reach God Himself who resides in the third level of heaven.

During those times, he and his staff communicated directly with Jesus in an unintelligible language. One staff member,[6] who is not a Pentecostal Christian, admitted that there was 'no pressure' to join in these prayer sessions and it was understood that an 'outsider' was unable to pray in tongues. But there was nonetheless a subtle understanding that every-one, 'regardless of his religious beliefs', should take time during every day to 'try to get in touch with God'. According to that same source, the only thing more offensive to the Attorney General than an atheist was a Christian who was not Evangelical or born-again. In the same spirit, when Ashcroft conducted interviews of prospective members of his staff, his first and foremost concern was not necessarily their judicial experience but rather their position on certain issues that, for him, separated the moral from the immoral or Good from Evil. According to one applicant, Ashcroft greeted him with the following questions: 'What are the rights of a fetus?' and 'What in the Constitution guarantees rights to homosexuals?' Though Ashcroft, when he served as Attorney General, made a feeble attempt to censor his pronouncements of the infallible links between church and state whenever he addressed the nation or the world in the mainstream media, his words remained pure religious emotion when spoken to those who shared his beliefs. One Evangelical Christian member of Congress I interviewed admitted that during those daily prayer sessions God often enabled Mr Ashcroft to resolve 'political dilemmas' which, in his opinion, non-believers would never have been able to do in time to protect the country from other horrific acts of terror.

In defence of his religious practices and beliefs, the former Attorney General claimed that as a gospel singer, lay preacher and popular speaker at Christian forums, he relied on his faith as his 'compass and his core' in making political decisions. In further defending himself against accusations that he often superseded civil law, he maintained that he was only 'exercising God's will'. 'We are a nation called to defend freedom,' he has said, 'a freedom that is not the grant of any government or document but that is our endowment from God.'[7]

A formidable individual, Ashcroft is intelligent, articulate and often charming, a man whose ambition matches his deep religious faith, allowing him to believe that all the trappings of his political achievements and power are a direct gift from God. In his autobiography *Lessons From a Father to His Son*, published in 1998, he writes about his campaign victories and failures in his home state of Missouri as 'resurrections and crucifixions', comparing his professional life with the trials and tribulations of Jesus Christ. He also adheres strictly to the rules of his faith, which include abstinence from smoking, drinking, pre-marital sex and dancing, which he believes to be sexually arousing; nor does he drive or use electronic equipment on the Sabbath. As proof of his deep commitment, Ashcroft ordered that the statue of Justice, a marble figure of a naked woman, be wrapped in a blue shroud to cover her bare breasts. Curiously, despite Ashcroft's departure from the Department of Justice, the statue remains covered.

For John Ashcroft, those who reject God's teachings must take the consequences He inflicts and consider them to be divine. For instance, he has always believed that those who have contracted, suffered and died from AIDS have been punished for their own 'misconduct' by the good Lord Himself. Those beliefs were made evident during Ashcroft's time as Governor of Missouri, when Senator Harry Wiggins, the spokesman for an apolitical group that was trying to get state funding for a hospice called the Good Samaritan Home for AIDS patients in Kansas City, came to him to try to change his mind, since the Governor had already twice vetoed a state grant for $900,000 for the hospice. After Wiggins had pleaded his case, explaining that if the home wasn't funded, indigent AIDS patients would be forced to die on the street, Ashcroft replied, 'I understand this would be the place that is cheapest for them to die, but they are in this situation because of their own misconduct.'[8] Ashcroft's position was that the state of Missouri was not financially responsible for those citizens who had rejected God's teachings and acted in an immoral way to bring upon themselves what he considered to be 'His just punishment for their sins'.

Whenever Ashcroft took a political position against homosexuality or abortion or any other act that he and his fellow Evangelicals opposed, he always backed up his arguments by pointing to the Bible and the infallibility of

Scripture. Throughout his political career in the Senate, as Attorney General of Missouri, as Governor, and later as Attorney General under President George W. Bush, he was always a staunch foe of gay rights. As a loyal member of the National Rifle Association, he continues to subscribe to their creed that the Second Amendment, which proclaims the right of the citizenry to bear arms in the context of citizen militias, justifies his opposition to any ban on the sale of assault weapons. Immediately following the events of 11 September 2001, Ashcroft supported ten additional amendments to the Constitution, including one which makes it less difficult to amend the entire document.

Ashcroft's determination to include God and religion in his political career was not unusual, as the Pentecostal church considers every one of its members a minister or missionary charged with the task of converting new souls. Because he took the edicts of his faith seriously, Ashcroft consistently promoted his personal theological beliefs in the form of legislative initiatives, implementing new laws rather than upholding and interpreting the Constitution and the laws of the land. As one of the main architects of the Patriot Act, which allows the Attorney General to arrest and hold suspected terrorists without charge and without benefit of legal counsel for an indefinite period of time, Ashcroft maintained, 'There is a higher calling than public service, which is service to God.'[9]

CHAPTER FOUR

A Vision of a New World Order

Let all the earth fear the Lord; let all the people of the world revere Him.

(Psalm 33:8)

PRIOR to the early 1970s Evangelicals were less active in politics than their present prominence would suggest. The emphasis on individual salvation and moral rehabilitation through Christ, as well as disenchantment with modern Godless society, meant that many remained aloof from secular politics altogether. Furthermore, they remained only a small fraction of the Protestant faith, although one that was growing fast. But the period before the Second World War gives some important indicators of their potential power and their likely political allegiances. For in the 1920s both Evangelical enthusiasm and political religion would leave their mark on the life of the Republic.

Throughout history, Jesus has been adapted to fit the social and cultural needs of the people. Just as readily, throughout American history, politicians have insinuated religion into most of the major issues of American life, beginning with slavery, civil and human rights, the Vietnam War, the environment, gay and women's rights, gun control, the death penalty, abortion and evolution versus creationism. In fact,

56

one of the main events that brought the term fundamentalism into the lexicon of the American public was the Scopes 'Monkey' Trial which took place in Tennessee in 1925.

John T. Scopes taught biology in a grade school in Dayton, Tennessee, a state where any reference to Darwin's theory of evolution was prohibited by law. Scopes intentionally challenged the law by testing his constitutional right to freedom of speech. His subsequent trial turned into a media circus between the 'intellectual elite' and the Christian Fundamentalists. Scopes was represented by Clarence Darrow, and the state of Tennessee was represented by William Jennings Bryan. Bryan, the prosecutor in the case, who had been the unsuccessful Republican candidate for President of the United States when he ran against William McKinley in 1900, went so far as to accuse Charles Darwin of being responsible for the atrocities committed during the First World War. Bryan said, 'German officers claimed that after reading Darwin, they decided to declare war, fighting to the end until only the strong survived which was Darwin's theory of the survival of the fittest.'[1]

Though Bryan won the case, Darrow forced him to admit certain facts that served to ridicule his beliefs in the process. By putting him on the stand, the famed defence lawyer managed to get Bryan to concede that the world was older than six thousand years and that God did not create the world in six days as told in Genesis. Since the trial was covered daily in newspapers throughout the United States, the intellectual elite became familiar enough with the new religious wave to recognize that Fundamentalist thinking was the antithesis of the natural progression of culture and scientific progress. H.L. Mencken, for example, denounced Fundamentalists as the ultimate 'scourge of the nation', and the enemy of 'science and intellectual liberty'.[2] Even today, the debate continues

57

with issues that are more complex, given the progress made in the fields of science, medicine and technology. President George W. Bush, when asked his opinion about Darwin's theory, replied, 'The verdict is still out on that one.'[3]

Alcohol and its devastating effects have also been a primary source of salvation and redemption which Evangelicals have used throughout the centuries. As they have always inveighed against the evils of drink, it is no wonder that George W. Bush's successful battle with alcohol has been used by them as proof that God not only forgives the sinner but rewards him with extraordinary gifts. His rise from alcoholic and failed businessman to President of the United States is no small example of the power of the Lord.

Decades before the creation of Alcoholics Anonymous, Evangelical preachers had helped poor addicts wean themselves off drink through the administration of the Holy Spirit. By the end of the First World War, American reformers had already succeeded in driving narcotic drugs to the margins of legality. Now an alliance of progressives, socialists and Evangelicals succeeded in outlawing the sale of alcohol through an amendment to the US Constitution and the passage of the Volstead Act in October 1919 outlawed the sale of beverages with an alcohol content greater than 0.5 per cent by volume from January of the following year. The Prohibition was by no means an exclusively Evangelical achievement. It enjoyed widespread support across the political spectrum. But it was the first time that Evangelical enthusiasm for confrontation with evil and its extirpation through changes in the law found decisive expression on the national stage in America. In alcohol they had an unambiguous enemy and for a while Prohibition must have seemed to be a spectacular triumph for the forces of righteousness. In fact, while the legal basis of Prohibition was both impressive and oppressive, the human thirst for intoxication proved stronger. The ban on the sale of alcohol lasted only until 1933, although the effects of Prohibition on the United States were lasting. Both organized crime and the federal government gained in power and prominence from the rise of a black market in alcohol. The inadvertent part played by private religious enthusiasm in the promotion of public vice did not, however, discourage later advocates of moral renewal from seeking to outlaw the inevitable. Popular desire to cast out various vices would continue to provide economic and political elites with mouth-watering opportunities for profit and power-grabbing, as we shall see.

In April 1935, Abraham Vereide, a Norwegian immigrant who made his living as a travelling preacher, founded the Family, a clandestine organization of devout Evangelical Christians whose goal was to introduce powerful men to Jesus Christ and to effect hidden acts of diplomacy. The Family, perhaps the most influential Evangelical organization of all time, like the Prohibitionists, appealed and continues to appeal, across party lines.[4] The Family was one of the principal benefactors of former Attorney General Ashcroft's prayer breakfasts held in the Department of Justice basement. In fact, the National Prayer Breakfast, established in 1953 by Ed McAteer and Mike Evans, a leader in the 'Mission-to-the-Jews' movement, an Evangelical enterprise to convert Jews to Jesus (Evans always preferred to be known as a Mid-East expert), is the Family's only publicized gathering. These prayer breakfasts, started during the annual convention of the National Religious Broadcasters, ultimately had enormous political influence in the 1980 presidential election. Held every February in Washington, D.C., with Congressional sponsorship, they continue today and are still supported by the Family. Each year, 3,000 delegates, representing many foreign countries, pay $425 each to attend the breakfast, which the Family considers an effective venue to recruit the rich and powerful and encourage them to 'participate in smaller and more frequent prayer meetings where they can further their political goals by counting on Jesus to take a personal interest in their affairs'.

One night, while lying in bed fretting about socialists, Wobblies, and a Swedish Communist who, he was sure, planned to bring Seattle under the control of Moscow, Vereide received a visitation: a voice, and a light in the dark, bright and blinding. The next day he met a friend, a wealthy businessman and former major, and the two men agreed upon a spiritual plan. They enlisted nineteen business executives in a weekly breakfast meeting and together they prayed, convinced that Jesus alone could redeem Seattle and crush the radical unions. They wanted to give Jesus a vessel, and so they asked God to raise up a leader. One of their number, a city councilman named Arthur Langlie, stood and said, 'I am ready to let God use me.' Langlie was made first mayor and later governor, backed in both campaigns by money and muscle from his prayer-breakfast friends, whose number had rapidly multiplied. Vereide and his new brothers spread out across the North-west in chauffeured vehicles (a $20,000 Dusenburg carried brothers on one mission, he boasted). 'Men,' wrote Vereide, 'thus quickened.' Prayer breakfast groups were formed in dozens of cities, from San Francisco to Philadelphia. There were already enough men ministering to the down-and-out, Vereide had decided; his mission field would be men with the means to seize the world for God. Vereide called his potential flock of the rich and powerful, those in need only of the 'real' Jesus, the 'up-and-out'.[5]

60

Vereide arrived in Washington, D.C., on 6 September 1941. Within a day or two, he organized his first prayer meeting in the nation's Capitol, which was attended by more than one hundred congressmen. By the end of the war, in 1945, one third of all American senators attended his weekly prayer meetings, determined to join Vereide in his vision of a 'new world order'. By then, he had already begun to organize prayer meetings for delegates to the United Nations as well, reaching an international audience, advising them on what he described as 'God's plan for rebuilding from the wreckage of the war'.

In 1946, Vereide toured the world, carrying with him letters of introduction from half a dozen American senators and congressmen as well as from Paul G. Hoffman, director of the Marshall Plan. In addition he travelled with a mandate from General John Hildring, Assistant Secretary of State, which listed those he considered to be 'good' Germans of the 'predictable type', who Vereide believed could be 'used in the tremendous task of reconstruction'. The only condition that Vereide required for their release was that these ex-Nazis or marginal figures within the Third Reich would swear to 'worship Jesus the way they had worshipped Hitler'.

In 1955, Senator Frank Carlson, a close advisor to President Dwight D. Eisenhower and a friend of Vereide, organized a meeting during which he stated that the Family's mission was to be a 'worldwide spiritual offensive', aimed at defeating, destroying and disarming the Soviet Union. By the time John Fitzgerald Kennedy was elected President of the United States in 1960, the Family's spiritual offensive had fronts on every continent but Antarctica, which they would visit in the 1980s to set up an office.

By the late 1960s, Vereide's speeches at local prayer breakfasts across the United States had become minor news events, and Family members, who travelled all over the world on behalf of Jesus Christ, began to garner media attention. In 1966, two years before Vereide died, he wrote a letter saying that the moment had come to 'submerge the institutional image of the Family'.

'No longer will the Family recruit powerful members in public,' he wrote, 'nor will we recruit so many. There must be, as always in the history of the world, one man or a small core who have caught the vision for their country and become aware of what a "leadership led by God" could mean spiritually to the nation and to the world . . . It is these men, banded together, who can accomplish the vision that God gave me years ago.' After Vereide's death, those politicians who were the most active within the organization – Dwight D. Eisenhower, John F. Kennedy, and George H.W. Bush – concluded that the Family would function under what they called 'biblical capitalism', which continues with the group's financial and political influence today.

During the 1960s, the Family forged relationships among American government and anti-Communist and dictatorial elements within Africa's postcolonial leadership. The Brazilian dictator General Costa e Silva, with Family support, was overseeing regular fellowship groups for Latin American leaders, and in Indonesia, General Suharto (who ordered several hundred thousand 'communists' to be killed, giving him the dubious honour of being one of the century's most murderous dictators) was ruling over a group of fifty Indonesian legislators. In 1978, the Family secretly helped the Carter administration organize a worldwide call to prayer with Menachem Begin and Anwar Sadat, and during the Reagan administration the Family helped build friendships between the United States government and such men as Salvadoran General Carlos Eugenios Vides Casanova, convicted by a Florida jury of the torture of thousands, and Honduran General Gustavo Alvarez Martinez, an Evangelical minister, who was linked to the Central Intelligence Agency (CIA). More recently, in 2001, it brought together the warring leaders of the Congo and Rwanda for a clandestine meeting, leading to an eventual peace accord in July 2002.

Today, membership into the Family consists mostly of politicians with close ties to foreign heads of state and businessmen in the oil and aerospace industries. One of the former members of the Family, a well-known senator from the Mid-West whom I interviewed in Washington in 2003, broke with the group because of what he describes as 'religious differences'. He nonetheless had only good things to say about the organization. The senator supports The Family's goal to forge 'relationships beyond the din of *vox populi*', although he claims that he cut off ties with the group because of their declaration that 'God's Covenant with the Jews has been broken and The Family is the new chosen-by-God Himself.' 'I just think on that point they went too far,' the senator explains. 'Everything else they are doing is great stuff for the good of democracy, but I just think their success rate has gone to their heads and made them believe they are holier than the Almighty and holier than the Jewish people [with whom] God made the Abrahamic Covenant.'

According to sources within the Family, its annual budget is more than $250 million, although those same sources claim that that figure is 'only a fraction of the Family's finances'. The money comes primarily from 'friends' of the organization, private donations from wealthy businessmen, foreign governments, church congregations, or mainstream foundations that 'may be unaware of The Family's activities'. Some of the largest donors include Michael Timmis, a Detroit lawyer and Republican fund-raiser; Paul Temple, a private investor from Maryland; and Jerome A. Lewis, a former CEO of the Petro-Lewis Corporation. Most recently, this secret organization has contributed more than $10 million to aid the Israeli government in the construction of the controversial fence dividing Israel from the Occupied Territories. They are also involved in financing the dismantling of Israeli settlements in Gaza and parts of the West Bank from which Israeli troops will withdraw and resettling those who have been displaced to areas of the Occupied Territories remaining under Israeli control.

The Family maintains a closely guarded computerized list of its members, issues no cards, collects no official dues, and asks its members not to speak about the group or its activities. The members of this secret organization, which crosses political party lines, have among them Senators Don Nickles (Republican, Oklahoma), Charles Grassley (Republican, Iowa), Pete Domenici (Republican, New Mexico), John Ensign (Republican, Nevada), James Inhoff (Republican, Oklahoma), Bill Nelson (Democrat, Florida) and Conrad Burns (Republican, Montana). Members from the House of Representatives include Jim DeMint (Republican, South Carolina), Frank Wolf (Republican, Virginia), Joseph Pitts (Republican, Pennsylvania), Zach Wamp (Republican, Tennessee) and Bart Stupak (Democrat, Michigan).

The organization has operated under many guises, including the National Organization for Christian Leadership, the International Christian Leadership, the National Leadership Council, Fellowship House, the Fellowship Foundation, the National Fellowship Council, and the International Foundation. These groups are intended to draw attention away from the Family and to prevent it from becoming, in the words of one Family member, 'a target for misunderstanding'.

While Vereide was busy saving Seattle from the Soviets, another religious politician was having a more spectacular, if less immediately lasting, impact on America's national life. Its success, though short-lived, provided a template for an activity that the Evangelicals would eventually make their own. Father Coughlin was a radio broadcaster in the 1920s and 1930s whose early support for Roosevelt and the New Deal shifted towards an apocalyptic anti-communism and growing sympathy for the path out of depression apparently offered by Mussolini and Hitler. At the peak of his popularity he was receiving 30,000 letters per week, and was a figure of considerable political power. His repeated claims that 'international bankers' were behind the rise of Communism gave a decidedly anti-Semitic tone to his broadcasts and had a lasting influence on the 'lunatic fringe'. More importantly, as Donald Warren argues in *Radio Priest*,[6] Coughlin was a pioneer of the broadcasting style that saturates American radio today.

CHAPTER FIVE

Spreading the Gospel

The nations have fallen into the pit they have dug; their feet are caught in the net they have hidden.

(Psalm 9:15)

IN 1934, Evangelical preachers discovered a way to be present in millions of American homes when the Council of Churches, a group representing the mainstream Protestant denominations, formed their own broadcasting units. General radio and television stations were reluctant to include a Christian agenda on their airwaves. As a result, separate religious stations were created to reach the general public, for the first time. The Evangelical community realized that if they were going to spread their message on the radio, their faithful listeners would ultimately be the ones to support this new enterprise. With millions of dollars pouring into these newly formed electronic ministries, those who preached the gospel on radio and eventually on television, became highly respected because of their new-found financial status. Converting souls to Jesus Christ became a multi-million dollar enterprise.

One of the first and most famous preachers on the radio during the 1930s and 1940s was Aimee Semple McPherson (1899–1944), certainly the first woman during the 1930s and

1940s to spread her religious message through the airwaves. Originally ordained as a Baptist minister, then a Pentecostal, McPherson was not only a pioneer in media Evangelism, but also the first preacher to be accused of sexual misconduct. Sexy, beautiful, extroverted, twice married and divorced, and with a slew of lovers among the Hollywood set, Aimee Semple McPherson knew exactly how to use the media for her own purposes. Throughout her career, her personal antics and escapades became as legendary as her faith. At one point during her career, she staged her own kidnapping. Weeks after she disappeared, she was found 'wandering and confused' on a California beach. In fact, she had not been kidnapped at all but rather had disappeared to have some 'private time' with a married lover, away from the public and the press. Other than her theatrics and her sex appeal, McPherson was also famous for healing people during her religious services at the Four Square Gospel Church at the Angelus Temple in Los Angeles, California, which she founded and which still exists today. In the course of her career, the beautiful Evangelical preacher amassed a multi-million-dollar fortune with her powers of healing.

Billy Graham, another pioneer in spreading the Evangelical message over the airwaves, has had a spiritual influence over every American President since Harry S. Truman was elected in 1948. Billy Graham began his career when he came to the attention of the press baron William Randolph Hearst, who ordered his newspapers to give the young preacher extensive coverage. By 1951, Graham had become a television celebrity throughout the United States and, later on, worldwide. Graham is credited not only with insinuating Evangelical religion into the mainstream media, spreading the gospel in the written press, radio and television, and eventually into political life, but also with helping George

W. Bush to give up drink and find Jesus. On his own, Graham is a fascinating figure, a man who is credited with influencing Harry S. Truman to recognize the State of Israel in 1948.

Before the creation of the State of Israel, when the nations of the world dismissed the Jews as a scattered people, the majority of the Christian world maintained that the homeless condition of the Jewish people was because the Jews had rejected Jesus as their Messiah. President Truman, a Democrat and a devout Baptist, first invited the Reverend Billy Graham to the White House to lead a prayer breakfast. Undoubtedly, Truman was influenced not only by his own adherence to Scripture but also by Graham when he defied the international community by recognizing the State of Israel. According to his daughter, Margaret Truman Daniel, her father not only had deep Christian convictions but also read and memorized the Bible during his entire life, which made Israel, for him, a moral imperative.

Michael Benson, author of *Harry S Truman and the Founding of Israel*,[1] wrote that by the age of fourteen Truman 'had read the Bible in its entirety four times. By the time Truman established a relationship with the Reverend Billy Graham, his conversance with the biblical history of the Middle East clearly played a significant part in his attempt to formulate his own presidential policy towards Palestine . . . Heavily influenced by a biblical upbringing with Judeo Christian themes, and by a Baptist training that stressed a Jewish return to Zion, Truman's favorite psalm was number 17, "By the rivers of Babylon, there we sat down, yea, we wept, when we remembered Zion".'

Further, as reported in Benson's book, in a conversation with Graham, Truman admitted, shortly after he recognized the Jewish State, that 'the Old Testament had been one

68

crucial factor in his commitment to the Jewish people that someday they would have a homeland of their own.'

After Israel became a reality, President Truman was both lauded and criticized by the Evangelical and Jewish communities. According to Benson, in response to non-Evangelical Christians who accused Truman of recognizing Israel only to curry favour with the Jewish voters in the United States, Truman claimed that he had always thought of himself as 'Cyrus, the Persian emperor who defeated the Babylonian ruler, Nebuchadnezzar, and allowed the Jews in 538 BC to leave their captivity and to return to Zion.' When a supporter of Truman's once complimented him for his importance to the creation of the State of Israel, he responded, 'Important, hell! I am the American Cyrus.'

Billy Graham is also someone who has managed to forge strong ties between Evangelical Christians and the Catholic Church.

With all the political and financial power the Christian Right in America has gained during the last twenty-some years, it is strange that their domestic agenda has focused primarily on issues that would result in sexual repression and diminishment of human rights. Even those born-again Christians who use their political and financial clout, rather than resorting to violence, have concentrated on topics that would regulate some of the most private feelings, emotions and opinions of their fellow human beings: prayer in school, pornography, adultery, euthanasia, stem-cell research that involves the harvesting of human embryos, the biblical 'eye for an eye' regarding the death penalty, as well as the all-encompassing topic that falls under their heading of 'family values'.

One of the peculiar aspects of the edicts of the Christian Right is their obsession with abortion. It is an issue about which the Christian Right agrees with the Roman Catholic Church. Given the Fundamentalists' fierce opposition to Catholic theological doctrine, the abortion issue has become the most obvious common ground for their joint political action. The Fundamentalists endorse violent civil action and extreme political measures to protect the rights of unborn children.

On a regular basis since at least 1972, Billy Graham has met with converts to Catholicism, whom he directs back to the Vatican for regular 'follow-ups'. Graham's gospel is often a Roman Catholic gospel. Throughout the years, Catholic leaders have learned they have nothing to fear from Graham's crusades and often use those crusades to retrieve non-practising Catholics, and even gain proselytes to their faith. During mass meetings led by Graham, when he calls for the audience to 'receive Christ' or make 'the step of faith', or 'to come to Christ', his words are helpful for Roman Catholic leaders, and are sometimes taken up by Roman clerics, to include their sacramental gospel. Graham, cooperating with his Catholic friends, ensures that no one leaves those mass crusades without some kind of commitment to God and religion. Once they are in the realm of the Lord, even as Catholics, they are open to a privileged encounter with Jesus that would give them 'born-again' status. In the revolving door of sinning and saving, Billy Graham has all the exits covered. The first step is to find common ground between Evangelicals and Catholics. The second step is to voice those issues which are dear to the hearts and minds of both born-agains and the Vatican. The third step is to approach Catholics, armed with support for the two biggest issues in their rhetoric – abortion and homosexuality – before nudging them gently over to the Christian Right. It is a temptation too glorious to refuse – a personal relationship with Jesus Christ.

This does not always sit well with the born-agains. In Wilson Ewin's book, *The Assimilation of Evangelist Billy Graham into the Roman Catholic Church*,[2] he writes (pp. 38-9): 'For some unexplainable or even mysterious reason, Billy Graham is unable to discern the theological, moral and spiritual soul of Roman Catholicism. Likewise, he has failed to grasp, or worse still, has chosen to ignore the historical character of the entire Vatican system. Instead, he has chosen to become attracted, impressed and finally to honor and follow the Holy See. The result has been a tragic failure on his part to understand the difference between the truth of God's Word and the utter blackness of Roman Catholicism.'

Graham's personal affinity for Catholicism has a long and often contradictory history, beginning during the early days of his influence. In an interview with the all-male religious bonding group Promise Keepers for their *New Man* magazine in March/April 1997, Graham said, 'Early on in my life, I didn't know much about Catholics. But through the years, I have made many friends within the Roman Catholic Church. In fact, when we hold a crusade in a city now, nearly all the Roman Catholic churches support it. And when we went to Minneapolis-St. Paul, Minnesota, for the crusade [in 1997], we saw St. Paul, which is largely Catholic, and Minneapolis, which is largely Lutheran, both supporting the crusade. That wouldn't have happened twenty-five years ago.' At the end of the crusade in Portland, Oregon in September 1992, the *Catholic Sentinel* made the following proclamation: 'Graham's message is for people to return to God and their churches . . . Graham offered special praise for the Catholic Church, saying "We're delighted that the Roman Catholic Church now cooperates with us wherever we go . . ." '[3]

In 1948, however, when he was asked what he thought the Four Square Gospel Church would do during their

August conclave in Copenhagen, Graham made the following statement on his weekly radio programme: 'I believe they are going to nominate the Antichrist.' Also in 1948, Graham called Roman Catholics 'one of the three gravest menaces facing orthodox Christianity'.[4] And yet, in 1961, he attended the World Council of Churches (WCC) assembly in New Delhi and later in Uppsala, Sweden in 1968. Today, Graham has become one of Pope John Paul II's biggest admirers, made evident when he concocted a plan in 1989 to award the Pope the 'Prince of Peace Prize' (which the Pope declined), and also described the Pope as 'the greatest religious leader of the modern world', and as a 'statesman, a pastor, and an Evangelist'.[5]

Similar to alliances that the Evangelicals make with the Jewish people, that with the Catholics is based both on the Bible and political expediency. Concerning abortion and homosexuality, way back in 1966 Graham already understood the benefits of embracing the Catholic church, especially when it came to taking a position against the mainstream Protestants who were socially, politically and culturally the polar opposite of the born–again Christian community. 'I find myself closer to Catholics than the radical Protestants,' Graham said in an interview with the *Philadelphia Evening Bulletin*. 'I think the Roman Catholic Church today is going through a second Reformation. I found my beliefs are essentially the same as those of orthodox Catholics. We only differ on some matters of later church tradition.'[6] Graham also found an ally within the Catholic Church as it concerned protecting its adherents throughout Eastern Europe during the heyday of the Soviet Union.

Another influential Evangelical who has used the media to promote the Evangelical message is the Reverend Pat Robertson. Robertson, the Evangelical preacher who ran unsuccessfully for the Republican presidential nomination in 1988 against George Bush, is most famous for having founded the Christian Broadcast Network which currently reaches 59 million homes throughout America. The idea was that Evangelicals would have their own Sunday services reaching hundreds of millions, to achieve which Robertson formed what he called the '700 Club', which allowed people to join only if they sent in an initial membership fee of $700 to the Robertson ministry. With all the millions that Robertson managed to get from his Evangelical listening audience, he was nonetheless unable to garner enough financial support to match the deep pockets of big business that supported George Bush in his bid for the presidency.

Throughout his career Robertson has always considered himself a friend of Israel, and was honoured in July 2002 by the Jewish State, which conferred upon him its 'State of Israel Friendship Award'. However, past statements and writings contradict his professed love for the Jewish people both in a biblical context and in everyday life. For example, in his book *The New World Order*,[7] Robertson wrote that there is an Invisible Cord that can be traced from European bankers in the nineteenth century who, he maintains, ordered the assassination of Abraham Lincoln. Also included in Robertson's Invisible Cord theory is the link between the Communist rabbi who, along with Karl Marx, the Trilateral Commission, the House of Morgan and British bankers, funded the Soviet KGB. Both these unholy links, according to Robertson, conspired to dominate the world under the aegis of Lucifer. According to writer and intellectual Michael Lind's review of Robertson's 1992 bestseller in the *New York Review of Books*, 'Robertson relies heavily on classic anti-Semitic texts such as the Protocols of the Elders of Zion . . .

73

Robertson's theories about Jewish bankers and Jewish revolutionaries are central to his conspiracy theory.'[8] Even today, on his Christian Broadcast Network, Robertson continues to preach that world Jewry will either be destroyed or converted in the End Times.

The advent of the Cold War produced a religious morality in the United States as Americans began to equate the evils of godless Communism with the sin of rejecting God and religion. The ultra right-wing John Birch Society was founded, named after a Baptist minister and American intelligence officer during the Second World War, who was ultimately murdered by the Chinese Communists in 1945. The ultra-conservative organization, the National Religious Broadcasters, led by Ben Armstrong, began combining religious messages with anti-Communist rhetoric that targeted Christians repressed in the Soviet Union and Eastern Europe. Bill Bright, who founded the Campus Crusade for Christ in 1967 in Canada, set up his organization by using the Communist formula of organizing separate cells throughout the world. At the height of the Cold War, the country had already learned from televised broadcasts of the Army–McCarthy Hearings, how the Communist party managed to infiltrate Hollywood by organizing secret revolutionary cells in America. By issuing what he called Four Spiritual Laws, Bill Bright used the same techniques to organize religious cells that would target people for conversion. The last three Spiritual Laws were even accompanied by a diagram indicating the relationship of God to man, God to the sinful man, God and man to Jesus, which resulted in Bright ultimately converting millions of souls by offering the choice between 'the self-directed life' and the 'Christ-directed life'.

Bright's Four Spiritual Laws are as follows:

Law Number One: God 'offers man a wonderful plan for his life'.

Law Number Two: 'Man is sinful and separated from God. Therefore he cannot know and experience God's love and plan for his life.'

Law Number Three: 'Jesus Christ is God's only provision for man's sin. Through Him man can know and experience God's love and plan for his life.'

Law Number Four: People must 'individually receive Jesus Christ as Savior and Lord; then they can know and experience God's love and plan for their lives.'[9]

Bright and his wife Vonett became one of the most successful Evangelical couples in the United States. They signed their now-famous 'Contract With God' in 1951, in which they promised to be 'Christ's slaves'. That promise ultimately resulted in the creation of their campus crusade for Christ. In fact, in 1988 President Ronald Reagan signed into law an annual Campus Crusade for Christ Day that eventually became an official date on the United States calendar. Today, Campus Crusade is active in 191 countries, and has a staff of 26,000 and an annual budget of $374 million. *Money Magazine* has repeatedly called it the 'most efficient religious group' in the United States.

During the 1950s, when America was engaged in a Cold War with the Soviet Union, Evangelicals considered it a silent war that signified the struggle between Good and Evil, between God-fearing Americans and godless Communists. In fact, during the ten years dubbed 'the fabulous fifties', the rhetoric put forward by President Eisenhower concerning the Cold War was that a 'normal' family and 'vigilant' mother were the 'front line' of defence against treason. In 1959, during his famous 'kitchen debate' with Nikita Khrushchev, Eisenhower's vice-president, Richard Nixon, asserted that the superiority of capitalism over Communism was 'embodied not in ideology or military might but in the comforts of a suburban home designed to make things easier for our women'. In the 1950s, those considering themselves the moral fibre of the country linked Communism to a deviant family, and sedition to perverted sexual behaviour. Fifty years ago, the natural tendencies of women were not only inspired by the Bible but were seen as the natural result of physiological, psychological and genetic traits and characteristics. According to sociologist David Riesman,[10] women who refused to bear children in the 1950s were considered peculiar, and women who could not or would not adjust to homemaking were considered unnatural, and diagnosed as perverted, neurotic or schizophrenic. According to Stephanie Coontz's book, *The Way We Never Were*,[11] women confined to psychiatric hospitals in the San Francisco Bay Area during the 1950s were given shock therapy as a way to force them to accept their domestic roles and their husbands' dictates. Shock treatments were also recommended for women who sought abortion on the assumption that failure to want a baby signified dangerous emotional disturbance. A 1954 article in *Esquire* magazine called working wives a 'menace', and a *Life* magazine author termed married women's employment a 'disease'. As for men, bachelors were categorized as immature, infantile, narcissistic, deviant or even pathological. Family advice expert Paul Landis argued that 'except for the sick, deformed, crippled, the emotionally warped and mentally defective, almost everyone has an opportunity and, by clear implication, a duty to marry.'[12]

America in the 1950s, or at least the example set by political and religious leaders for the typical American family, was scandal-free and steeped in a love of God and country. The motto back then was 'a family that prays together stays together.' Evangelicals, born-again or Fundamentalist Christians were determined to infuse a dose of morality, based on the literal interpretation of Scripture, back into the lives of all Americans. One of the leaders of that movement was a powerful and revered Evangelical preacher who has wielded considerable political power in America for more than thirty years – the Reverend Jerry Falwell.

CHAPTER SIX

On the Lord's Side

The Lord is close to the brokenhearted and saves those who are crushed in spirit.

(Psalm 102:13–14)

JERRY Falwell found Jesus Christ on 20 January 1953 at the Park Avenue Baptist Church in Lynchburg, Virginia, on the same night that his best friend, Jim Moon, converted. Years later, Moon would become Falwell's co-pastor at the Thomas Road Baptist Church, which Falwell founded in 1958. Back then the church was housed in an abandoned soda factory, and had only a few members. By 1959, the congregation had grown to three times its original size, and by 1988 it had 18,000 members and 60 associate pastors. Today, the total income of Falwell's Thomas Road Baptist Church is more than $160 million a year, and its service, the Old Time Gospel Hour, is the longest running uninterrupted church service on television, reaching millions of 'lost souls' every Sunday all over the world on 392 television outlets and 600 radio stations in the United States alone. The service is also available twenty-four hours a day on Falwell's website.

Falwell's conversion story is nothing less than inspiring.[1] In 1957, he claims, God let him know that his true calling was to become a pastor himself. 'My heart was burning to serve Christ,' Falwell explains, 'and so I transferred to the Baptist Bible College in Springfield, Missouri to prepare myself for whatever God wanted me to do.' According to him, during his years at that Bible college, God 'literally turned' his life around. 'During my final year of school there, I prayed earnestly for wisdom about what to do with my life, and one night, I had an epiphany while I was driving the usual two hundred miles that I drove every weekend to intern as a youth pastor at Kansas City Baptist Temple. It was on that particular occasion, only several weeks before graduation in May, that the pastor at Kansas City advised me that he would be absent for Sunday service and asked if I would bring the Sunday morning message at the church. I had never done that before, and obviously I was scared, so I prayed and fasted during the week and asked God to let that sermon be a sign if He wanted me to be a pastor or not.' That Sunday Falwell saved nineteen souls who converted to Christ. One of the people whose souls he saved was an elderly lady who told him that she had been a charter member of the church for over twenty years, and had only come to realize when Falwell spoke that she had been born-again. 'I took that to mean that God had sent me a sign,' Falwell continues, 'that being a pastor and saving souls was my true calling.'

Despite Falwell's personal faith and his influence on other Evangelicals, things were changing in America. From the mid-1950s on, people began to look for something different to liberate them from the constraints of tradition. Daring literature with sexually explicit themes, along with confessional art, exploded. Poets like Robert Lowell published their most private thoughts and feelings, while Vladimir Nabokov wrote *Lolita*, the story of a grown man's sexual obsession for his pre-pubescent stepdaughter. In 1960, the

birth control pill was put on the market, which spurred a
nascent sexual revolution, making women equal to men, no
longer forced to pay the ultimate price of pregnancy and
shame because of their libido. The sexual revolution spread
to college campuses throughout the country when women
burned their bras and derided virginity and second–class status
in marriage. Gender roles became a prevalent topic and
eventually included homosexuality when cult figures like
Allan Ginsberg and Robert Mapplethorpe treated their own
homosexuality in their respective writings and visual art. Also
during the 1960s the Cold War receded into the background
to be replaced by the unpopular war in Vietnam. The result
was a further chasm within society between the God-fearing
segment of the population, who equated religion with
patriotism, and those who opposed American involvement
in Vietnam, who were considered to be not only unpatriotic
but sinners in the eyes of the Lord. The radical Evangelical
paper *Sojourners* (formerly *Post-American*), started during the
days of the anti-Vietnam War protests, viewed history as the
struggle between light and darkness.

Ironically, John F. Kennedy, the first Catholic President,
was the one everyone worried about most in terms of not
upholding the separation between church and state, because
he belonged to the most powerful church in the country.
However, the vast bureaucracy of the Catholic Church made
it much less efficient than the small independent businesses of
Evangelical Christianity. When the latter united to mobilize
and influence votes, it made a difference. As for Kennedy and
his awareness of public concern, he was always cautious
about introducing religion into the White House. Still, back
then, the press treated the presidency with reverence and
discretion and was reluctant to delve into the personal lives
of political figures. When President Kennedy summoned

cardinals and bishops to the White House, ostensibly for baptisms and convivial dinners, it was not reported whether or not they also prayed with him during the Cuban missile crisis.

Following President Kennedy's assassination, a different kind of religion and faith once again became part of the political language when Lyndon B. Johnson encouraged the American people to return to God to help them through the 'black period in history'. President Johnson's religious credentials were beyond reproach. A member of the Disciples of Christ Church, which has approximately 800,000 members in the United States and Canada, Johnson believed that his mission was to share the 'good news of Jesus Christ', loving, witnessing and serving 'from our doorsteps to the ends of the earth'. He and the other church members believed that God called upon them to be a faithful growing church that demonstrates true community, deep Christian spirituality, a passion for justice, and above all, to put their faith 'not in creeds, but only in Jesus Christ'.

In 1962, God spoke to Jerry Falwell again, this time about saving the soul of America. The United States Supreme Court, in 1962 and 1963, had taken prayer and Bible reading out of the public school system. Ten years later, in 1973, *Roe* vs. *Wade* opened the door to state-by-state policies on abortion. As far as Falwell and the other Evangelicals were concerned, those decisions amounted to banishing God from the hearts and minds of Americans and declaring open season on the unborn. For them, the United States, supposed to be 'a nation under God' for 200 years, was suddenly completely abandoning the God of America's founding fathers.

The Religious Right was equally incensed that courts and judges were determined to make all religions equal in the

United States, putting Christianity on the same level with Buddhism, Islam and Judaism. Since the other religions were false, in the Fundamentalists' view, that meant that Christianity must also be considered equally false under the law. Legislation even limited the spanking of children by their parents, even though Fundamentalists claimed that the Bible advocated physical punishment, calling it 'a duty for a father to spank his children'. As far as the Evangelicals were concerned, the government was invading the inner sanctum of the family. According to Jerry Falwell and his Evangelical followers, the country began losing its soul when prayer was expelled from the schools, abortion became legal, the divorce rate rose above 50 per cent, and there were approximately one million teenage pregnancies, despite sex education and contraception being taught in the public schools, contrary to Evangelical beliefs that abstinence should be taught instead. Equally offensive to Falwell were the increased use of recreational drugs, acceptance of the gay and lesbian lifestyle, gun control, and Hollywood's influence promoting the portrayal of violence and sex, on television and in the movies. When the Equal Rights Amendment, which supported the feminist revolution, became a viable issue throughout America, the Christian Right believed it challenged the Bible's teachings that a woman's place is in the home. Finally, when the Internal Revenue Service threatened to withdraw tax-exempt status from Evangelical schools and colleges, the Christian Right took that as a declaration of war. Even the United Nations was part of a global plot, bent on creating a one-world socialist government they (the Evangelicals) were convinced would redefine global moral structure.

By 1964, riding on a platform of patriotism and fear of the Soviet threat, Evangelicals nonetheless failed in their attempt to enter national politics when Barry Goldwater, the conservative Republican candidate for President of the United States, was defeated. Goldwater, though not an Evangelical Christian, was their choice because he was a fierce opponent of Communism and an advocate of morality. According to Falwell, even then, there was a positive side to the moral decay of America. In the 1970s, while the Christian consensus was that America was heading rapidly towards the End-Times scenario or Armageddon, there was also the feeling that the disintegration of moral and biblical values would lead Americans to a spiritual awakening that would ultimately translate into concrete political change, in order to save the world from Evil. Rather than being discouraged, Falwell was heartened. 'God and those who are His faithful followers,' he said, 'must never be concerned about popularity or polls. We must only be concerned about God's approval.'

In 1973, when Israel once again defeated the Arab armies during the Yom Kippur War, Falwell and other Evangelical leaders not only stood staunchly behind the Jewish State as the last bastion of democracy in a sea of Soviet-armed Arab nations, but officially clashed with the mainline Protestant churches. It was then, as well, beginning in the 1970s, that an alliance was formed between Evangelical Christians and the Jewish people.

In reaction to the Israeli victories of 1967 and 1973, one of the most virulent anti-Israel campaigns since the post-Second World War era began. While the Evangelicals remained constant in their opinion that the Jewish State was a prerequisite for the second coming of Jesus to earth, mainstream Protestants sympathized with the plight of the Palestinian people, the newly oppressed, displaced victims of Israel, which was seen as an occupying force throughout the West Bank and Gaza. The liberal Protestant church, defining itself in terms of a 'liberation theology', believed Israel had lost its status as victim, given the years that had passed, the Holocaust became a distant memory. The mainstream Protestant churches justified their position because Protestant Americans had defeated the Nazis and therefore bore no guilt for the systematic slaughter of the Jewish people.

By 1975, a United Nations resolution had equated Zionism with racism, while the right-wing Likud party was in power in Israel, supported to a large degree by the Orthodox Jewish community. Though Israel had been founded on the basis of secular Zionism, world disapproval of Israel's behaviour towards the Palestinians contributed to a gradual inclination on the part of Israelis to lean to the religious and political right as a means of turning inward for self-protection. The Jewish community in the United States, seeking new allies to support Israel, gravitated towards Evangelical Christians who, like the Orthodox in Israel, were also politically right wing and fearful of Islam, while opposed to relinquishing any biblical land to the Palestinians. Given their Fundamentalism and political compatibilities, Evangelical and Jewish ties deepened even more through the late 1970s and early 1980s when staunchly anti-Communist Evangelical Christians helped Jews in their struggle to free Soviet Jewry and guarantee them safe passage to Israel. In what is perhaps the first example of how the Fundamentalist Christian community changed laws or pushed through amendments, the Jackson-Vanik Amendment to the Constitution was passed in 1974, calling for the limitation of trade between the United States and the Soviet Union because of the restriction of immigration of Soviet Jews to Israel.

In the 1970s, journalists and other political pundits in the United States began noting that more and more religious activists were appearing, motivated by their determination to bring Judeo-Christian values back into the psyche of the American people. The time was right for them, since Americans were not quite over the tumultuous decade of the 1960s, when people looked for leaders to spearhead such social causes as free love, abortion, open marriage, drugs, gay and women's rights, and pacifism. Communal living, collective thinking, socialist ideals, the sharing of wealth, and rejection of all the materialistic trappings that America had become used to, had reached its peak during the Vietnam War. By the middle of the 1970s, the United States was in fiscal, political and spiritual turmoil. As a backlash to the tumultuous 1960s, people were ready to substitute their 'godless' icons for those who were God-fearing.

John Nelson Darby was back in vogue.

CHAPTER SEVEN

The Politics of Prayer

President Carter inherited an impossible situation . . . and he and his advisors made the worst of it.

(Gaddis Smith, historian)

DURING the 1970s, various radical theologies were in fashion. For some Christians, the basic questions had to do with the need for drastic reinterpretation of traditional beliefs. For others, the fundamental question was not how to adapt to modernity but, rather, how to counter the forces of conformity. People sought a rational definition of a 'Christian lifestyle'.

In 1976, James Earl Carter III was elected President of the United States. A month after his inauguration, both *Time* and *Newsweek* magazines proclaimed 1976 to be the 'year of the Evangelicals'. Carter, who had started life as a peanut farmer and became Governor of Georgia, was an avowed born-again Christian and an outsider to Washington politics. His sister, Ruth Carter Stapleton, was an Evangelical minister who 'laid on hands' to cure people, including those who were well known for their rejection of God. Eldridge Cleaver, for example, the former leader of the Black Panthers, a militant group who believed that only revolution would achieve racial equality, claimed to have found God under Ruth Carter Stapleton's guidance while he was in exile in the south of France. Larry Flint, the pornography king who owned an X-rated publishing empire, was another convert, who told the world that he had been 'healed' by President Carter's sister. Paul Stookey, formerly of Peter, Paul and Mary, a folk-singing group popular in the 1960s, also found God because of Stapleton.

In the beginning of his religious career, Jerry Falwell had involved himself only with domestic issues that were dear to the hearts and minds of all Evangelicals. His justification was that since the world was doomed, there was no point in trying to involve his followers in foreign affairs or even in national political elections. Eventually, as the power of the liberals seemed to increase, especially in their protests against the war in Vietnam, Falwell and other Evangelical leaders came to believe that because 'secular humanists were destroying the world', Christians had to become more involved, or they would share responsibility for the world's demise. 'Unless we Christians were willing to become more assertive in the moral and religious defense of the world,' Falwell announced, 'we would be somewhat responsible for the death of democracy and the disappearance of Christian values.'[1] More significant to this change of policy, a born-again Christian was in the White House and Jerry Falwell and other Evangelicals were inspired to take the Christian Right even further.

In response to this call for biblical politics, in 1977 Falwell founded Liberty University, an Evangelical institution of higher education and, even more crucial to his cause, the Moral Majority, a group meant to broaden the Fundamentalist agenda, with the intention of actively involving his followers in politics. Falwell's goal was to create a spiritual army of young people who were pro-life, pro-Christian morality and pro-America. His rationalization was that during the tumultuous twentieth century, America had been through two world wars and several smaller ones and yet did not lose her 'character or her soul'.

In his capacity as an esteemed religious leader, Falwell not only raised the issues of abortion, prayer in schools, and pornography, but he also called for a strong defence to counter Soviet designs. This call bolstered Fundamentalist support of Israel, considered a democratic outpost in the Middle East.

In the United States, the Moral Majority became the central focus of the Religious Right, a reaction or revolt against the radical climate many Americans considered to run counter to traditional religious and cultural values. In addition to the committed Christians who embraced Falwell's movement, millions of Americans, who were not particularly religious but who feared a collapse of all moral values, felt sympathetic towards certain positions the Moral Majority stood for, most specifically their hatred and fear of Communism. These were the same people who had lost control of their children during the radical 1960s and looked towards the new Religious Right, not as the Kingdom of Righteousness, but as a means to turn the trend or tendency back to family values. Only then could they hope to regain control of their children, who had been lost in an atmosphere of drugs and anti-American rebellion. Rather than considering themselves as 'cohorts' in a right-wing revolution, they regarded themselves as part of a movement back towards tradition.

But as President Carter's first term drew to an end, the Christian Right grew disenchanted with him and his political platforms. Eventually, it was the peace accord between Anwar Sadat and Menachem Begin that turned out to be the beginning of Carter's political demise. For Evangelicals,

Carter was a born-again in humanist clothes, less because he was for abortion and homosexual rights and steadfastly determined to uphold the separation between church and state, than because he was instrumental in giving away biblical territories that had been recorded as having been promised to the Jews in an inerrant biblical text.

While opinions coming from either side of the political spectrum are based on a subjective vision of the world today, two events which occurred in the past three decades have been pivotal in changing the internal texture of the United States. These two separate events were also largely responsible for Evangelical involvement in the Israeli–Palestinian conflict and, to a larger extent, for their increasing influence on American foreign policy.

The first was on 4 November 1979 when Iranian Fundamentalists took Americans hostage in Tehran. The second happened on 11 September 2001 when Islamic terrorists attacked New York and Washington, D.C. In both instances the culprits were foreign, which mobilized not only the Christian Right on the basis of religion, but the rest of the country on the basis of patriotism. As well, on both occasions, the terrorists were Muslims, which reinforced the belief that Islam was evil.

The American hostage drama in Iran has become pivotal in Evangelical Christian lore as well as in their political renaissance. For them, a direct attack by Islamic Fundamentalists against American Judeo-Christian democracy began a Holy War that continues to rage today. Those separate terror attacks acted as a catalyst that fuelled an Evangelical belief that eventually seeped into the consciousness of the secular portion of the country. The 1979 attack was a moment in American history that made all Americans aware that they were not exempt from the violence sweeping the world. The

Evangelicals were able to grasp the significance of the event because of their deep belief in Scripture, knowing that terrorism would ultimately shift American policy towards the rest of the world. By sensing this potential policy shift, and incorporating the inevitability of terrorism into Evangelical rhetoric, they transformed the randomness of the attack, and made it into a harbinger of things to come. As a result of those two terrorist attacks, the United States experienced a religious rebirth that has and will forever influence the political, social, economic and cultural life of all its citizens, regardless of their religious persuasion. Even more significant is that this climate of religious fervour and all-consuming fear brought Evangelical Christians from the periphery of American politics to its centre.

In 1979, when the American hostages were taken from the United States Embassy in Tehran, I was working for CBS television in New York. I remember the moment precisely: 4 November 1979 was a Sunday, and a play-off football game leading up to the Super Bowl was taking place. A group of my colleagues from CBS were at my Manhattan apartment, watching the game, which we never saw to its finish. The studio called with the news that seventy Americans were being held captive, a situation that would last for exactly 444 days.

For more than a year, we covered the story without let-up, following events in Iran and waiting to hear that some kind of negotiations had begun. We learned that 4 November was a significant date in Iran, a double anniversary: Student Day, and the day that the Ayatollah Khomeini had gone into exile in Turkey in 1964. To commemorate those two events, the students planned a demonstration, which was to begin at the University of Tehran and continue on an east–west route through the city, passing in front of the

American Embassy. The demonstrators, steeped in anti-American sentiment, quickly turned violent. When the mob passed in front of the Embassy and saw the American flag, their rage and hatred escalated to the point that they stormed the gate and took over the building, and so the drama began.

Several days after the hostages were taken, during a respite in the coverage of the story, I finally sat down at my desk in the newsroom and began leafing through the pile of newspapers that had been sitting there unopened since the crisis began. The usual photographs of blindfolded hostages being paraded through the streets of Iran were not what shocked me. Rather, I was stunned by an image that appeared on the front page of the *New York Times*. Jimmy Carter, surrounded by some of his closest advisors, was on his knees in the Oval Office. The caption read, 'President Carter and his Cabinet pray for the release of American hostages.'

The President of the most powerful country in the world was not pictured calling out the Marines, or telephoning other heads of state to mobilize some kind of a coalition to liberate seventy American Embassy workers. Instead, he was drawing upon his faith to turn the situation around and give the United States back its dignity, and the families back their loved ones. Something extraordinary was happening in the country. One of the most prestigious and respected newspapers, known for its liberal tendencies and support of the Democratic Party, had printed a photograph of the American President trying to solve humiliation and trauma with prayer. What this signified to the American people was that their President apparently believed that God was the answer to what had become a national tragedy. More than that, relying on religion to solve a political crisis had somehow become acceptable to mainstream America. It was a symptom of a profound change in the very texture and atmosphere of the United States. The American people, rendered impotent and humiliated, craved God and religion to soothe their fears and comfort their souls. Within days, Evangelical voices were heard, condemning the evils of Islam and citing biblical references to Islam's Holy War against Christianity.

Enmity between Christians and Muslims dates back to the Crusades of the eleventh century. Now Evangelical scholars and leaders began citing both historic and current reasons for their belief that Islam encompassed all that is Evil. Deeply woven into the subconscious of the Western Christian world through its culture and literature, Islam is seen as the only religion that ever threatened the existence of Christianity, with the fall of Byzantium to the Turks and the conquest of Spain by the Arabs. While the hostages were kept in captivity, born-again Christians claimed that the situation was significant of the profound differences between the civilized Christian world and the barbaric tenets of Islam:

Muslims reject the Christian concept of a Trinitarian God: Father, Son and Holy Ghost;

Muslims reject the belief that Jesus is the Son of God;

Muslims are violent, even during their annual pilgrimage to Mecca when their own people lose their lives;

Friday, the day of communal prayer in the Mosque, is a day of rage;

Moslems pray to 'get points' rather than to communicate with God.[2]

During the weeks and months that followed, long after the Super Bowl game had been played, Carter's popularity rating in opinion polls fell drastically. Images of hooded Americans

being marched from one hiding place to another still dominated the front page of newspapers, and the Iranian hostages
were the lead story on television news. Angry crowds of
young bearded men, fists raised and voices shouting, 'Death
to America', were also a constant staple of the news, as were
those same young zealots flagellating themselves until they
were bloody as they paid homage to Allah. Eventually, other
images evoked equal fascination from the American public –
photographs and news footage of the fragile, dying Shah, his
family struggling along with dozens of Louis Vuitton bags, as
the Iranian leader moved permanently into a penthouse suite
at New York Hospital to receive treatment for the cancer
that would kill him. This was a human-interest story filled
with everything Americans devoured: incredible wealth,
pathos, brutality and suffering. The imminent demise of a
once-omnipotent leader only made the story more dramatic.
Photographs of his beautiful wife Farah Diba, suddenly
looking as bedraggled and exhausted as any suburban house-
wife with small children and a dying husband, were juxta-
posed with images of her in better times, covered with
priceless jewellery and wearing her ill-fated crown.

Other American journalists, less concerned with 'human
interest' stories, wrote in depth about the inhuman practices
of the SAVAC, the Shah's secret service, that had tortured
and killed thousands of Iranians. Either viewpoint of the
drama made Carter look ineffectual. As a result, his popularity continued to plunge as rapidly as Fundamentalist Islam
pervaded Iran.

Average Americans did not understand the significance of the
Islamic revolution in Iran, nor did they grasp the degree to
which the United States was perceived as the enemy. To
most Americans, Iran was just one more example of an ally

that had fallen under the control of a dictator, the Ayatollah. Dying for God had little meaning for the average American in those days. Up until then, when America had been exposed to Arab terror, the perpetrator did not die along with his victims. Further, for the American people, the religious convictions of those who had overthrown the Shah and their ultimate political agenda were not considered to be a direct threat to the United States. Communism remained the big evil, and a revolution implemented by Islamic Fundamentalists was simply too far-fetched and a little too vague to comprehend. For the vast majority of Americans, the centre of conflict remained Eastern Europe. Even some of the most sophisticated political pundits in the United States were unable to anticipate or even imagine the implications of an Islamic revolution on the other side of the world. The irony was that the Iranian Revolution, by bringing Fundamental Islam to power in Iran, had as a counter-reaction encouraged Fundamental Christianity in the United States.

Unfortunately for Carter and for the hostages, their families and the rest of the country, the President's prayers did not help to end the crisis, nor did they help his own political career. Since their prayers and several failed military attempts to rescue the hostages did not work, Falwell and other powerful Evangelical Christians took the situation as a sign from God that the time had come to involve themselves in the upcoming presidential election of 1980. As Jerry Falwell said at the time, 'while President Carter is a good Christian, he does not read Scripture carefully enough to understand the crucial place that Israel and the Jewish people play in God's plan, and, above all, he does not realize the threat of Islam against Christianity.'[3] Within months of the collective trauma that touched the entire country, the re-

94

ligious right wing officially entered the political arena, resolved to make America 'a new Jerusalem'.

Several weeks before campaigning began for the 1980 presidential election, a Gallup poll indicated that one out of every three Americans had experienced a religious born-again conversion: nearly 50 per cent believed that the Bible was without error, and over 80 per cent saw Jesus as a divine figure. The poll also revealed that there were 1,300 Evangelical Christian radio and television stations throughout the country with an audience of about 130 million listeners, making annual profits estimated between $500 million and 'billions' of dollars. One leading Fundamentalist, the founder and director of the Christian Broadcast Network, Pat Robertson, got on his airwaves to proclaim, 'We have enough votes to run this country!'

As it turned out, he wasn't wrong.

It was a curious time in America, especially for those who viewed Carter as one of the most religious leaders the country had ever elected. It seemed incomprehensible that the Christian Right was suddenly in opposition to one of their own. But they were and the focus of their affections was Ronald Reagan, a former actor and once the popular Governor of California who believed more in astrology than he did in the Bible. But Reagan was affable, flexible and ambitious, qualities that, when coupled with his acting ability, made him able to say all the right words that would satisfy a growing constituency.

Ed McAteer was not only against Jimmy Carter and in favour of Ronald Reagan but he was, more than any other Evangelical leader, responsible for orchestrating Carter's defeat for a second term in the White House. In one of several interviews shortly before his death,[4] Ed told me,

'From the beginning, I just knew that the presidency surpassed Carter's abilities. It was too big a job for him. He never understood how to govern a country like America and he never understood that any political mandate is God-given and God-inspired.'

It was Ed McAteer who, in 1979, introduced Jerry Falwell to the presidential candidate Ronald Reagan, whom he groomed to win the 1980 election. According to McAteer, it was because of his relationship with Reagan and his ability to 'guide him into being perfect presidential material' that Falwell threw the Moral Majority behind his candidate which resulted in Reagan's victory over Jimmy Carter. Actually, if Jimmy Carter had not rejected the overtures of his born-again constituency, McAteer's goal would have been far more difficult to achieve. Still, Reagan was a quick study. Within days of having been approached by McAteer and Falwell, Reagan began making statements in support of Israel that had their genesis in the Bible. 'The Redemption is not only the Redemption of Israel,' the future President said, 'but the Redemption of the entire world, since the Redemption of the world depends on the Redemption of Israel.'[5]

According to McAteer, the most defining moment of his relationship with Reagan occurred at a campaign event that he arranged in October 1979, which was held in the Coliseum in Dallas, Texas. Because his organization, the Religious Roundtable, is non-profit and therefore under law cannot actually support a political candidate, McAteer was obliged to invite both presidential contenders to appear before the group. It was a crucial event for any candidate who needed to convince the Evangelical community that he was their best choice for President of the United States. The audience was composed entirely of Evangelical Christians, a good proportion of them members of the Dixiecrat Party as well as part of the more right-wing segment of the Republican Party whose domestic issues included their opposition to abortion, to gay and women's rights, and to gun control, their support of prayer in schools and a rejection of First Amendment rights when it came to a separation of church and state. Even more significant was that the group was profoundly patriotic and understood, perhaps more than the mainstream portion of the country, how Carter had contributed to the hostage crisis – an event they considered the 'greatest humiliation of America thus far'.

During that same interview, McAteer recalled the events leading up to what he termed 'Carter's political demise'. 'Carter, who was a born-again Christian, decided not to attend the rally because his advisors told him that he should court the mainstream votes and not "pander to his fellow born-agains",' McAteer explained. 'I got a call from one of Carter's advisors who told me that they had no intention of playing a "ring around the roses" game with the Christian Right. After several years of Carter, having been elected by the Evangelicals for his first term, I realized that when he refused to endorse anti-abortion measures or come out against separation of church and state, or refused to invite Evangelicals to the White House, that he was not going to bat for us. It's not that there was any hatred towards him, just plain old discouragement that he didn't know how to handle things to protect God and this country.'

Primarily because of the President's human rights policy and his attitude towards Israel, McAteer and his fellow Christians blamed Carter for having contributed to the creation of one of the most 'repressive regimes in modern history'.

'Carter ushered in the most totalitarian regime, which was

Khomeini's Iran,' McAteer declared, 'which ultimately financed terror throughout the world against the United States and Israel which is continuing today.'

While Carter declined Ed McAteer's invitation to appear before the major figures of the Evangelical community in Dallas, Reagan accepted. 'It was at my urging,' McAteer said, 'that Ronald Reagan attended our rally and not only showed the group of more than 20,000 Bible-believing Christians his recognition and respect, but he uttered one phrase that I had written that ultimately clinched the election for him.' Minutes before Reagan was to appear on stage having been primed and rehearsed with exactly what he was to say, McAteer suggested that they pray together. 'I told him that it would be a good thing if he consulted the Lord and Mr Reagan said, "OK, Ed, let's do it." So we gathered in a circle, me and about five or six other Evangelical preachers, and we all joined hands with Reagan and we prayed that God would bless this man and make all the American people see the wisdom in electing him our leader.'

Ronald Reagan, who had never professed to having been 'born-again', or to having any particular Evangelical leanings, nonetheless understood from his friend and political mentor, Ed McAteer, that the group he was about to address represented one of the most crucial keys into the White House.

After the prayer ended, Ronald Reagan stepped out on the stage and waited until the applause had died down. When the auditorium was silent, he looked over the crowd and said the words that Ed McAteer had primed him to say: 'I know that you cannot endorse me because of your non-profit status,' the future President said, 'but I do endorse you and what you believe.'

According to McAteer, the auditorium erupted in cheers

and applause. 'That was the moment when I knew that we had a potentially powerful voting block that would include the Dixiecrats and all the Evangelicals which at that time were more than 50 million strong in the United States.'

To further shore up Christian support, Reagan, coached by McAteer, knew exactly how to respond to their questions. When one Evangelical minister raised his hand and asked Reagan how he felt about prayer in schools, the future President replied, 'No one will ever convince me that there's anything wrong with little children praying in the school house.' The crowd went wild. Similarly, when another preacher queried him on his position against abortion, Reagan said, 'Well, the only people I have ever met who were for abortions are those who have already been born.'

Reagan's responses may have lacked depth and intellect, but they certainly did not lack emotion. Rather, by the simplicity of his words, Ronald Reagan touched the hearts of born-again Christians everywhere.

William J. Murray, an Evangelical Christian and the founder and head of the Religious Freedom Coalition, is an energetic man whose commitment to Israel and to the domestic agenda of the Christian Right in America has earned him accolades from his peers. During an interview in Washington in 2004, Mr Murray shared with me his impressions of President Reagan.[6] 'I first met him right after his election when I was invited to an event in the Rose Garden at the White House. It was then that he announced that his administration would try to pass an Amendment to the Constitution to allow school prayer.' According to Murray, President Reagan's effort was 'doomed from the start by a Congress controlled by liberal Democrats out of touch with the people of this nation'.

'One thing is certain,' Mr Murray adds. 'He [Reagan] was

the first true pro-life President this country ever had. He even wrote an anti-abortion book, *Abortion and the Conscience of the Nation*.' It is interesting to note that William J. Murray and many other Evangelical Christians believe that had Ronald Reagan not taken this public stand on abortion, the country would not have a pro-life President today. 'It was Ronald Reagan who sat down with then Vice-President George H.W. Bush, showed him a video of the destruction of an unborn baby, and convinced him that abortion was wrong.' It was a significant moment, not only for the pro-life movement, but also for George H.W. Bush who, up until then, had always followed his wife's lead on abortion rights, which was clear. In her autobiography, Barbara Bush wrote, 'For me, abortion is a personal issue – between the mother, father and doctor. Abortion is not a presidential matter.'[7]

Shortly before he left office in 1988, President Reagan made an official proclamation which not only made his depth of concern for the unborn known to the world, but also made the pro-life movement the core of social conservatism.

Now, therefore, I, Ronald Reagan, President of the United States of America, by virtue of the authority vested in me by the Constitution and laws of the United States, do hereby proclaim and declare the unalienable personhood of every American, from the moment of conception until natural death, and I do proclaim, ordain, and declare that I will take care that the Constitution and laws of the United States are faithfully executed for the protection of America's unborn children. Upon this act, sincerely believed to be an act of justice, warranted by the Constitution, I invoke the considered judgment of mankind and the gracious favor of Almighty God. I also proclaim Sunday, January 17, 1988, as National Sanctity of Human

Life Day. I call upon the citizens of this blessed land to gather on that day in their homes and places of worship to give thanks for the gift of life they enjoy and to reaffirm their commitment to the dignity of every human being and the sanctity of every human life.

To this day Christian leaders work tirelessly to get 'Reagan-type candidates' elected throughout the country, those men and women who believe in smaller government, lower taxes and the fervent support of a Greater Israel. Those who have studied Reagan claim that what he stood for has not changed since his days in the White House, and they consistently defend him against charges that he was 'intellectually lazy'. According to those who still revere him and hold him up as the quintessential conservative President, Reagan had three goals: to defeat Communism, to lower taxes, and to recover the economy. And, as far as they are concerned, he succeeded in all three.

The captive Americans of the 1979 Iranian hostage crisis were released the day after President Ronald Reagan was sworn into office. Falwell and McAteer had the impetus to make Americans aware that Ronald Reagan had been blessed by God. Almost a decade later, when Reagan presided over the collapse of the Soviet Union, an event America celebrated, the President continued to pander to the Evangelical community. Speaking in the language of Fundamentalism, Reagan said that the demise of Communism was 'proof of God over the godless'.

CHAPTER EIGHT

A Covenant-Keeping God

I will bless those who bless you, and whoever curses you, I will curse; and all peoples on earth will be blessed through you.

(Genesis 12:3)

THROUGHOUT Ronald Reagan's first administration, Americans witnessed several crucial events in the Middle East that raised their consciousness about religious fanaticism – in case they had forgotten the Iranian hostage drama. The war in Lebanon brought images of suicide bombers ramming trucks and cars into American Marine installations, embassies and tourist centres. Missionaries, journalists and academics were kidnapped by Hezbollah, the radical Islamic terror organization or Party of God in Lebanon, while the Iran–Iraq War brought images of Iranian soldiers determined to die for Allah, wearing the key to paradise around their necks. Slowly but surely, religious fanaticism became synonymous with extreme Islam, whose soldiers were young men determined to destroy Western civilization by giving their own lives for Allah. With a growing awareness of the Middle East, the relationship between Evangelical Christians and the Jewish population in Israel grew even more solid.

Benjamin Netanyahu, the right-wing Israeli politician,

was one of the more visible catalysts in uniting the Religious Right in America with the ideological Right in Israel and eventually with the more secular mainstream in both countries. In 1983, Netanyahu referred to Jordan as 'eastern' Palestine, suggesting that the most valid Palestinian state was not the West Bank and Gaza, but rather the Hashemite Kingdom. While it was a daring statement, it was not the first time that the right wing in Israel had suggested that Jordan, with nearly 90 per cent of its population Palestinian, was the most logical state for the Palestinian people. Almost immediately, Netanyahu's popularity soared not only in Israel's right-wing Likud Party and in Orthodox circles throughout the Jewish State, but also among the right-wing Christian population in the United States. Netanyahu's main genius, however, when it came to uniting the more liberal Jewish segment of the American population with the conservatives, was his stand on the global threat of Islamic terrorism. The ideological religious right wing in Israel, along with the secular Right, had a common area of interest with the majority of Americans when it came to defending themselves against terrorist attacks perpetrated by militant Islamic groups. For the secular, keeping Israel's borders intact was a matter of strategy – to have room to defend themselves against Arab attacks. For the United States, it still meant a guarantee to keep Israel militarily superior in a region where Arab nations were armed and economically subsidized by the Soviet Union. For the religious, it was solely to uphold God's word as written and interpreted in Scripture.

Equally significant of the increasingly strong bond between Evangelical Christians and the Jewish people was the influence of Jerry Falwell and Ed McAteer on the Israeli–Palestinian conflict. Shortly after Reagan was elected President in 1980, Falwell commented to the *New York Times*:

'The United States government should not be a party to any pressure that could create a peace that is not lasting, equitable, and scriptural.'[1] Obviously, the key word, one that spoke directly to the Christian Right, was 'scriptural'.

Influenced by Evangelical leaders and beholden to them for his presidential victory, Reagan supported the right-wing Israeli government under Menachem Begin, including Begin's policies not to make any 'territorial concessions'. Jewish–Evangelical relations became so close during the 1980s that immediately after Israel bombed Iraq's nuclear reactor in 1981 Prime Minister Begin telephoned Jerry Falwell even before calling President Reagan.[2] According to Reverend Falwell, Begin had asked him to intercede with his good friend President Reagan, to explain that what might seem to have been 'unwarranted aggression' against Iraq was actually a precise strike to destroy its nuclear reactor. That same year, Jerry Falwell received Israel's prestigious Jabotinsky Award in recognition of his support for the Jewish State.

During the first Reagan administration, Begin's right-wing Likud Party sought even closer ties with the leaders of the American Christian Right, who publicly supported Likud's settlement policies in the West Bank and Gaza and also endorsed Israel's invasion of Lebanon in 1982. Falwell's close ties with the Reagan White House prompted him to invite Moshe Arens, then Israeli Foreign Minister, to speak at the fifth annual convention of the Moral Majority in Jerusalem, during which Arens described the Lebanon War as 'a great victory, not only for Israel but also for the free world'. With focus on the Middle East, the relationship between Evangelical Christians and the Jewish population in Israel was firmly established. A formerly abstract connection with its basis in the Bible was now transformed to a desire to 'walk the land where Jesus walked'.

104

Ed McAteer's self-professed love for Jesus and his 'un-equivocal love for the Jewish people and the State of Israel' made him the most influential 'Christian Zionist' in America. During the Reagan years, McAteer was more forgiving of those who had erred morally according to Scripture than of those Christians who did not wholly support Israel and the Jewish people. 'The best friends that Israel has are those people who believe the Bible does not *contain* the word of God,' McAteer told me during an interview, 'but that the Bible *is* the word of God.'[3]

In 1982, the Anti-Defamation League in New York published a book entitled *The Real Anti-Semitism in America*, in which they made the case for a strong Evangelical–Jewish alliance, arguing that anti-Israel sentiment among the main-stream Protestant community posed the greatest threat to American Jewry. Even more emotive was the accusation that the mainstream Protestant community's support for an in-dependent Palestinian homeland threatened the very exis-tence of the Jewish State. The response from the Evangelical community was an increase in private donations that allowed them to open offices in Jerusalem and to begin working to support existing settlements, finance Jewish emigration and subsidize the fledgling Israeli economy, in tandem with the Israeli government.

David Parsons comes from the outer banks of North Carolina where he grew up in a Southern Baptist family.[4] A handsome and articulate man of forty-four, with a good sense of humour, his story of finding Jesus would impress even those who don't believe in miracles. As a child, Parsons was aware that his mother was an invalid and expected to die from an untreatable cardiovascular disease. By the time he was eleven, he was doing all the cooking for the family and caring for his younger siblings. When his mother wasn't bed-ridden, she was in and out of hospitals as one doctor after another told her that there was nothing more they could do for her. 'They basically told my mother, who was only thirty years old at the time, to go home and die peacefully in her own bed,' he says. In April 1971, the family was told that she had only one month to live.

Parsons remembers what happened shortly afterwards, while he was in bed in the room he shared with his two brothers. Without their knowledge, their mother had managed to go to a healing service at an Evangelical church. 'I remember it was a school night,' Parsons says, 'and she came into the room and began jumping on the bed, crying and shouting how Jesus had healed her.' According to Parsons, his mother claimed that Jesus gathered up all the disease in her body and expelled it from below her left ribcage. 'Today, at sixty, she is younger than she was at thirty, and she travels the world. That was the turning point for me. I still have my mother today and I have to thank Jesus for it.'

After finishing law school, Parsons joined a prestigious firm in North Carolina, and became a junior partner after several years, with an impressive client list. When he wasn't meeting with corporate executives or advising corporations on hostile takeovers, he was on the company yacht, fishing in the Gulf Stream, or taking off on ski vacations in the firm's private plane, always accompanied by young executives like himself with brilliant futures, and beautiful women. Yet with everything he could possibly want materially as well as the respect of his peers and colleagues and with the guarantee of becoming a full partner before his thirty-fifth birthday, David Parsons still wasn't content. 'I had it very good,' he says, 'but I just had a sense that God had other plans for me. I knew that if I didn't move to Israel, I would regret it for the rest of my life.' So Parsons began travelling to Israel for his vacations. During one visit, there was a bombing and as he rushed to the scene to try to help the injured, he found himself standing next to a Dutch flight-attendant for KLM Airlines, who had also come to Israel because of a belief: that she, on behalf of all Christians, had to atone for the Holocaust. Over the next few years, the couple stayed in touch, meeting each year in Jerusalem. By 1990, David Parsons had decided to leave the law firm, sell his condominium, and draw the curtain on a life that most men would have envied. He went to Washington, D.C., and began working for the Christian Israel Public Action Campaign (CIPAC), the Evangelical Christian lobby for Israel on Capitol Hill. From the beginning of the Gulf War in 1991, through the Madrid Peace Conference, which eventually led to the Oslo Accord, Parsons spent his time trying to organize support against the peace conference, because he believed that 'Israel was at risk if another Arab state was created on another of its borders.' Parsons also believed that he had embarked on a journey. 'Some people are called into the ministry,' he explains, 'but I had a calling from God to get involved in modern Israel.'

Around the time Parsons began vacationing in Israel, a group of charismatic Pre-millennial Christians (followers of John Nelson Darby) led by Malcolm Heddings and Timothy King were busy founding an organization called the International Christian Embassy in Jerusalem. The foundation of the Embassy was fundamentally religious; it was also a formal stand against the Jerusalem Bill of 1980, which had resulted in more than a dozen countries moving their embassies from Jerusalem to Tel Aviv, in support of the creation of an eventual Palestinian state with East Jerusalem as its capital.

As early as 1980, the Director of the Pilgrim Promoting Division of the Israeli Ministry of Trade and Tourism estimated that 100,000 of the 250,000 annual American visitors to Israel were Christian tourists who visited the biblical sites in Judea and Samaria, otherwise known as the West Bank. During the 1970s and 1980s, Evangelical bookstores sprang up in the United States, stocked with books arguing that the fullest understanding of the origins of the Christian faith was open only to those who had an informed appreciation of the Jewish religion and the Jewish people. A new sort of deep connection and unconditional love for Judaism and the Jewish people were permeating the Evangelical community. Many born-again Christians moved to Israel to set up facilities for learning Hebrew and for studying the Jewish religion. This sympathetic interest in Judaism and Israel continued to grow throughout the 1970s and 1980s and was eventually reinforced by another trend, the proliferation of End Times literature. In an interview Heddings, currently the international director of the International Christian Embassy, said of the organization's efforts, 'When the Embassy opened in 1980, it was a difficult time in terms of how the Jewish people in Israel viewed Christians. They were fearful of our trying to convert them rather than understanding, as they do now, that we are merely trying to show another face of Jesus that does not pressure or intimidate. Our goal is to ease Jesus in so He will eventually be embraced by the Jewish people with joy.'[5]

Eventually, David Parsons went to work for the International Christian Embassy in Jerusalem as the editor of their various publications and, most recently, as their spokesperson. It is because of Parsons' work that the Embassy has expanded into Europe, and has branches and representatives in eighty countries.

When I visited David Parsons at the Embassy in Jerusalem, I asked whether the Bible gives the Jews *carte blanche* in the

Holy Land. Parsons and every one of the men and women I spoke to who work at the International Christian Embassy in Jerusalem answered: 'If King Solomon looked down through the ages and saw the Christians and their new role and place here in Israel, he would encourage them to remain even more boldly in the prophetic picture, to play out the part that was set down for them so long ago.'

Malcolm Heddings, an Assembly of God preacher, discussed the Embassy's position on converting the Jewish people to Christianity. 'It is not up to us to convert the Jewish people; it is up to God, and it will happen, because Jesus is the ultimate word on this issue. It's not my job to condemn those who don't believe in Jesus as the Savior. That's the work of the Holy Spirit, and He will take care of that. My job is to have a growing relationship with God.'[6]

Parsons, Malcolm Heddings and Timothy King are all close friends of President Bush, Congressman Tom DeLay and Newt Gingrich. In his capacity as director of the Embassy and as a Pentecostal minister, Heddings travels the world in an effort to get governments to change their negative impressions of Israel's measures to control Palestinian rebellion. An eloquent speaker, he lectures foreign heads of state on the Bible as a historical document and on the importance of not allowing Israeli security to be compromised, given the 'track record of the Palestinians'. 'President Bush is a sincere man,' Heddings says, 'and we are thankful he is a man who reads the Bible. We pray that Bush and other leaders will eventually understand how they have underestimated the Islamic agenda. I try to explain to the President and to other leaders that unless we deal with the Islamic issue head-on, there will never be world peace.'[7]

My meeting with Mr Heddings at the Embassy in Jerusalem was coincidentally on the day before he was scheduled to leave for Washington to meet DeLay. He stated that the purpose of his trip was to 'derail' the Road Map. Heddings was going to the White House armed with several million signatures from Evangelical Christians, as well as from prominent Jewish leaders in the United States, denouncing President Bush's 'push' for an Israeli–Palestinian peace accord. Included on that petition were signatures of the heads of such mainstream Jewish organizations as the Anti-Defamation League, AIPAC (American Israel Public Affairs Committee – the main pro-Israel lobby in Washington), the Congress of Presidents, and the American Jewish Committee, all of whom understand the potential power that Christian and Jewish lobbying forces have when it comes to influencing American foreign policy.

Heddings, Parsons and those who are in charge of the Embassy's activities believe that regardless of who is President, God's plan 'will win out and the Jews will make their peace with Jesus and have peace within their borders'. 'But the struggle over the land right now, even in the Abrahamic Covenant,' David Parsons explained, 'allows for struggle in the borders, because the Jews have not yet embraced Jesus. We like to consider ourselves a ministry of comfort to comfort the Jewish people in their time of need and to remind them of God's promises to them. We know they are confronting a nasty enemy, and we know the answer lies with the Israeli people and their ability to call on God and not rely on the idea that the United States is here to prevent another Holocaust, because the only one who can prevent that and the only one we can all rely on is God.'[8]

The building that houses the International Christian Embassy in Jerusalem is an imposing granite and stucco structure, once the home of a wealthy and powerful Palestinian family, which later became the Ivory Coast Embassy, and subsequently the Embassy of Pinochet's Chile. The men and women on staff there come from America, Scandinavia, England, Australia, Canada and South America. Their demeanour is joyous, with cries of *Hallelujah* and *Praise the Lord*. Their pilgrimages to the Jordan river for baptism ceremonies, their indoctrination films and literature that instruct Christians to embrace and protect the Jewish people as the 'chosen ones' of God are promoted as 'good works'. The precept they live by and preach to their followers is that 'getting high on prophecy' is not enough, that 'keeping busy with prophetic charts and theologizing about Israel will not do.' Instead, they follow Isaiah 40:1 – 'Comfort ye, comfort ye, my people!' – which they interpret as a call to action. Rather than merely professing to love the Jewish people or having a desire to visit the Holy Land to walk where Jesus walked, the people at the Embassy are involved in such concrete activities as facilitating the immigration of Jewish settlers from around the world and donating all of their $80 million annual budget to social and political activities and programmes within Israel.

David Parsons was very careful to point out that the Evangelicals' love and support for the Jewish people are not altogether altruistic. 'I want to see God's promises to the Jewish people and this land fulfilled,' he explained, 'because it does something to my faith. If God can't keep His promises to Israel and the Jewish people, and He's the same faithful loving God, how can I expect Him to keep His covenant with me as a Christian?' Parsons answered his own question when he continued, 'That would be impossible. By His nature, God is a covenant-keeping God, and by being here as an observer or witness or as someone praying in this ministry of comfort, we will be here to watch God fulfill His promises to Israel and the Jewish people. It is the bright side of prophecy. A lot of Christians are obsessed with the dark side of prophecy, but there is something about God's promises to Israel that is very faith-fulfilling.'[9]

As for the question of expecting the Jewish people to accept Jesus and convert to Christianity as a condition of the return of the Messiah, Parsons says,

> This is not a matter of any Jew converting to anything, it is a matter of God fulfilling His promise. It is that simple. Conversion is, after all, part of God's plan. It's not up to us to convert anybody. God loves the world, but He chose Abraham for the world's redemption, not just for the Jews, so we are supporting the Israeli State and the Jewish people for our own redemption as well. The Jewish people are key to that redemption. There are so many Jewish sages and rabbis who understand, as we do, that when the Jewish people are in exile, the land will not give its fruit. When they are away from this land, it is like it says in the New Testament, that they 'got spanked for my sake'. In the end, God will vindicate the Jewish people because they are the chosen people and because He chose Jerusalem and will choose it again as his throne. Often Israeli settlers come here and try to engage us to fight the Road Map and I tell them all these things about God and how in the end He will not let anything bad happen to the Jewish people as long as they embrace Jesus, and they go away challenged. This is the basis for Christian Zionism.[10]

Part of the equation in that troubled part of the world involves the Palestinian people, and it is on its support for the Palestinians' cause that Evangelicals like David Parsons break with the mainstream Protestant Church.

Christians think Israel should take Syria and Jordan because it was promised in the Bible. We don't think that should happen until the millennium when Messiah is reigning here in Jerusalem. Don't forget that His reign is one of peace, and also with a rod of iron, and He will call the shots. But in the meantime Israel must live by these principles that God set out, knowing in the end that Israel will keep to the borders as set down in the Covenant with Abraham. As important is that the Lord said, 'If you are walking towards me, there are rewards, but if you are walking away from me, there are repercussions.' The Jews must right their relationship with Jesus.[11]

While the American Evangelical community was building a solid presence in the Holy Land, mainstream Protestants from around the world also began to arrive in Israel. As recently as April 2002, the basic differences between the two groups, especially as they affect the Middle East, were obvious. The traditional Protestant Church issued a statement through the Council of Churches Communications Committee, in cooperation with two other mainstream Protestant Christian bodies. They had adopted what they called a 'Code of Fair Practice' for coverage of the Israeli–Palestinian conflict. Their message was clear. They maintained that the attacks on the United States by Islamic Fundamentalists should not be compared with suicide bombings committed by Palestinians against Israelis, since terrorist attacks within Israel were a reaction to occupation and should therefore be viewed as legitimate acts of revolution and revolt. The Council of Churches called for journalists to be 'balanced, fair and accurate' concerning images used on television and in newspapers, and warned journalists about using loaded words such as 'gunmen, terrorists, Islamic bombers and fanatic Moslems' when covering the conflict. However, the position taken by the mainstream Protestant community only helped to further cement the relationship between the Evangelical churches and the Jewish population, both in America and in Israel.

In terms of policy, even back in 1980, the Evangelicals called for the transfer of Palestinians out of Israel and the West Bank and Gaza and into Jordan or other Arab lands, while the Protestant Church's philosophy was to achieve a 'melding' together of all religions and cultures throughout the Holy Land. Protestant leaders called for the right of Jews to live in Hebron, Gaza and all other areas of the West Bank and for Palestinians to be allowed to live freely in Tel Aviv, Jaffa, Ramla and all other Israeli cities with the same rights as the Jews. This philosophical rift remains today, and one of the best examples of the differences between the International Christian Embassy in Jerusalem and its mainstream Protestant equivalent is the Kibbutz of Nis Ammim in the Galilee.

Nis Ammim literally means a 'sign from the nation', which in the Bible is a sign from the prophet Isaiah. The kibbutz, which is run by a German Protestant pastor called Andreas Griffin, is founded on the principle that there must be mutual acceptance without conversion between Jews and Christians. Nis Ammim was financed by a multinational company based in Switzerland, and the company remains its principal backer. The shareholders are predominantly Christians from Germany, Switzerland and Holland. The basic premise was that the Reformed Calvinists from Europe would create a haven where Jews, Bedouins, Muslims, Druze, Christians and visiting Europeans could work and live together in peace. The original idea was that Christians would come to Nis Ammim for a limited time in order to learn about Judaism and the history of Christians and Jews. 'Not only because of what is written in the Bible,' Pastor Griffin explained, when I visited him at Nis Ammim in spring 2003, 'but also because of the painful history between Christians and Jews, in fact, two thousand years of Christian contempt for Jews.'[12]

The differences between David Parsons and Andreas Griffin are not merely theological but also glaringly physical. While Parsons is articulate and sophisticated in Polo shirts and Gucci loafers, Griffin wears heavy leather sandals and nylon t-shirts, and is a plodding, extremely cautious individual. His sense of political correctness when it comes to his relationship with the Jewish people is evident. Even the church on the kibbutz grounds is devoid of any cross or statue of Jesus Christ. 'Our church is called a house of prayer and it is built like a Quaker Meeting House,' Pastor Griffin explains. 'The only religious symbols we have are twelve windows on each side of the structure and twelve small tiles on the pulpit which are symbolic of the twelve tribes of Israel and the twelve Apostles.' During the Sunday services, the pastor adds that there is never any mention of Jesus Christ in an effort not to offend 'our Jewish friends'. 'Jesus remains in our hearts,' he says, 'so it isn't necessary to flaunt our beliefs. We put our own religious convictions aside out of guilt and atonement, for the sake of making amends to the Jewish people whose parents and grandparents were slaughtered during the war.'

While the Evangelicals believe that they bear no responsibility for the Holocaust, though they think the Catholic Church and European politicians were instrumental in organizing it either by omission or commission, Andreas Griffin and those who own Nis Ammim take responsibility and make it their mission not to try to convert the Jewish people to their faith. 'We at Nis Ammim focus on learning and teaching the people who come here about the Holocaust, so they will take that knowledge back to Germany or Holland and share it with others.' According to Pastor Griffin, he only accepts visiting Germans between the ages of twenty-five and forty-five, those who carry no direct guilt for the slaughter of six million Jews in Europe. 'For us, it's impossible to try and convert the Jewish people because Christians received their belief in God from them. Discussing the Shoah here is a very important part of our activities. We have mostly German and other European youngsters coming here during school vacations or for civil service work to learn about Jews, Israel and the Shoah, but they are not allowed to stay longer than six years maximum.'

Lately, Pastor Griffin admits, it has become increasingly difficult to entice European youngsters to come to Nis Ammim because of all the negative press about Israel. 'Europeans are still taking the part of the Palestinians as the underdog,' Pastor Griffin adds, 'and it is getting worse, since the Holocaust happened more than sixty years ago, and so there are very few survivors. Soon there will be none.' Griffin is often amazed at how little those young people who still come actually know about what happened during the war. 'I always ask them if they know about the Shoah and they always tell me that they do. But the truth is that they really don't know anything from the Israeli or Jewish perspective, which is what I concentrate on when I teach them about the atrocities committed against the Jewish people.'

Pastor Andreas Griffin has experienced the resistance of certain Europeans to visiting Nis Ammim because they feel the Palestinian people are being treated unjustly. He considers this objection a thinly veiled remnant of the anti-Semitism still present in a Protestant community which embraces 'liberation theology'. When Protestants claim that their opposition to Israel is because they see 'Zionism' as racism, and view Israel as using 'apartheid politics' and forsaking equality, Griffin thinks it is a pretext to come out against Israel in an acceptable way. He has the same view of the 1975 United Nations Resolution that formally equated Zionism with racism. The mainstream Protestant community and Nis Ammim have difficulty attracting tourists and visitors because Israel is seen as an occupying force and Palestinians as victims.

Evangelical Christians in Jerusalem, specifically the International Christian Embassy, have no problems attracting visiting constituents. Every autumn, during the Christian Feast of Tabernacles, which corresponds with the Jewish holiday of Succoth, the International Christian Embassy in Jerusalem plays host to thousands of American Christians who travel to the Holy Land to participate in the festivities. Most of these visitors have been given airline tickets and hotel accommodation by Christian organizations in their home states in order to 'walk where Jesus walked', and to solidify an already fervent belief in the importance of the survival of the Jewish State. This fact alone denotes the difference between the enormous financial support that the Christian Embassy continues to receive from Evangelical Christians in America, and the struggle that Nis Ammim faces each year in trying to get financial support from its donors in Europe.

CHAPTER NINE

To Walk Where Jesus Walked

He has sent Me to bind up the brokenhearted.
(Isaiah 61:1)

JAN Morrison, a friendly American woman with short hair and glasses, is a devout Evangelical Christian who has integrated her religious beliefs with a concrete political agenda. Smiling constantly as she talks, she explains that she writes about sexual molestation, and that she votes for any candidate who is determined to oppose the creation of a Palestinian state. 'Israel is important to me,' Morrison says, 'because this is the only land ever promised to a people by God. And He chose this land for His home, for His son to be born in, to live in and die. He chose the Jewish people as His people, and nothing will ever change that, because it is an everlasting covenant for now and forever more.'[1]

While almost all Evangelical Christians can recite the Bible verse by verse and know exactly where any one phrase comes from, they often have a befuddled sense of history and American foreign policy that they spout without any hesitation or reticence. For Morrison, this trip to participate in the Feast of Tabernacles was her first experience outside the United States. According to her, coming to Israel was the 'most moving and emotional moment in my life'.

118

'Everything I ever believed in,' she said, 'suddenly took on a different perspective. There's a special peace about this land that isn't anywhere else I've ever been. When you step off the plane, it's like something that you don't expect to happen to you. Every experience you have here takes on a special meaning. As small as Israel is, the world revolves politically around this land, all war begins and ends here, and that's amazing to me. This is the place where my soul comes to rest. And even though there's a lot of turmoil here that won't end until the Messiah sets His foot on the Mount of Olives, there is still a kind of peace here that you don't find anywhere else.'

For Jan Morrison and others like her, the events of 11 September 2001, while horrifying and shocking, only solidified her faith and her connection to the Jewish people. They also justified her inherent mistrust of Islam. 'After 9/11,' Morrison begins, 'whenever I would meet an Israeli, they would ask me if I was American, and then right away, they would assure me that we would be safe, me and all the other Americans, and of course the country as a whole. All of them would even tell me that they would pray for us. But whenever I met an Arab, they told me that we, the United States, had gotten what we deserved. The big difference between the Arab people and the Jewish people is that the Arab people strap bombs to their children and send them out to die and kill others, while the Jewish people have a different concept of life and how important it is to save lives and to live in peace.'

Since she returned from Israel, Morrison has taken to acting as an unofficial travelling Ambassador of Good Will for the Jewish State in the United States. She has made it her mission to inform her fellow Evangelicals about what she defines as the 'truth' behind the Israeli–Palestinian conflict. When we met during the festivities, she was anxious to

119

describe her experiences, especially the time she was able to talk directly with Jesus Christ.

> Now Jesus said to me: 'Jan, the Galilee is where I walked and talked with my disciples. That's where they got to know me and I got to know them.' It was incredible but, you see, from a Christian perspective, seeing Israel, and talking directly with Jesus, made me return to the States and start telling everyone I met how they don't know the truth about Israel. They truly don't. People say there is calm here when a few weeks pass without a terrorist attack, but there is never really calm because people are always wondering when the next attack will take place . . . I tell people the truth and I tell them to pray for the Jewish people because God says to pray for the peace of Jerusalem. Personally, I pray for them because I love them so much. But I always pray for the Arab people too. Some Christians consider there's a veil over the eyes of the Jewish people in some respects because they haven't accepted Jesus yet, but there's a whole quilt over the eyes of the Arab people, because it's a religious thing with them that is teaching the Arabs to kill. It's their religion that is teaching them to hate.

Carlyle Anderson, an accountant from New Hampshire, travels to Israel once a year for the Feast of Tabernacles. When describing his love for Israel, he relates a personal encounter that he had with Jesus. 'When I actually was able to meet Jesus down near the Galilee and actually talk to Him, He assured me that it be would like it's written in Ezekiel in the Bible, that He would bring the people back to the Lord, and help the people here be brought to the Lord. But Jesus also warned me that Bush is only a president. He's not a king, and he's not God, so he can't be perfect and accomplish everything the Bible says.'[2]

Rita Angela, a secretary at a high school in Lexington, Kentucky, is just as crucial to the Evangelical movement as those Evangelicals who actually travel to Israel. When a group of students from Somalia came to her school as exchange students for a semester, she saw these new arrivals as a 'virtual mission field'. Standing on the Mount of Olives with tears in her eyes as she looked at the Old City below her, she talked about her trip to Israel and how she tries to instill Christian values in everyone she meets back home in the United States. 'I felt I had an obligation to save these kids from an eternity in Hell,' Angela said. 'I devised a list of tips on what to do and not to do to reach these youngsters for conversion:

Don't approach them in groups.
Don't bring them to your church, because they will misunderstand the singing and clapping as a party.
Do invite them home for a meal.
Do bring them chocolate chip cookies.
Do talk about how, in order to get saved, they must accept Jesus.

'Our job is not just to make someone a Christian. Our job is to show them the love of Christ,'[3] she tells me.

Like other Evangelicals who were in Jerusalem for the Feast of Tabernacles, Rita Angela attests to a personal encounter with Jesus. 'I was in the Galilee and it was 3.30 in the morning and God woke me up and told me He wanted to talk to me down at the shore and if I followed Him, my life would never be the same,' Angela explains. 'So, naturally I got up and went down to the shore, and of course, it was Jesus speaking to me. He held out His hand like that and I walked down and He was just pouring things into me about the land and the people and I just couldn't keep things straight there was so much of it.'

On the opening evening of the celebration of the Feast of Tabernacles on 12 October 2003, Prime Minister Ariel Sharon made a speech welcoming the thousands of American Evangelicals who had come to Israel for the festivities. Malcolm Heddings, director of the International Christian Embassy, was more direct during his speech: 'When you came in you were given a blue pen and a piece of paper,' Heddings told the crowd. 'We want to keep track of who you are. We want to know your address and have it correct. Fill it out and give it to us either in the offering bucket or later in the week. There is a second section on this paper that's very important. Israel is facing a very difficult economic time. We as Christians need not only to stand with Israel in prayer, but also to stand with Israel in finance. We need to help the infrastructure, giving to the needy of this land whenever we can. And it takes a lot of money. As you know it is not a cheap place to visit, but I can assure you it is equally not a cheap place to live here. And Israel needs our help. So please, on the second section of the form, give us a pledge. Tell us what you can do throughout the year. Help the International Christian Embassy help Israel. We challenge each and every one of you to pray, to think, and to dig deep into your pockets. Please join me as we thank the Lord for His abundant provision in our lives.'

At that point, ushers walked around the crowd, carrying black buckets. In the background, joyful music blared and men dressed in prayer shawls and skullcaps danced the traditional Jewish *hora* as cheques, banknotes and change landed in the buckets.

Gina, an Evangelical Christian, lives in a rural farming area of New Jersey. Although she is only in her mid-thirties, her face is lined with fatigue, and her hands are red and rough from hard work. Married to a man who has been out of work for the past four years, Gina has eight children, seven biological and one that she and her husband recently adopted. Like a growing majority of born-again Christians, Gina home-schools her offspring, teaching them the basic required subjects in addition to a very concentrated study of the Bible. In between running the home, keeping her husband's spirits up and overseeing the care and education of her large brood, Gina also holds down a menial job as a waitress at a nearby truck stop. Despite all the financial hardships that she and her family have endured these past few years, she faithfully gives a stipend of her meagre income every month to an organization called On the Wings of Eagles. On the Wings of Eagles is run by Yechiel Eckstein, an American Orthodox rabbi, and Richard Land, an Evangelical Christian, who use a portion of their $100 million budget to bring Jews currently living in Russia to Israel. Gina says, 'God has put a love in my heart for the Jewish people, and I know it's the love that He has for the people Himself. Through Him, it's the desire of my heart to see good come to these people and to their land because of God's desire and prophecy.'[4]

Standing in the crowd that evening, Gina reached into her pocket when the black buckets came around. When asked about the personal sacrifice she makes each month when she sends money to help Russian Jews, Gina only wishes that she could give more. 'I give monthly to the Eagles' Wings Ministry. It was through the man who is the head of that ministry that I became aware of the needs of the Jewish people. Almost all of what I give every month – and it's not a lot because I have so little, but at least I give consistently – is sown into the land of Israel.' Admittedly, Gina is not particularly political nor is she well versed in the intricate nuances of the Israeli–Palestinian conflict, but what she does know and understand through her religion is that God has a purpose for the Jewish people and the land of Israel. 'Probably the purpose is salvation for the entire world, because God revealed Himself first to the Jews and it is the Jewish people who will bring that revelation to the Gentiles.'

Following the contributions, Ehud Olmert, who at the time was serving as Deputy Prime Minister under Ariel Sharon, addressed the group, and his words only added to the religious frenzy that was so palpable in the convention centre. 'Jerusalem *is* the Temple Mount,' Olmert began. 'Twice in our history we lost the Temple Mount. It's the heart of Jewish existence and the United States knows that Jerusalem can only be one united, undivided capital. There can be no other basis for future political developments. I don't think Islam encourages terror, but these groups of terrorists all across the world are giving extreme violent interpretations of their religion. You cannot escape this conclusion. You have to fight terror without any particular restraints. You can't fight terrorists with words. You do what you need to do.' Later, outside the conference hall, Ehud Olmert spoke to me about the continuous support of major Christian organizations when it comes to Israel's existence. 'It's not the only basis,' he said, 'but it's a very important basis for our existence, no doubt about it. America is a Christian society and has been the most supportive of all the countries in the world to the existence of the State of Israel.'

CHAPTER TEN

The Almighty('s) Dollar

*There's a Bible on that shelf there. But I keep it next to Voltaire –
poison and antidote.*

(Bertrand Russell (1872–1970),
British philosopher)

DESPITE Ronald Reagan's re-election in 1984 and the awareness of Israel as God's chosen nation throughout the Evangelical community, the mood throughout America shifted during the late 1980s. Any continued political success for the Evangelicals in the United States would prove to be brief. The country grew complacent, concerned less about moral values than about financial gain. Communism had been vanquished and the economy enjoyed an extraordinary boom. As a result, even the Evangelical community began to crave something more exciting than the sober Fundamentalism and militant piety preached by Jerry Falwell and born-again Christian leaders. This need to escape the grim components of Evangelical Christianity brought forth a new breed of charismatic preachers like Jimmy Swaggart, whose speciality was healing people over the airwaves, while taking an extremely hateful position against the Roman Catholic Church, homosexuals and the Supreme Court. Probably more than anything else, he offered his public relief from their dreary lives, which accounted for their fidelity and their donations to his television ministry which, in its heyday, added up to more than $150 million a year. His prayer meetings were nourishing because he reached people by recounting how he had known poverty and misery first-hand and therefore could understand their own frustration and pain. He also preached against fornication and pornography and, at least in the beginning of his career, appeared to be honest, especially when he voluntarily released financial statements for his television ministry to the press. In the end, Swaggart was disgraced and exposed as having trysts with prostitutes in a run-down motel in Louisiana and a life-long addiction to pornography. One of the prostitutes with whom Swaggart was involved eventually posed for *Penthouse* magazine and, for a high six-figure fee, recounted her affair with the born-again minister in lurid detail. The media turned on him immediately, as did his audience, and after he was reprimanded by his peers and 'defrocked' for one year, his financial empire dwindled to a mere $4.5 million a year and his faithful viewers diminished by 80 per cent.

Oral Roberts was another Evangelical minister who not only healed people live on air but who also founded the Oral Roberts University in Tulsa, Oklahoma in 1965 after receiving what he described as a 'command from God'. The university groomed future generations of televangelist ministers to preach and convert new souls to the born-again Christian faith. Roberts, who had only about two years at college, where he studied the Bible, reported in 1980 that he had had a vision of a 900-foot-tall Jesus who encouraged him to raise money to build what eventually became his 'City of Faith Medical and Research Center'. The Center, which opened its doors in 1981, had constant financial problems and in March 1986, at the height of Roberts' fiscal woes, he

126

announced to his television congregation that he had spoken directly to God who told him that he would be 'called home [die]', if he was unable to raise $8 million by 31 March 1987. On 1 April Roberts once again got on the airwaves to tell his faithful listeners that the $8 million had indeed been raised and his life spared. Shortly afterwards, still in 1987, Roberts claimed that he had raised the dead and would return after his own death to rule on earth beside Jesus Christ. Roberts' son Richard, who is part of the Oral Roberts ministry today, claimed that he had actually witnessed his father raising a child from the dead. Despite the miracles that Roberts claimed he had achieved and the money he had raised 'by God's grace', the Medical Center became too costly to maintain and eventually closed in 1989. The sexual antics of Jimmy Swaggart and the incredible claims of Oral Roberts, however, paled by comparison with Jim and Tammy Bakker, who have the distinction of being the most notorious of all the televangelists.

The Bakkers called their ministry the 'Praise the Lord [PTL]' cable network and it operated out of Charlotte, North Carolina. PTL also was the name of their television ministry, which made instant inroads into the highest echelons of society. Industrialists, actors, sports and media figures and politicians appeared with them on their religious broadcasts. The first conservative politician who openly embraced the PTL and who had admitted links with the Fundamentalist and New Christian Right was Senator Jesse Helms, a Southern Republican most famous for his segregationist position long after integration had become a reality throughout America. Using the religious platform of Praise the Lord, Senator Helms campaigned against taxation of private schools and the withdrawal of American troops in South Korea, and on other political and social issues sponsored by the Christian movement. The followers of Tammy and Jim Bakker sent in millions of dollars which were mostly used for Tammy's ridiculously expensive wardrobe, wigs, jewellery and beauty care, and their extravagant homes adorned with marble, *faux* Versailles crystal chandeliers and ersatz Louis XIV furniture. The amazing thing was that while their fans and followers knew about their extravagant lifestyle, they adored them and were mesmerized by their particular brand of consumer Evangelism, which preached that 'God loves those who succeed.' It gave all the have-nots, average and underprivileged an escape from their dreary dead-end lives. More amazing was that even the poor, living on fixed welfare incomes or meagre pensions, sent money faithfully every month to Tammy and Jim, although the PTL network received considerable contributions from the rich and famous as well. Jim and Tammy Bakker were not only the epitome of the American way of capitalism and the free market, but they encouraged a mass recognition of God who, according to them, preached that faith was the best way to achieve eternal happiness which, of course, meant being surrounded by all the luxuries that money could buy.

Eventually the Bakker movement was unmasked as a monumental fraud. In September 1989, Jim Bakker went on trial for financial irregularities and immoral conduct. The story was a matter for scandal and glee throughout America. Those who were not Evangelicals were shocked and disgusted by the Bakkers' incredible vulgarity, although their faithful public, while horrified by the swift and undignified fall of the Bakkers, were nonetheless shocked that their link to the Almighty had been silenced by mere mortal law-makers.

The national and international media followed Jim's arrest, Tammy's hysteria, and the subsequent sex scandal when it was discovered that Bakker had been carrying on a lurid affair with one of his church secretaries. What brought about Bakker's downfall in the eyes of the law was not so much his ostentatious lifestyle, nor his penchant for encouraging the millions of Evangelicals who faithfully watched his religious services on television to send in money to maintain the couple's opulent lifestyle, but the fact that when he was caught with his secretary Bakker used church funds to keep the young woman quiet. While Jim was led off in handcuffs, his legs in shackles, head bowed and tears streaming down his cheeks, Tammy elevated grief and outrage to an art form. Simpering and whining and with a total lack of dignity, she was seen countless times on national television, her cheeks streaked with black mascara streaming from her false lashes, her bleached blonde hair teased to the hilt and standing up in spikes, and her high-pitched voice whining from coast to coast as she evoked Jesus and swore that her husband would be vindicated. In fact, in one particularly shameful interview, Mrs Bakker claimed that Jim was being sacrificed for his beliefs much the same as Christ had been crucified on the cross.

In the end, Tammy was forced to sell her jewels, cars, furs and homes. Still, the American public, similar to their reaction after Jimmy Swaggart fell from grace, had a profound need for the kind of religious awakening and one-on-one contact with God that the Bakkers had offered them every Sunday. Even after Jim Bakker was carted away from the spiritual stage to the bowels of a California prison, billions of dollars continued to pour in to other television ministries that were still operational. It was proof that a great portion of the American public needed to believe the claims that those televangelist preachers made: that they could heal the sick, raise the dead or turn a miserable and destitute life into one of satisfaction and riches. The most prevalent message of all these Evangelical preachers, however, was that God was the answer to everyone's economic problems. As Pat Robertson said, 'In the Kingdom of God, there is no recession or shortage of anything.'[1]

Late-night talk shows featured comedians who made the disgraced religious leaders the butt of their humour, all of which ultimately affected the social, moral and political agenda of President Reagan's successor, George Bush.

Ed McAteer was always the quintessential super-salesman, his shot-gun delivery peppering his listeners with anecdotes that let them understand instantly that during his lifetime he had been at the centre of numerous high-level policy government decisions. Just as easily, he could underscore his privileged connections by mentioning that he also happened to have a direct line to the Almighty. There is no doubt that McAteer was a Washington insider who had the ear of many of those who run the country. He had been asked by two Presidents, Ronald Reagan and George Bush, and two presidential hopefuls, Jack Kemp and Pat Robertson, to act as their advisor or as a member of their administrations. Despite his lifetime loyalty to the Republican Party, he always had a somewhat ambiguous relationship with the Bush family, beginning with George Bush.

Ed McAteer's first contact with George W. Bush was during the elder Bush's presidential campaign in 1988, when Bush Senior asked him to 'come on board' to act as the liaison between the Christian community and the Republican Party. At the time, Doug Wead, an Assemblies of God Evangelical who belonged to the Pentecostal Church, was in charge of 'grooming' the younger Bush as the political link to the Christian community on behalf of his father. Despite the fact that Wead's background was also in sales, he needed the king of salesmanship to help him educate George W. in the ways of the Evangelical community. No one was better suited for the job than Ed McAteer. 'As soon as Doug approached me and I agreed to work with him and with Bush Junior,' McAteer told me, 'I was immediately asked by Bush Senior to take a more visible and permanent place in the campaign. I refused, because I believed I could do more good as someone who was not identifiable but who worked behind the scenes to get things done. And the first thing I did was to fly down to Dallas and meet with W.A. Criswell, the Reverend Billy Graham's preacher at the First Baptist church in Dallas. I spoke there in front of all those Baptists and I plugged the young Bush – made him a hero so all my Christian friends would listen to him when it came down to pushing for their votes for his daddy.'[2]

Shortly afterwards, McAteer arranged for the younger Bush to speak before the most influential group of Evangelicals at the National Religious Broadcasters conference. 'Both Bush and his daddy knew they needed the South if they were going to win the election,' McAteer explained. 'Once they won the primaries in the southern states, they knew they would win the election. It was all over for Mr Dukakis, the Democratic opponent.'

After George Bush became the forty-first President of the United States, Ed McAteer got a beautiful letter from him. 'He just about told me if I couldn't actually walk on water,' McAteer said, 'then I could get ankle deep and not sink. He was just very grateful to me for that great victory and how I had organized everything so that my fellow Christians knew he would come out strong against abortion – saving those little babies – and against the evils of homosexuality and all

131

the other topics that are so dear to us, especially our concern for Israel and the Jewish people.'

On the day of President George Bush's inauguration, Ed McAteer watched with pride as the newly elected President, with his wife Barbara at his side, was sworn into office. Afterwards, McAteer cheered as the new President and First Lady led a parade down Pennsylvania Avenue towards the White House. 'The only thing that struck me back then was that Bush Junior couldn't make eye contact with me. He just about avoided me every time I approached.'

After the festivities were over and Bush Senior was comfortably ensconced in the Oval Office, McAteer heard from various contacts that the President had decided 'to distance himself from the Christian Right on those issues which would alienate the more liberal or mainstream members of the Republican Party'.

'Let me just say,' McAteer said, 'that it was the Christian Right that brought the President the southern states and got him elected. And it was the Christian Right that caused him to lose the election the second time around. But after that message, I had no further contact with Bush Senior or anyone else in the White House until two years ago, when I happened to be on the same speaking program in Dallas as the current President, George W. Bush. After the speeches were over, I noticed young George heading my way to shake some hands. I'm not even sure he saw me until he was right next to me.' According to McAteer, the President paused, looked a bit startled before he leaned over and squeezed McAteer on the shoulder. 'We had some good times, didn't we, Ed?' he said, before moving on to work the crowd.

In 1988, the United States entered into a dialogue with the Palestinian Liberation Organization (PLO). The humiliating events of 1979 in Iran seemed to have been all but forgotten by the American people, although Ed McAteer and others who believed as he did remembered only too well. They were very aware that contrary to what he had promised the Christian Right, George Bush did not make morality, God and religion the dominant aspects of his presidency, because they did not dominate the psyche of the country. To further demonstrate his desire to court the secular portion of America, President Bush, on 2 October 1990, appointed David Hackett Souter as Associate Justice of the Supreme Court. Historically, Souter's opinions had always supported the constitutional rights of privacy and choice, which only served to alienate the American President from the Christian Right. From then until now, Souter has always been considered as one of the three 'swing' justices of the Supreme Court, who acknowledged that the Constitution protects a woman's right to choose.

Despite the opprobrium heaped on him by the Evangelical community, there was nonetheless a brief moment during his one term as President of the United States when George Bush regained some of his support with the Christian Right. In 1991, the United States expelled Iraqi forces from Kuwait, which contributed to an atmosphere throughout of business, political pragmatism and oil. For the Christian Right, however, the Gulf War was symbolic of the Christian battle against the evils of Islam. The irony, however, was that the Arab world was separated in the minds of a good portion of Americans as being either 'for us or against us' – a familiar slogan that was re-used during the second Gulf War when Bush Junior invaded Iraq.

During the first Gulf War in 1991, I was in Tel Aviv doing a story for *Elle* magazine on Christiane Amanpour, who had recently started working for CNN. Every evening without fail the sirens wailed, signalling another incoming SCUD, compliments of Saddam Hussein. The reaction was swift. Putting on gas masks and slinging our emergency medical kits over our shoulders, we all walked swiftly down a cement staircase to the basement of the hotel, where we waited. Usually the Patriot missiles supplied by the United States intercepted the SCUDs, although there were several deadly exceptions. Often we would hear the explosion which seemed to miss us by inches, and while we waited for the all-clear, special squads of Israeli soldiers inspected the missile fragments to see if the Iraqi leader had sent in chemical weapons, which he never did. And always we learned of Israeli casualties.

During that war, President George Bush had formed a coalition with Arab nations to liberate Kuwait on condition that Israel would not enter into the fray, even if attacked directly by Saddam Hussein – which was exactly what happened. In Tel Aviv for the duration of the war, I became friendly with an Evangelical Christian who had come to Israel with a group of born-again Christian Pilgrims to work at the International Christian Embassy in Jerusalem. When the war broke out, he, along with his group, travelled from Jerusalem to Tel Aviv and stayed on in a gesture of solidarity with the Jewish people.

Before the sirens began, which was virtually every evening, I had many lively conversations with this man, which always focused on his love for the Jews and for the Jewish State. Eventually, I broached the subject of a double standard that had always been imposed on Israel when it came to defending itself against Arab aggression. I wondered how my new Christian acquaintance felt about the American President making a deal with the Arab coalition that prevented Israel from responding militarily to the nightly SCUD attacks. I also wondered how he felt about the United States of America risking the lives of its soldiers to liberate Kuwait, an Arab nation that was the sworn enemy of Israel. At the time, his response struck me as no different than the opinions of the mainstream American population who supported the war for a very specific and pragmatic reason – oil. 'We have to do what's good for the country,' he told me. 'We have to liberate Kuwait so Saddam doesn't bring America to its knees. Everyone knows he'll blackmail us by raising oil prices and causing a shortage and then we'll have lines at the gas stations the way we had back in the 1970s.' And Israel? 'God will take care of the Jewish people,' he assured me. 'It says so right in the Good Book.'

At the time, I remember thinking about those long gas lines in the late 1970s and how, while waiting in my car to fill up, I had seen bumper stickers which read: 'Need Heat? Burn A Jew.'

Despite the fact that this particular Evangelical had come to Israel to work voluntarily at the Christian Embassy, and had stayed on as a show of support for the Jewish people, his reaction to the war was based on his sentiments as an American citizen. Never did he express any hatred for Arabs in general or Islam as the embodiment of evil; rather, he articulated a plausible opinion about the Iraqi leader who had marched into a sovereign country with the intention of taking over the oil fields and bringing America 'to its knees'. The fact that Israel had been restrained from responding militarily to Iraqi SCUD attacks or the fact that Kuwait was an enemy of the Jewish State did not enter into the equation. It was apparent that this American Evangelical considered himself to be American before he identified himself as a born-again Christian.

Still, in a nod to the Christian Right who had helped put

him into the White House, President George Bush called upon the Reverend Billy Graham to guide the nation in prayer. On the night the Gulf War began, Billy Graham was a guest at the White House during which time he talked to Bush Senior about the importance of 'turning to God as a people of faith, turning to Him in hope'. His words did not include hatred for Arabs or Islam. The following morning, while the war was in full swing, the Reverend Graham went to Fort Myers in New Jersey, where American troops were waiting to be shipped overseas, to conduct a religious service. According to President Bush, 'We had a lovely service where Dr Graham led our nation in a beautiful prayer with special emphasis on the troops overseas. We prayed that we would vanquish Iraqi forces.'[3] On 31 January 1991, George Bush said, in a speech to the American people, 'Across this nation, churches, synagogues and even mosques are packed with record attendance at services, filled with people who are praying for our success in this military operation against the evil of Saddam Hussein.' Back then, the enemy was limited to a brutal dictator who had not only tortured and killed his own people but had invaded a neighbouring country. According to Ed McAteer, the reason that the Evangelical community withdrew its support for George Bush had everything to do with the Gulf War as it concerned the President's lack of support for the Jewish State. 'The President turned his back on the Christian Right,' McAteer told me in 2004.

The first Palestinian uprising, or Intifada, began in December 1987 and lasted until September 1993. The Intifada took its toll on the Israeli population and was the impetus for the American Jewish community to accept the notion of 'land for peace', and the creation of a Palestinian state in the West Bank and Gaza. In 1991, under the sponsorship and encouragement of President George Bush who believed his constituency was in the secular portion of the country, the Madrid Peace Conference began with Israeli and Palestinian negotiators making an initial effort to set the parameters for a comprehensive peace accord. At the same time, secret negotiations were in progress in Oslo, Norway, and parallel open negotiations were taking place in Washington, D.C.

Whether or not the born-again community made a conscious political decision to concentrate on foreign policy because they were unable to push through laws in the United States based on the Ten Commandments and the religious and moral imperatives of their beliefs is debatable. What is clear is that Bush's appointment of David Hackett Souter to the Supreme Court sent a clear message to the Christian Right.

As the 1992 election campaign began, George Bush held a commanding lead in the polls. For a brief moment, the Religious Right held hope that their candidate, Patrick J. Buchanan, a top aide in the Nixon and Reagan administrations, would be a viable challenge to the incumbent President. A former television commentator who had severed his life-long ties to the Republican Party to declare his candidacy for the Reform Party presidential nomination, Buchanan was primed to set off a bitter battle between forces loyal to the founder of the Reform Party, Ross Perot and Minnesota Governor Jesse Ventura, a former wrestling star. But when Buchanan entered into the Reform Party, he was greeted with accusations of anti-Semitism by Conservative Republicans who cited several passages in his book which demeaned America's role in fighting Adolf Hitler. It was a telling moment in the United States, since Buchanan was firmly against abortion and gay rights, and soundly for the death penalty, prayer in schools, and all the other domestic issues

137

dear to the hearts of the Religious Right. Clearly, the crucial religious importance of the Jewish State and the biblical Covenant between God and Abraham were far more important to Evangelical voters than any right-wing domestic agenda. Not only did Ross Perot win the nomination of the Reform Party but he forced a three-party race for President of the United States.

For the majority of secular Americans, George Bush's popularity was based on the fact that he had been the Commander-in-Chief during America's most decisive military victory since the Second World War – the Gulf War. As a result, most of the favourite Democratic candidates were reluctant to challenge him as the country geared up for the elections. It was only after the then Governor of Arkansas, a young and eager politician named William Jefferson Clinton, who was not considered a Washington insider, was nominated on the Democratic ticket, that the polls showed Bush losing the presidential race. America responded to Clinton not only because of his youth but because he was symbolic of a new breed of politician who was prepared to meet the challenges of a new world order. Within days of his nomination, Clinton had surged to the top of the polls. Even more damaging to Bush was Ross Perot, a self-made billionaire, who ran on one issue only – reducing the deficit. As a result of the country's floundering economy, the campaigns of all three candidates focused around the country's economic problems. The irony of the situation was that George Bush, who had been Vice-President during the Reagan administration, which could claim responsibility for the decline of the Soviet Empire and the end of the Cold War, was suddenly recreated as Bush-the-candidate, a man without any cause at all except a dangerously moribund economy. For the secular portion of America, no longer could the

Republicans rely on the tired adage about not trusting a Democrat to stand up to the Russians, while the Evangelicals, who had the potential to swing the vote to the right, were sufficiently disenchanted with Bush either to vote for Perot or simply not to vote at all. The problem in the 1992 election was not only that Ross Perot took votes away from Bush, but that the Religious Right were neither prepared nor sufficiently united to guarantee a Republican victory.

The majority of Americans usually elect politicians who have brought their religious convictions to any government post they hold. Americans have taken it for granted that, in addition to military might and high technological superiority, God has been instrumental in protecting the very freedoms upon which their country was founded. As a result, the attitude of the President has always been a good indicator of the level of religiosity in America: seemingly, every President has considered God to be his closest advisor and spiritual guide while he occupied the White House. Even Bill Clinton, who represented the antithesis of religious morality for the devout segment of the population, conducted his campaigns more as revival meetings than any other mainstream candidate did. From his first campaign in 1992 when he transformed himself into full preaching mode in black churches, and throughout his two administrations, he peppered all his speeches with phrases from the Bible, the one book he knew by heart, chapter and verse. The discrepancy only appeared at the end of his tenure. During his inauguration, President Bill Clinton not only swore to God to uphold the oath of office of President of the United States, but he also swore on a Bible – 'I have never had intercourse with that woman' – when he denied his relationship with the White House intern Monica Lewinsky. Clinton again made God part of his defence after it was discovered that he had lied, confessing his 'sin' by quoting from the New Testament and the Yom Kippur liturgy at an annual Washington prayer breakfast. 'I have turned my life over to a higher power and asked God to absolve me from my sins,' the President said. 'My sin is the result of my having lost my way and forgotten the Ten Commandments.'[4]

Despite Bill Clinton's attempt to become the P.T. Barnum of any public show of faith, what is certain is that after George Bush lost the presidential election in 1992, the Christian Right had reached a low in their financial and spiritual influence on the American public.

CHAPTER ELEVEN

The Resurgence of the Christian Right

Politics give guys so much power that they tend to behave badly around women. And I hope I never get into that.
                                        (Bill Clinton, to a woman friend
                                        while a Rhodes scholar at Oxford)

THROUGHOUT the Clinton years in the White House, from 1992 until 2000, Evangelicals had little success in pushing through any of their domestic policies, nor did they have any significant influence on US foreign policy. In fact, during both Clinton administrations, they considered morality and Christian values to be at a low point in their history and Israel to have been virtually abandoned by a President who did not believe in the words of the Lord as written in the Abrahamic Covenant.

While the vast majority of baby-boomers saw the new President Clinton as one of their own – young, ambitious and fun, and with a wife, Hillary, who was an accomplished woman, liberated, successful and independent, in her own right – the Evangelicals were convinced that the devil himself had taken up residence in the White House. And Mrs Clinton was the antithesis of what a God-fearing wife and mother should be. For the Christian Right, their goal of bringing America back to the moral standards that had been set after the Iranian hostage crisis in 1979 seemed impossible to attain. As Jerry Falwell said, after the terror attacks of 2001, 'There was a positive side to these unfortunate events of someone like Clinton in the White House. It produced a spiritual re-awakening of our youth who were on fire for God and burning to make a difference in America.'[1] Falwell even had a response when confronted by Clinton's over-whelming popularity in the polls. 'Jesus Christ was never concerned about polls or popularity,' he said. 'He wasn't concerned about anything except getting God's approval, and Bill Clinton does not have the approval of our Lord!'[2]

The defeat of President George Bush in 1992, and the election of Yitzak Rabin as Prime Minister of Israel on a platform that called for a gradual withdrawal of Israeli troops from the West Bank and Gaza, both signalled a real first step towards an autonomous Palestinian state. In September 1992, President Clinton received the Palestinian and Israeli leadership on the White House lawn for the signing of the Oslo Peace Accord. The absence of any religious leaders at the ceremony had been a conscious decision on the part of the American President. The religious aspect of the conflict was considered as complicating an already sensitive situation. Ignoring the religious issue, however, did nothing to solve the on-going question of whether the conflict was a terri-torial disagreement or a blood feud steeped in religious beliefs. Failing to define the Israeli–Palestinian conflict in more than political or historical terms only exacerbated extremism in the three religions concerned – Judaism, Christianity and Islam.

On 5 November 1995, the dream of peace died when Rabin was assassinated in Tel Aviv by a Jewish extremist from the right-wing Israeli Kach Party. After his own re-election in 1996, however, and in tribute to his fallen friend, President

Clinton was even more determined to pursue a viable peace accord. As usual, Clinton's agenda was contrary to everything the Christian Right believed in. Further, Shimon Peres, one of the architects of the Israeli–Palestinian peace accord, was designated interim Prime Minister until the Israeli elections could take place in June 1996. As it turned out, the Israeli population was no more ready for peace with the Palestinians than the American Evangelical community, which resulted in the defeat of Peres and the election of Benjamin Netanyahu as Israel's new Prime Minister. That same year, Jerry Falwell formed the National Committee, a platform to arouse, inform and mobilize religious conservatives in America in order to combat what he called the 'moral and spiritual collapse of the nation'. The threat of the Jewish State's relinquishing what the Christian Right considered biblical holy land was a real and present danger.

Under the auspices of the National Committee, Falwell travelled all over the country organizing patriotic and inspirational 'God Save America' rallies. Each month he published the *National Liberty Journal*, with a readership of more than 250,000 religious leaders. The *Journal*'s goal was to alert and inform the conservative and religious constituencies about bias in 'liberal news outlets' that encouraged the abandonment of strong traditional values. Preaching Christian values and evoking biblical images to support the notion of a one-state solution in the Middle East, Falwell inspired his followers to embrace the premise that Jesus was the epitome of Good, while Allah represented all that was Evil. In addition, shortly after Netanyahu's victory, he formed the Israel Christian Advocacy Council. To celebrate the creation of Falwell's organization, Netanyahu brought seventeen Christian leaders to Israel to sign a pledge that 'America [would] never, never desert Israel.'[3]

In response to Netanyahu's initiative, the Third International Christian Zionist Congress proclaimed that, 'the truths of God are sovereign and it is written that the Land which He promised to His People is not to be partitioned . . . It would be further error for the nations to recognize a Palestinian state in any part of Eretz Israel.' Immediately following the conference, the International Christian Embassy in Jerusalem published a survey that showed most Christians throughout Israel and the Occupied Territories – Maronites, Catholics, Assyrians, Copts, Armenians, Evangelicals – supported Netanyahu because of his anti-Muslim position. That survey indicated that 30,000 Christians had voted for Netanyahu, the exact number of votes that had decided the election in his favour.

At the same time, in the United States, a well-funded public relations campaign, bolstered by support from powerful Washington insiders like former Assistant Secretary of State Elliot Abrams and prominent Orthodox Jewish Rabbi Daniel Lapin, head of Toward Tradition, a neo-conservative group based in Washington State, was launched to convince Jews that the Christian Right was not anti-Semitic, but rather the best friend that Israel had at a time when the nation was being ostracized by most of Europe and the Arab world.

In 1994, Toward Tradition funded a number of full-page advertisements in the *New York Times*. One, signed by Abrams, Midge Decter and more than seventy other neo-conservatives, defended the Christian Right from criticism by Jewish groups and sought to persuade Jews to overcome their mistrust and suspicion of Christian conservatives associated with the Republican Party. In a surprising turn of events which heartened the Conservatives and the Evangelicals, on 4 January 1995 the Republican Party took control of both the United States House of Representatives and the

Senate for the first time in more than forty years. At the time, many Republicans saw the victory as the beginning of a 'Republican revolution', and certainly it was a harbinger of things to come. In response to the victory led by conservative Republican and Evangelical Christian Newt Gingrich, who was also the House Majority Leader, Toward Tradition bought an ad in the *New York Times* to congratulate conservative Republicans and especially Newt Gingrich. Signed by Elliot Abrams and others, the ad read 'Mazel Tov', and reiterated its support for Gingrich's 'contract with America', which promised to bring moral values back to the country.

In 1999, President Clinton was reaching the end of his second term and had already been impeached, negotiations presided over by the United States had begun and ended, and territory had been offered and rejected and was being renegotiated. Ultra-religious Jewish settlers, supported primarily by Evangelical Christians, refused to relinquish one iota of Jewish soil based on doctrine they found in the Old Testament. On the other side of the conflict, the radical Islamic factions gained great popularity in the West Bank and Gaza and eventually garnered the majority of the popular vote over what had seemed to be the more mainstream Al-Fatah movement, led by Yasser Arafat. With the involvement of the Evangelicals and their physical presence in the Holy Land, yet another religious component had entered into the conflict with the intention of impeding the creation of a Palestinian state.

In September 2000, the second Intifada or Palestinian uprising erupted throughout the West Bank and Gaza. Suicide bombings by Palestinian terrorists were justified by the Koran's call to *jihad*, as the duty of every Muslim man, woman and child. The word *jihad* means 'struggle', and can mean anything from 'inner struggle for righteousness' to 'violent Holy War', depending on the context and the interpreter of the text. In December 2000, Ariel Sharon, the newly elected Israeli Prime Minister, addressed a group of 1,500 Christian Zionists who had travelled to Jerusalem. 'We regard you to be one of our best friends in the world,' the Prime Minister told a cheering crowd. In January 2000, a large group of influential Jewish scholars and rabbis signed a theological statement calling on Jews to relinquish their fear and mistrust of Christianity and to acknowledge church efforts in the decades since the Holocaust to amend Christian teaching about Judaism. The statement is called *Dabru Emet*, a biblical phrase that means 'to speak the truth to one another'. It was printed in paid advertisements in the Sunday *New York Times* and the *Baltimore Sun*, and was released by the Institute for Christian and Jewish Studies, an independent interfaith organization in Baltimore.[4]

The opening paragraph in the document speaks of an unprecedented shift in Jewish and Christian relations. In what is probably its most controversial point, the document states 'Nazism was not a Christian phenomenon.' The document claims major commonalities between the faiths, saying that Jews and Christians worship the same God, seek authority from the same book, the Old Testament, and accept the moral principles of the Torah. The second paragraph of the statement claims that it is time for Jews to learn about the efforts of Christians to honour Judaism, since both faiths worship the God of Abraham, Isaac and Jacob, and that 'through Christianity' hundreds of millions of people have entered into a relationship with the God of Israel.

This call for forgiveness and love asks the many Jewish leaders in the United States who, though supportive of Israel, remain committed to a liberal Democratic agenda domestically and internationally, to reject their 'habit of swearing loyalty' to every item on the Democratic Party platform. Moreover, it assumes that all Jews unconditionally support Israel's current position in the Palestinian conflict. Behind such statements is a longstanding and more calculated neo-conservative goal: to shift as much as possible of the overwhelmingly Democratic Jewish vote to the Republican column. As it turned out, it was an agenda which had an enormous effect on the outcome of the presidential election in 2004.

In a news release dated 20 June 2000, Rabbi Lapin called on Jews to defend the Christian Right and to stop supporting Jewish organizations that systematically attack Christian Evangelical organizations. In essence, Lapin encouraged American Jews to 'put aside their objections to the Christian Right's domestic agenda', and to 'regard the Evangelicals' love and support for Israel as something positive for the Jewish people'. His rationale was that the Jewish State was currently in peril, while abortion rights or gun control were items that could stand debate. 'Take care of your own' became the motto of a major portion of the Jewish community. By demanding that American Jews do what he thought was good for Israel, rather than what was good for the United States, Lapin's implication was that American Jews' primary duty was to Jewry and Israel, and only secondarily to the United States. The primacy of their obligation to Israel would not only trump their domestic concerns, but also lead to American Jews making Israel the sole consideration in their judgment of American foreign policy.

The resurgence to power of the Christian Right, therefore, at the end of President Clinton's eight years in the White House, was less the result of the Evil of Islam and more because a surprising majority of citizens viewed the Clinton years as having been morally bankrupt. In 2000, George W. Bush was elected President of the United States, largely because of the support of the Evangelical Christians and their disdain for opposition candidate Al Gore, who was considered tainted by his connection to the Clinton White House. For the first time since they had elected Ronald Reagan, the Christian Right was able once again to put 'one of their own' in the White House.

The 2000 Bush–Gore race was not only the most contested and bitterly fought election in American history, it was also the most God-fearing election campaign of the last hundred years. During the 2000 campaign, Elaine Kamarck, a Democratic advisor, declared, 'The Democratic Party is going to take back God this time.'[5]

James Robison, a television Evangelist who once led stadium crusades to convert people into accepting Jesus in their lives, is now the host of a Christian talk show in Dallas. Shortly before the 2000 presidential campaign began, after the news that Al Gore had enough votes to garner the Democratic nomination, Robison received a phone call one Sunday from a believer who asked if they could pray together. It was George W. Bush, looking for help in preparing for a 'tough road' ahead. Robison told Bush that he was not going to know every answer to every 'woe that America is suffering'. They prayed together on the phone and asked God to grant Mr Bush 'calm, confidence and the wisdom to know when to speak and when not to speak, and the serenity to make good judgments for the sake of God and the American people'.[6]

During the 2000 campaign, and again immediately after

his State of the Union address in January 2004, whenever George W. Bush was asked which political philosopher he admired the most, he always replied, 'Christ, because he changed my heart.' During an interview in 2000 at his ranch in Crawford, Texas, the just-elected President quoted verbatim the existential question WWJD (What Would Jesus Do?) found on a special bracelet worn by thousands of Christian teenagers, before announcing: 'Faith is the center of my life.'[7] In the 2004 election, George W. Bush continued to maintain that God had told him directly that he was His preferred choice for President of the United States. 'God has chosen me to fulfill this duty for all Americans, whether they are Democrat or Republican, Christian or Jew, and so I am in God's hands.' By July 2004, he had revised God's message somewhat, telling a group of reporters in Dallas, 'I think God knows I've done the best job that I could, but only because I allowed myself to be guided by Jesus Christ.'

Despite the support of the Christian Right, George W. Bush's presidency had no real direction in the beginning other than reducing taxes which would benefit the rich, cutting social welfare programmes for the poor, and imparting a godly moral directive. The moral agenda limped along without any measurable success.

The Bush presidency became defined and took form one year into the new century, on 11 September 2001, when the unthinkable happened. Islamic Fundamentalists attacked the United States, resulting in the deaths of more than three thousand people. This time, the catastrophe surpassed even the Iranian hostage crisis of 1979, and was interpreted by the Evangelical community as a message from God Himself. Apparently, President Bush also heard that message because his presidency suddenly became defined by its fight against terrorism, which brought faith, God and religion to the forefront of American politics and served as the basis of his political agenda. The attacks also caused a renewed form of militant piety that slowly crept into the consciousness of the American people.

If 1979 was the beginning of the last crusade for Evangelical Christians to rid the world of an Islamic threat, 2001 was further proof that the war was far from over. If 1979 was the storm that drove Americans to seek shelter with the Lord, 2001 was the moral earthquake that made them realize that the Lord Himself was at risk. The Israeli–Palestinian conflict was once again viewed as a microcosm of a larger war, no longer between the two superpowers, but a holy war that pitted the Judeo-Christian world against Islam.

In the years following 1979, when Evangelicals were briefly catapulted to political prominence, compromise was never an option when it came to their domestic agenda. Neither was making certain issues a priority over others. After the tragedy of 11 September 2001, the Christian Right realized that their potential for influencing foreign policy was far greater than their ability to change laws that infringed on the private lives of individuals. Fear and hysteria swept the country. The extent to which Evangelicals have always focused on local and state domestic issues in the United States became less important to them than their ability to change the outcome of national elections, the purpose of which was to direct American policy throughout the Arab world, most specifically as it shaped the Israeli–Palestinian conflict.

The concept of *priority* rather than *compromise* began brewing in the Evangelical cauldron.

After the destruction of the World Trade Center and the partial destruction of the Pentagon, the Christian Right rose from obscurity to political power. Emotions peaked, and national grieving and shock permeated the entire nation. Even the average secular citizen was willing to accept the premise that America was engaged in a holy war, one not of its own making. But the Evangelicals went even further. By making the Abrahamic Covenant a priority over other biblical teachings that are interpreted as God's wrath against homosexuals or God's opposition to abortion, they made their presence known to all sides of the political spectrum. It didn't take long for Democrats as well as Republicans to understand that the Evangelical community was growing more powerful every day. Regardless of the outcome of any election, the Religious Right would not disappear. Nor would its leaders make the same mistakes as their predecessors had during the 1980s.

Unlike the previous generation of Evangelical leaders, a new breed of Christian leaders was well poised to mobilize not only their followers but the secular segment of the country as well. Between 1979 and 2001, they had had sufficient time to re-organize and re-define their approach to save as many souls as possible, especially those who had not yet entered into the kingdom of heaven. Self-confident, educated, sophisticated and assertive, the new Evangelicals could no longer be dismissed as Bible-toting, itinerant, greedy preachers. The majority were respected pillars of the American mainstream and were highly sophisticated about garnering support within their own community as well as within the Jewish community to work together to save democracy and, above all, to preserve Judeo-Christian values. Across party lines, voters expected politicians and political candidates to make national security a priority. Americans, even those who were not religious, became familiar with the inclusion of God in any candidate's political rhetoric. They grew to accept many politicians' claims that they knew what God wanted them to do, that it was His will, not their own, that would save Christianity and preserve democracy. For Evangelicals, God had always been a prerequisite for a safe America. For the secular segment of the population, evoking God could only help to guarantee that America would continue to exist.

CHAPTER TWELVE

Fear and Loathing in America

Why of course the people don't want war . . . But after all it is the leaders of the country who determine the policy, and it is always a simple matter to drag the people along . . . whether it is a democracy, or a fascist dictatorship, or a parliament, or a communist dictatorship . . . Voice or no voice, the people can always be brought to the bidding of the leaders; that is easy. All you have to do is to tell them they are being attacked, and denounce the pacifists for lack of patriotism and exposing the country to danger.
(Hermann Goering at the Nuremberg Trials)

THE Patriot Act became law in the United States on 25 October 2001, only six weeks after the terrorist attacks. It expanded the guidelines of the Foreign Intelligence Surveillance Act (FISA) which already gave the government the power to search and spy on American citizens. The purpose of FISA was to identify and capture international spies by implementing wire taps and breaking into suspects' homes and offices to photocopy suspicious documents or to plant 'bugs' to monitor their activities. In response to the terrorist attacks in September 2001, surveillance requests in 2002 by the federal government under FISA outnumbered all those under law for the first time in American history. Many believed there was ample reason for the government to be over-cautious since the events of 9/11, but the danger, of course, was that government officials like John Ashcroft misused their privilege and responsibility to protect the United States from radical Islamic terrorists bent on destroying not only the United States but Christianity itself.

The United States Patriot Act has given the country's law enforcement agencies the power to exercise random searches, unwarranted seizures and arbitrary arrests. Almost everyone detained under the Patriot Act has been accused or suspected of a connection to Middle East terrorism. Since 9/11 there has been a whole new class of criminal cases in which technicalities in the law have allowed the indefinite and secret detention of American citizens or legal residents in solitary confinement and without access to a lawyer, if the President of the United States designates a detainee an 'enemy combatant'. Though the detainee can technically force the court to hold a *habeas corpus* proceeding requiring specific charges to be made, the Justice Department has only to state its suspicions about the person being held, without having to offer concrete evidence or be subjected to cross-examination by the subject's attorney, for that person to continue being held without any specific charges. This means that the *habeas corpus* hearing (the most fundamental of all legal rights, established by Magna Carta in 1215) is an exercise in futility. FISA, in conjunction with the Patriot Act, had and has the potential to apprehend spies and terrorists, but can also be used to monitor the private activities, such as sexual practices, of American citizens considered by those in power to be behaving contrary to the Bible. According to FISA under then Attorney General Ashcroft, the agency could gain entry into the homes and offices of American citizens without informing them, and can conduct an investigation without advising suspects that they are the focus of that investigation. From 11 September 2001 until his resignation shortly after the November 2004 elections, Ashcroft approved more than 22,000 anti-terrorist subpoenas and search warrants, aimed at American citizens and foreign residents. In May 2003, he admitted that the Justice Department, under his direction, had on 248 occasions delayed notifying a target that he or she was under investigation. During the past two years, a plan has been under consideration to put microchips in the new digital subway fare cards so that anyone using the public transportation system can be monitored from the moment he or she puts his or her card in the turnstile to the moment he or she gets off at a particular station. What this microchip would do is to increase the ability of the government to watch any citizen far beyond the method now in use, of random checks in the subways by police with hand-held metal detectors.

Another aspect of this increase in the government's power to invade the privacy of ordinary citizens is the Total Information Awareness Program or TIA, a Pentagon project led by Rear Admiral John Poindexter. Although Congress has curtailed TIA activities, the purpose of the project was to allow the government electronic access to the private affairs of all Americans. The opinion was that the advantages of government access to credit card statements or medical records was more intrusive on the rights of citizens than warranted by the expected benefits. This does not mean that opinions won't change in the future, especially if there is a consistent threat of terrorist attacks. When Congress curtailed the activities of the TIA, it did not completely stop the agency's activities and has reserved the right to 're-activate' or 'expand' its powers at any time. Agents can still examine the private life of any foreigner, and there are rumours that installation of a system to monitor all intruders who attempt to reach American shores, resembling one along the Israeli coastline, is in the works.

After the attacks of 11 September 2001, President George W. Bush created the Department of Homeland Security, with an annual budget of $36 billion. The money has been spent on a variety of security efforts, including $5.8 billion spent hiring, training and equipping federal airport screeners and $3 billion allocated for 'bio-terrorism preparedness'. The remaining billions are being spent on sophisticated radiation sensors and surveillance systems that have already been installed in some cities, as well as on financing the Federal Bureau of Investigation (FBI) to create files on those individuals who, for example, take scuba-diving courses, considering them suspect because of a possible 'underwater' attack.

Because of the fear and paranoia that gripped the country after the 9/11 attacks, President Bush was able to focus on the domestic agenda of his benefactors within the Christian Right. During his first four years in the White House, Bush kept his promise to the 80 million Evangelicals who helped elect him, by clouding the separation between church and state as set down by the Founding Fathers in the Constitution. President Bush's 'compassionate conservative' agenda became a euphemism for faith in God and unquestioning belief in the Bible

Evangelical Christians believe that any action taken on the basis of faith eliminates any chance of error, since God is the last word on any and all decisions. In the hearts and minds of those devout Americans, it would be disastrous in times of conflict and terror to incur God's wrath. Following that logic, Evangelicals believe that the sin of abortion, when innocent unborn babies – whom they regard as complete human beings with souls – are killed, will result in the eventual massacre of other innocent human beings in more advanced stages of their lives. Murder is murder as far as they are concerned, whether the victims are civilians who die in terrorist attacks, soldiers who die fighting the terrorists who commit those acts, or aborted unborn babies.

One striking ambiguity in the tenets of the Religious Right is their ferocity against abortion coupled with their enthusiasm for the death penalty. According to a Gallup poll taken in December 2003, 99 per cent of the people who uphold the tenet of 'pro-life', are also in favour of capital punishment.

When George W. Bush was Governor of Texas, a state that performs more executions than any other, he presided over the executions of one sixth of all of those killed there since the death penalty was re-instituted in 1976. Louisiana, another state whose legislators have a majority voting record against abortion, is second only to Texas in the number of executions carried out every year. Two of the chief prosecutors in the District Attorney's office in Jefferson County, which has put more people to death in recent years than any other parish in Louisiana, have not only defended the rights of unborn babies, they also wear ghoulish neckties while trying capital cases, to illustrate their keenness for the death penalty. Two of the more popular designs on the ties are a dangling rope and an image of the Grim Reaper. Wearing the ties in an open courtroom is not just bad taste, but typifies the racist-tinged, bloodthirsty culture that permeates the Jefferson County District Attorney's office, since most of those tried for murder are African-Americans. They seem only one step removed from lynch mobs in their zeal for 'an eye for an eye' within the criminal justice system. Their love for execution does not abate even when the trial is over. Every time a prosecutor wins a death sentence, the entire staff takes up a collection for a plaque with a needle on it (executions are by lethal injection), and the condemned man's name is proudly displayed on the winning prosecutor's office wall.[1]

While the death penalty is an emotional subject, legalized abortion in the United States probably evokes the most passionate feelings among born-again Christians. Demonstrations are commonplace throughout America during which those opposing abortion often carry graphic photographs of aborted foetuses or hoist new-born babies in front of television cameras, pointing to those infants who are 'survivors' of abortion as opposed to those who were 'targeted for murder'.

On 13 December 1971, the Supreme Court first heard the now-famous *Roe* vs. *Wade* argument, brought by a pregnant single woman (Roe) who instigated a class action suit challenging the constitutionality of the Texas criminal abortion laws, which made any abortion, except one on medical advice for the sole purpose of saving the mother's life, a crime. The case was re-argued before the Supreme Court on 11 October 1972 and finally decided in favour of Roe on 22 January 1973. Abortion was made legal on demand throughout the United States if done by a qualified physician and performed not later than twenty weeks into any pregnancy, before foetal viability. Exceptions were made where the abortion could be performed even later into gestation if the mother's life was at risk. In reality, however, the question of abortion has never been settled.

Abortion, for President Bush, has always been an important issue. Since he took office, while he has taken steps to blur the lines between the holy and the powerful, his appointment of John Ashcroft as Attorney General on the anniversary of *Roe* vs. *Wade* – 22 January 2001 – was not lost on the Evangelical community. Ashcroft, whose religious adherence to Scripture and his Pentecostal moral compass make George W. Bush look like a heretic, is known for his opposition to abortion. On the day of Mr Ashcroft's appointment as Attorney General, President Bush said, 'We share a great goal, to work towards the day when every child is welcome and protected in law.'

On his first day in office, President Bush reinstated a ban on federal funding of any group associated with abortion or abortion counselling. The non-governmental organizations or NGOs were hit the hardest as they are the ones who habitually deal with the urban poor, who count on public funding to pay for their abortions. At the same time, the White House office of Faith-Based and Community Initiatives set out upon a programme of redistribution, taking funds from existing social programmes in favour of abortion, and transferring them to individual church organizations to help them fund their own local social programmes, such as drug or alcohol addictions. The only condition for participation in the church group was mandatory attendance at prayer and Bible readings, regardless of faith or lack of faith. In response to his critics, President Bush maintained that, 'without faith in God, it is impossible to overcome anything, including alcohol or drug addiction – reason enough to insist that all participants in those social programs join in prayer.'[2]

During the Texas legislative session in 2003, the same state that was the testing ground for *Roe* vs. *Wade*, a bill was passed, authored by State Representative Ralph Corte, which required the following protections for the unborn: first, a pregnant mother must be shown her baby's characteristics with colour pictures during each two-week period of gestation; second, the mother must be informed that there is a theory that links abortion with breast cancer; third, a

159

twenty-four-hour waiting period is required before an abortion can be performed; fourth, there must be face-to-face communication between the pregnant mother and the abortionist before the procedure; and fifth, no state funding will be paid to any organization which either performs abortions or refers patients for abortions.

Although many Republicans have offered the 'pro-life' (anti-abortion) movement rhetorical tributes, Bush's policy has been the biggest political victory for the pro-life movement since Ronald Reagan was President.

On 7 November 2003, President Bush signed into law a ban, which passed first in the House of Representatives (Congress) and then in the Senate, on 'partial-birth abortion', a term that has entered into the Evangelical lexicon. The term is not only a law that prevents aborting a foetus at more than three months in all cases, even at the expense of a mother's life, it represents an acknowledgment of President Bush's loyalty to the Christian Right.

When the bill was signed by President Bush in the Oval Office, seven prominent Evangelical 'pro-life' Christians who had been instrumental in lobbying to pass the law were present. Two of those witnessing the event were the Reverend Jerry Falwell and Ed McAteer, the 'godfather' of the Christian Right. Another man who witnessed the event was Charles Colson, the Watergate felon who found Jesus while serving time in prison for his illegal activities leading to President Richard Nixon's resignation. During the meeting that preceded the signing, Bush announced that his administration would put all its resources behind the partial-birth abortion ban. Then he asked the group if everyone would join hands and 'pray that God will bless our efforts to preserve life in our land'.[3] 'What an astounding moment for me personally,' the Reverend Jerry Falwell said. 'Standing there in the Oval Office I felt suddenly humbled to be in the presence of a man – our President – who takes his faith very seriously and who seeks the prayers of his friends as he leads our nation.' Following the prayer, Reverend Falwell told President Bush that the seven people present in the room that day represented about 200,000 pastors and 80 million believers nationwide who considered him 'not only to be our President but also a man of God'. In response, Bush turned towards Falwell and said, 'I'll try to live up to it.'[4]

Another witness in the Oval Office that day was Jay Sekulow, a lawyer for the Christian Right and the principal defender of the constitutionality of the partial-birth abortion ban. 'The law is constitutionally sound and we're hopeful it will survive the legal challenges which are already underway,' Sekulow said. 'We will work aggressively to assist the United States Department of Justice in defending this law as it makes its way through the courts and ultimately to the Supreme Court.' In response, President Bush called for another prayer. 'Please join me in praying for Jay and his team,' the President said, 'and the Justice Department attorneys and the many other attorneys who will be defending the partial-birth abortion ban.' After the prayer ended, Falwell added, 'Let us put our hands on this fine man and pray. May God keep President Bush at the forefront of our prayers as he leads this important battle, because this is one fight that deserves our vigilant prayers.'[5]

When the prayer ended, the President's eyes were filled with tears. After the Reverend Falwell emerged from the Oval Office, he made the following statement about George W. Bush's level of faith. 'The Scriptures say God is the one who appoints leaders,' Falwell said, 'and if a leader truly knows God, that would give him a special anointing. At certain times, at certain hours in our country, God has had a special man to hear His testimony and more than anything else, God loves leaders who have overcome adversity by finding their life's mission. Our President has gone from drinking too much to building a new world architecture.'[6]

The United States is a country founded on religious freedom. It would, therefore, be wrong to take someone to task, even the President of the United States, because he considers God and his religion central to his existence. It would be equally unjust to criticize him or anyone else because they had occasion to gather together for a moment of prayer people who happen to share their religious faith. The question that begs a response, however, is: when does a religious moment in the Oval Office interfere with the separation of church and state as structured explicitly in the Constitution? When are domestic and foreign policy issues succumbing to religious interests?

In the United States the people elect their leaders to make their voices heard. In any democracy, the debate between church and state is not always a black-or-white issue. For example, the debate falls into a grey area when a religious individual is elected by the people to run a school board, and, based on his or her religious convictions, is in favour of Bible study. In that instance, the debate should be not whether school prayer should be a mandated law, but whether or not those who wish to have Bible study should be allowed to use public school facilities, paid for by public monies, rather than using a facility paid for by private donations. The debate falls into a dark shade of grey, however, when that same school board official, who happens to adhere to a particular religious conviction, violates the spirit of the Constitution by forcing students to participate in prayer, whether on school premises, or in a separate privately funded facility. Finally, the debate moves into a black area of controversy when a particular religious group exerts influence over the President of the United States in domestic issues such as prayer in schools or in foreign policy issues concerning the workings of any sovereign state.

The events of 11 September not only unleashed America's war on terrorism, but also brought to the forefront of government certain religious ideas that have become the basis for the Republican domestic policy agenda.

Ironically, while Ronald Reagan has become the *de facto* example of the best kind of conservative Republican in recent American history, he suffered for over a decade, not only from Alzheimer's, but because he was one of the millions of victims of a law that prohibits federal funding for embryonic stem-cell research which doctors believe will provide a cure for Alzheimer's and other terrible diseases.

When the former President was ninety-three years old and in the last stages of the illness, his wife Nancy took to using her influence to push for federal funding of embryonic stem-cell research. President George W. Bush, who certainly has some of the good-natured traits that his predecessor Ronald Reagan had, has gone far beyond Reagan's stand against abortion given the new technological advances at the forefront of modern medicine. Bush has incorporated his stand against abortion to include stem-cell research, which involves the cloning of cells and destruction of early human embryos in the laboratory. For religious conservatives, harvesting embryos represents a horrifying industrialization of abortion. For scientists, stem-cell research offers the possibility of treating horrific diseases, replacing damaged human organs and conceivably even halting the ageing process.

Changing her opinion in front of the many pro-life conservatives who remained her husband's staunchest supporters, Mrs Reagan said, 'This is not the same as abortion.

This is about giving life.'[7] In fact, in 2001 she wrote a personal letter to President Bush in which she pleaded that he change his position on stem-cell research. President Bush did not make any effort to take Mrs Reagan's pleas into consideration.

Gary Bauer is an influential and powerful Evangelical who served in President Reagan's administration for eight years, beginning in July 1985 as Undersecretary of Education and, in that capacity, was named Chairman of President's Reagan's Special Working Group on the Family. A slight elfin man with wisps of fair hair and large blue eyes, he served as the President's Chief Domestic Policy Advisor during the last two years of President Reagan's administration. Most recently, Bauer challenged President George W. Bush for the Republican nomination for President in the 2000 election and currently heads American Values, a right-wing Christian group based in Washington, D.C., whose goals are to elect 'Reagan-type candidates' who will 'uphold the moral values of the Bible'. And yet Gary Bauer, despite his love and respect for President Reagan, did not change his position against harvesting embryos for medical research. Bauer believes that conservatives will 'no longer tolerate the politicians they elect to surrender on cultural or moral issues'. 'What will we have gained,' Bauer asked rhetorically, 'if we defeat the "axis of evil" abroad and lower taxes, but at home abandon our Founders' conviction that only a virtuous people can remain free?'[8]

During an interview at his offices in Washington, D.C., Bauer maintained that people who are in church on Sunday and in voting booths on Tuesday comprise at least 40 per cent of the Republican coalition, the largest faction in the party. 'If you were an alien,' Bauer explained, 'and you landed on earth the day after the last presidential election and you met Americans on the street and you wanted to find out how they had voted, but you couldn't ask them their party affiliation, the question you would want to ask them is if they are regular church attendees. Because people who said yes voted overwhelmingly Republican, and people who said no, voted overwhelmingly Democrat.'

Critics of the Bush administration have claimed that those topics that are dear to the Christian Right have taken attention away from employment, economic growth, education, health-care, child-care and a social-welfare system – all usual concerns of any enlightened Western democracy. Nonetheless, this climate of religion is exactly what President Bush promised he would instill in America when he was on the campaign trail, courting the nearly 80 million Evangelical Christians who voted him into office in 2000 and who re-elected him in 2004. Other issues that President Bush has embraced are the legal battle about whether the words 'under God' should remain in the Pledge of Allegiance to the flag. Millions of public school children are compelled to recite the Pledge with those words before the school day begins, even those among them who are atheists, agnostics, or Hindu, Buddhist, or Muslim.

Originally the Pledge, in keeping with the Constitution, was devoid of any religious references. In 1954, in the aftermath of the Korean War, President Eisenhower signed into law an act adding the words 'under God' to the Pledge of Allegiance. By way of justifying his decision, Eisenhower told the American people, 'In this way, we are reaffirming the transcendence of religious faith in America's heritage and future; in this way we shall constantly strengthen those spiritual weapons which forever will be our country's most powerful resource in peace and war.'[9] Immediately following the signing ceremony, Eisenhower wrote, 'From this day forward, millions of our school children will daily proclaim . . . the dedication of our nation and our people to the Almighty.'[10]

Some thirty years after President Eisenhower incorporated those words into the Pledge, George Bush, father of the current President, made the Pledge with the words 'Under God' a key issue in his 1988 campaign against Democratic presidential candidate Michael Dukakis.

Another issue that has pitted the Evangelicals against the secular segment of society has to do with the Ten Commandments. In late 2003, Justice Roy Moore of the state of Alabama approved the construction of a massive monument, on which the Ten Commandments are engraved, to be placed as a permanent exhibit in the Alabama Judiciary Building in the state's capital, Montgomery. Supporters of the monument declared that the Ten Commandments were 'universal', although more than 15 per cent of the population does not adhere to the laws of God given to Moses. The stone monument was removed, but the battle continues to wage in the Supreme Court.

Another emotive topic is gay marriage. During the 2004 presidential campaign Gary Bauer was also one of the most vocal and active Evangelicals against gay marriage. It was as crucial an issue to that election as abortion was in 2000. Bauer, along with many other powerful Evangelical leaders, warned President Bush well before the beginning of the campaign that if he failed to support an amendment to the Constitution that banned same-sex marriages, he risked losing their support. 'We understand,' Bauer told me, 'the dilemma for any Republican President or presidential candidate who supports an amendment that bans gay marriage – he risks alienating a major portion of his more moderate Republican electorate. We understand, but we don't accept it.'[11]

The message from the Evangelicals to the White House has become even clearer. A slogan on the back of the Republican Convention programme in 2000 and again in 2004 read, 'What Can 80 Million Evangelicals Do For America? Anything They Want!'

CHAPTER THIRTEEN

With God on the Campaign Trail

They say you can't legislate morality. Well, you certainly can.
(John Ashcroft, 25 May 1998,
quoted in the *Chicago Tribune*)

KARL Rove, George W. Bush's strategist, took the message seriously during the 2004 campaign. He remembered how in 2000 Bush nearly lost the election because four million Evangelicals simply did not vote. Robert Knight, director of the Culture and Family Institute, who was also important to helping George W. Bush win re-election, says, 'Jesus taught us that the value of teaching young children charity, peace, and kindness is indisputable.'[1] Knight claims that radical homosexuals and civil libertarians are the ones adamantly opposed to religious values in public schools.

The debate about gay marriage was an emotive issue during the first four years that Bush was in the White House, and became even more crucial in the 2004 campaign when the Massachusetts Supreme Court approved homosexual and lesbian unions. Evangelical Christians were deeply involved in overturning the ruling to prevent any other states attempting to legalize gay and lesbian marriages, quoting Deuteronomy: 'God did not intend for men to lie with men or women with women.' That is eerily similar to the slogan used by segregationists in 1958 when they, too, quoted from Deuteronomy 7:3 condemning interracial marriages: 'Almighty God . . . did not intend for races to mix.' It was only in 1967 that the Supreme Court banned laws concerning interracial marriage.

On 12 February 2004, marriage licences were issued in San Francisco to more than 3,300 same-sex couples. And in a small upstate New York town called the Village of New Paltz, a young mayor – a member of the environmentalist Green Party, a Democrat and a likely candidate for Governor of New York in 2006 – began officiating at a series of short afternoon ceremonies for same-sex couples. President Bush responded to the situation in all three states by claiming that the 'digression from law' was the result of a 'handful of activist judges'. He made it clear that he considered marriage to be 'the most fundamental institution of civilization'. In support of the President, David Huizenga, pastor of the Sunshine Community Church, the largest Christian Reform Church in Michigan, claimed that he received daily numerous e-mails from such Christian conservative groups as the American Family Association. 'If we allow this, then marriage is in danger in our country,' Huizenga said. 'I think marriage would be a joke in this country. It would further the breakdown of our society and our schools.'[2]

Fundamentalists almost all believe that gay marriage 'goes against God's plan'. One woman, a member of an Evangelical Church in Connecticut, said, 'Homosexuals are disillusioned [sic] by lies from Satan.'

Whether or not Satan plays a part in the debate about homosexuality, what is certain is that God entered into the polemic when He took His place on the campaign trail. For President Bush to have stated that God opposed homosexu-

169

ality should not come as a surprise to the American people. In 2003, President Bush proclaimed the week of 12 October 'Marriage Protection Week', a move, as he explained it, 'against those gay lobbyists whose aim is to get activist judges to accord the status of marriage to same-sex relationships'.[3] Congressman Tom DeLay, the House Majority Leader and a fervent born-again Christian, denounced what he called a 'runaway judiciary', and vowed to seek a constitutional amendment prohibiting marriage between gays. 'This is not going to stop here – this is going to be in the forefront for a long time to come,'[4] he said. According to Ed Gillespie, chairman of the Republican National Committee, the American public is 'overwhelmingly opposed to gay marriage'.[5] A poll of 1,515 Americans conducted between 15 and 19 October 2003, by the Pew Research Center for the People and the Press, found that 59 per cent of respondents opposed gay marriage.

The Defense of Marriage Act (DOMA) was proposed into law on 7 May 1996. It cleared the Congress by a vote of 347 to 67 and the Senate by 85 in favour and 14 opposed, and was signed into law on 10 September 1996 by President Bill Clinton. In brief, DOMA denied the federal government the authority to decide for individual states concerning same-sex marriages. Rather, the bill provides that each state be 'required to give effect to or law of any other state with respect to same sex marriage'. At the same time Congress and the Senate voted (50–49) against a law which would ban employers from discriminating on the basis of sexual orientation. Senator John Kerry, Democratic candidate for President in 2004, was only one of fourteen senators who voted against DOMA. Recently, Congress used its power under the full faith and credit provision in the Constitution to legislate that 'no state can be forced to give effect to any other state's recognition of same-sex relationships.'

During the 2004 campaign, Evangelicals claimed that Kerry not only supported homosexual marriage, but advocated the 'homosexual relentless quest to gain governmental and social endorsement of their lifestyle(s)'. Reverend Jerry Falwell claimed, 'Homosexual advocates are invading our public schools to secure gullible disciples of their dangerous social agenda.' He further maintained that the Gay, Lesbian, and Straight Education Network has printed a 'curriculum guide' for public school teachers that presents a six-point lesson plan, designed to 'convince students that homosexual relationships are the equivalent of traditional man–woman relationships'.[6]

'The lesson plans range from discussing the historical parallels of same-sex marriage,' Falwell claimed during an interview on the *Travis Smiley Show*, 'to providing students with the chance to read books about homosexual relations and then consider what it would be like to be in a same-sex wedding.'[7]

The danger in such propaganda – that homosexuality can be taught and is even possibly contagious – is that teachers suspected of being homosexual will be fired or worse. Linda Harvey of Mission America, another Evangelical organization, wrote an article for her organization's internal newspaper which detailed how students across the nation are being 'inundated with pro-homosexual material'.

'At the same time,' she claims, 'students of faith are often ridiculed in these classes.'[8]

Claude Allen is another critic of homosexuality. Allen came to media attention as a religious and political conservative when, as the spokesman for the 1984 re-election campaign of Senator Jesse Helms, he was quoted as saying that their Democratic opponent was vulnerable because of his links with 'queers'. Allen, who is active in a Christian group that works in the United States and in Israel to encourage homosexuals to 'take the road to Jesus', was recently nominated by President Bush to the United States Court of Appeals for the Fourth Circuit Court in Virginia. Coincidentally, another member of that Christian group is Bill Pryor, the Alabama Attorney General who is also a nominee for the United States Court of Appeals for the Eleventh Circuit in Atlanta. Bill Pryor is best remembered for his brief to the Supreme Court in 2003 in defence of a Texas law that criminalizes sexual relations between gays. The brief puts sexual relations between gays in the same category as necrophilia, bestiality and paedophilia, and argues that states have the right to punish people who engage in gay sex as criminals. In support of Pryor's point of view, President Bush opened the 2003 summit with Russian President Vladimir Putin by saying, 'We need common-sense judges who understand that our rights were derived from God, and those are the kind of judges I intend to put on the bench.'

Notwithstanding their position on gay rights and same-sex marriage, Evangelicals have been known to compromise, defend and show loyalty to their own, even if one of their own goes against their biblical beliefs. One past example of that loyalty involves the Reverend Billy Graham. During Lyndon B. Johnson's administration, one of President Johnson's closest advisors, Walter Jenkins, was caught in a compromising position with a bartender in a men's room at the YMCA. Upon learning of Jenkins' arrest, the first person President Johnson called was Billy Graham. Five days after the scandal broke in the media, Graham visited President Johnson to offer his support. 'You know,' Graham said, 'when Jesus dealt with people with moral problems, like dear

Walter, he always dealt tenderly. I just hope if you have any contact with him, you'll give him my love and understanding.'[9] As it turned out, Johnson never saw Jenkins again. After a few days in a Washington psychiatric hospital, Jenkins returned to Texas, his career in politics finished.

A more recent example of tolerance concerns a woman, an avowed lesbian and political activist within the gay and lesbian community, who stood proudly beside her father in January 2000, as he was sworn in as Vice-President of the United States in 2000 and was proudly present when he won re-election in 2004.

Mary Cheney, Vice-President Cheney's daughter, worked as the Gay Relations manager for Coors Brewing. She has been fortunate that those on the far right have chosen to 'respect her personal privacy'. The details of Mary's life are vague, although she and her 'life partner' Heather Poe live in the Denver, Colorado area in a house they jointly own. All those who know her and her father note the unusually close relationship between them. 'They would go on vacation together, just the two of them,' a close friend relates. 'It's rare for an openly lesbian daughter and her father to be so close. The two have traveled to Russia and South America and enjoy hunting and fly-fishing together.'[10]

Elizabeth Birch, executive director of the Human Rights Campaign, a gay political action committee, believes that Mary Cheney's sexuality remains an important issue to all campaigns. 'It is relevant because Mary's presence is precisely what we have been saying for years,' Birch said. 'Gay people live inside of American families.'[11] In fact, the Vice-President's daughter is fairly conservative when it comes to political issues other than gay rights.

Democrat or Republican, the gay community is comprised of men and women who consider issues other than same-sex marriage when voting for a political candidate. For example, Margaret Leber, a lesbian, a registered Republican and a member of the Pink Pistols, an organization of gay and lesbian gun owners, considers the Democratic position on gun control to be contrary to her profound beliefs. 'Somebody with my values and beliefs cannot be a single issue voter.'[12]

The Log Cabin Republicans, founded twenty-five years ago, is a group of gay and lesbian Republicans who, aside from their sexual preferences, embrace all the other right-wing issues of the mainstream Republican Party. Patrick Guerriero, executive director of the group, estimates that a million people identify themselves as gay Republicans who voted for Bush in 2000. Though George W. Bush has always been in favour of family values and, as Governor of Texas, supported laws that made homosexual activity between consenting adults a crime, he faced a dilemma during the re-election campaign. An openly gay family friend of George W. Bush, Charles Francis, arranged a meeting between Bush and gay Republicans, focusing on such subjects as gay siblings, gay marriage and AIDS. Francis has since founded the Republican Unity Coalition, a group of prominent Republicans, including former President Ford, dedicated to making sexual orientation a non-issue in the Republican Party. He maintains that the one million gays and lesbians who voted for Bush in 2000 would not do so in 2004 if the President pushed for the Marriage Amendment to the Constitution.

During a series of interviews with gay Republicans, the majority of them voiced their concern that people seem to assume that only heterosexuals worry about taxes or national security, while homosexuals are concerned only about their own sexuality. Jim McFarland, a member of the Pro-Life

Alliance of Gays and Lesbians and an active gay Republican, has always supported President Bush because he believes that the President 'would handle foreign policy much better and fiscal policy much better. I certainly don't want that big tax cut reversed that he passed,' McFarland said. 'There are other issues that have a big impact on my life other than my being gay.'[13]

To some there are more crucial issues, but not to all.

On the issues of abortion and homosexuality, both the Catholic Church and the Evangelicals have been unable to relinquish the traditions of sexual repression and misogyny which have existed in all the monotheistic religions.

For leaders of all religions and denominations, abortion and homosexuality are considered sins against God and His commandments, partly because controlling the sexual activity of believers is a strong factor in social control. Traditional family values, as expounded by the Christian Right, call for women to be the guardians and caretakers of the home and family, subservient to their husbands.

Traditionally, Christianity, while controlled by men, has prospered largely through the faithful adherence of women – it was mostly women who went to church, made novenas, and inculcated the children. But a new attempt by Fundamentalists to engage fully the men of America is off to a running start.

One of the more radical groups of Evangelical men is Promise Keepers, an organization that is Catholic in its roots and charismatic to its core and supported without reservation by Billy Graham. The Promise Keepers are a group of men whose goal is to 'celebrate biblical manhood and motivate men towards Christ-like masculinity'. Founded in 1990 by Bill McCartney, head coach of the University of Colorado football team, Promise Keepers was born out of his commitment to 'unite men through vital relationships to become godly influences in their world – by making promises to Jesus Christ and to one another that last a lifetime'.

Although McCartney is credited with founding Promise Keepers, Randy Phillips, a senior pastor who led the Denver Broncos Bible study group for two years, is Acting President and administrative head of the organization. Both McCartney and Phillips are former Catholics affiliated with the charismatic Vineyard movement which emphasizes the validity of 'signs and wonders' for today and views miraculous displays of divine power as essential to the growth of the church. Mel Gibson, another Vineyard adherent, produced and starred in the film, *Signs*, about bizarre and unexplainable crop delineations that are purported to come from either God or aliens.

Promise Keepers have a range of programmes and self-help seminars geared to 'maximize' Christian manhood by encouraging men to share their problems, to weep openly and embrace one another as a means of offering comfort and support through the trials and tribulations of trying to be a 'good Christian male in today's ungodly world'. Some of the events that the group organizes are stadium rallies, pastors' conferences, national television advertising spots, a newsletter and an Internet website. Thomas Nelson Publishers, an Evangelical publishing group in the United States, has produced nearly two dozen Christian titles for Christian men, including a revised version of Bill McCartney's autobiography, *From Ashes To Glory*.[14]

Many Evangelical claims and activities are clouded by hypocrisy and ambiguity, beginning with their professed love for the Jewish people, and ending with their abhorrence of homosexuality. A former member of Promise Keepers, who dropped out because of what he called blatant 'homosexual advances' by other members that 'distressed and disturbed his sense of godly equilibrium', described to me some of his experiences during his ten years as a faithful follower of the group, on condition of anonymity. He said that the Promise Keepers believe that men, by 'walking away from their family duties, are responsible for much of society's dysfunction . . . And that dysfunction [causes] high school dropouts, a soaring crime rate, racism, divorce, homosexuality and abortion.' Promise Keepers believe that the only way to restore America to a moral God-fearing country is by recruiting men to be 'promise keepers' instead of 'promise breakers'. 'The Women's Liberation Movement,' he continued, 'was a reaction to the pain and abuse that women suffered at the hands of men. What [Promise Keepers] are searching for is not only another purpose for the male in society but a new male identity in a world that is conflicted and constantly changing.'

Promise Keepers has formed separate partnerships with various Evangelical denominations, such as the Assemblies of God (John Ashcroft's Church) and the International Pentecostal Holiness Church. In fact, the Assemblies of God Church has appointed a liaison between its ministry and the Promise Keepers in an effort to increase membership. Recently, the group was achieving agreements with the Southern Baptist Convention and the Christian and Missionary Alliance. Not unlike Billy Graham, Promise Keepers views the Catholic Church as just another Christian denomination with a few differences, rather than an apostate organization that advocates salvation, extra-biblical revelation, the worship of idols, and dozens of other false doctrines. During its 1994 National Convention, Promise Keepers prayed for total 'Christian unity'. In response, the Catholic Archdiocese

177

of Los Angeles under Cardinal Mahoney has welcomed Bill McCartney and his friends, all lapsed Catholics, back into the 'fellowship with Romanism'. 'Promise Keepers began among more Fundamentalist and Evangelical Christian communities,' Mahoney stated, 'but is now being expanded to include Catholic congregations . . . at the Catholic parish level.'[15]

Jack Hayford, another charismatic Baptist preacher whose congregation, The Church On The Way, based near Los Angeles in Van Nuys, California, boasts members among the Hollywood elite, is a frequent speaker at Promise Keepers seminars. A Charismatic Christian or Pentecostal, who speaks and prays in tongues, Hayford usually entices people to 'dance with the Lord'. According to a member of Hayford's church, at the beginning of one Promise Keepers seminar, Hayford explained that the 'dance' that he teaches was one that he had learned in Africa when the Lord spoke to him directly by asking, 'May I have this dance?' As Hayford began doing an African folkdance around the podium, suggestive of the dances associated with African witch-doctoring, he was joined by several Promise Keeping men, who danced along with him.

One of the other beliefs that Jack Hayford promotes stems from yet another *tête-à-tête* he apparently had with Jesus, when he had a vision of Him seated in heaven, and Jesus told Hayford why God required circumcision in the Old Testament. 'God wants to touch your very identity as a man,' Hayford explained to the group, in an effort to encourage adult circumcision of those men who had not yet experienced the ritual. 'He wants to reach out and touch your secret and private parts. This enables Him to better perform surgery on the heart. God wants to touch man's creative parts.'[16]

178

In keeping with their spirit of pagan worship, the Promise Keepers have a warm connection with a group of Cherokee Indians who reside on a reservation in North Carolina. During one joint event, the group walked with the Indians approximately 168 miles, at the end of which there was a name-giving ceremony. The Indian Chief, in keeping with the honour of bestowing an Indian name on those worthy of having one, gave to Bill McCartney the name Victorious Warrior, and to Randy Phillips God's Eagle. Both men were also given Indian headdresses and a poem called 'No More Broken Treaties'.

One of the men on the Board of Directors of Promise Keepers is Pentecostal pastor James Ryle, a former convict who served time in prison on drug-related charges. Ryle, who claims he is a modern-day 'prophet', maintains that God instructed him to reveal to the church that both the Beatles and their music were the results of a special anointing of the Holy Spirit, and that God was looking for others upon whom to place that anointing, supposedly to bring about a worldwide revival through music. 'The Lord has appointed me as a lookout,' Ryle said, 'and shown me some things that I want to show you. The Lord spoke to me and said, "What you saw in the Beatles – the gifting and the sound that they had – was from Me . . . It was My purpose to bring forth through music a worldwide revival that would usher in the move of My spirit in bringing men and women to Christ."' Ryle also claimed that God gave him 'a vision of a Beatles' concert during which the audience, instead of screaming the name of the Beatles, was screaming the name of Jesus'.[17]

While Promise Keepers do not allow women or young boys to be members, there are several offshoots of the group which cater only to women and teenage boys. For example, Young Warriors is a group that only targets teenagers, and features seminars offering Christian contemporary music and Bible study. Heritage Keepers is another group that caters to women, usually wives, sisters, mothers and girlfriends of Promise Keepers. It teaches a woman how to be 'godly with her family, God and community'. Deborah Tyler of Morristown, Tennessee, organized something called 'Four Keys for Abundant Living: A Promise Keeper's Counterpart', to 'provide opportunities for women to be challenged, inspired and encouraged, and to lead each woman to a personal commitment to God's Word as the ultimate authority for successful living'.[18]

Perhaps the best definition of Promise Keepers was offered by Bill McCartney himself. 'We are macho men for Christ,' he said.[19]

In the political, cultural and social atmosphere of America today, unlike that of previous generations, the Right wing draws support from young people. Unlike the elitist Republican youth movement of the 1950s–1980s, this new breed of college conservatives are poised to inherit the responsibility of shaping the future of America and the Republican Party in the years to come. They are rising in number to spread the conservative gospel. Even at those colleges and universities which have historically been liberal, such as the previously all-black Howard University in Washington, D.C., Berkeley in California, or the University of Wisconsin at Madison, students have started groups that are now called Hip Hop Republicans.[20] The Campus Leadership Program has, by their own count, helped set up 256 conservative campus groups in less than three years. The College Republican National Committee, a group that mobilizes students to campaign, has tripled its membership since 1999 to an all-time high of 1,148 chapters. The impact has been felt far from the campuses where, Scott Stewart, Chairman of the College Republican National Committee, says, campus conservatives were instrumental in the success of the Republican Party in the last midterm elections. 'Students provide the enthusiasm, the excitement and the legwork for knocking on doors and giving out pamphlets.'[21]

To the older generation, it seems odd that the young men and women who are members of this new conservative youth movement actually look like the hippies who rebelled against the right-wing establishment in the 1960s. Unlike the preppies who came out in support of Ronald Reagan in the 1980s, dressed in sports jackets, knee-length skirts and button-down shirts, these young right-wingers wear torn jeans and tee shirts and have straggly hair. Some of them even smoke grass and listen to hard rock. But they are in constant rebellion on campus against what was called earlier 'anti-establishment', and is now called left-wing liberalism. Today's rebellion is against any liberal political label, especially political 'correctness', which attempts, sometimes ludicrously, to be non-judgmental. These young people are judgmental.

The change is extraordinary, and was crucial to the 2004 presidential election.

Throughout history, younger generations have instinctively rebelled against the establishment, whether conservative in the 1960s, or liberal in the 1990s. Add to that the fear after the events of 9/11, the need to believe in an all-protecting God, and the belief that the new Evil Empire is no longer Communism but Islam, and the shift to the Right among the young is not surprising.

Campus conservatives are being funded by an array of conservative interest groups, such as Young Americans for Freedom, Young America's Foundation, Leadership

181

Institute, Collegiate Network, and the Intercollegiate Studies Institute. These groups spend money in various ways to push a right-wing agenda on campuses: some make direct cash grants to student groups to start and run conservative campus newspapers; others provide free training in conservative leadership, donating money for these young people's travel to their publishing programmes. Other groups subsidize hefty speaking fees for celebrity right-wing speakers on campus. Through coordinated efforts and activities in the last three years, groups have embarked on a concerted campus recruitment drive to turn temperamentally conservative youngsters into organized right-wing activists. Exhibitionist patriotism has become the new trend. The American flag has become a symbol of uncritical support for the United States against its enemies. In most conservative college dormitories, there is a picture of Hillary Clinton on the doormat, which means that people entering or leaving literally wipe their feet on her face, whether for her lack of submissiveness or her politics.

Another new Christian Right tendency is found in the American workplace, where 'faith-based morality' has become integrated into many employers' and employees' daily routine.

A programme run by the Ellington Wesleyan (Methodist) Church in Ellington, Connecticut, is part of this growing movement, offering a variety of group meetings to encourage religion in offices throughout the country. In 2003, there were more than 1,200 Christian groups devoted to 'workplace ministries' in North America alone, twice as many as five years earlier, and at least two hundred more were organized in 2004. David Miller, head of the Center for Faith and Culture at Yale University, believes that religion is no longer a private matter. 'After a long period of people saying that religion was a private matter,' Miller says, 'many people are intent to integrate these two parts of their lives.'[22]

Some of the religious groups offer prayer or Bible study in offices, as a substitute for the once-popular 'coffee break', while others meet in churches where people are taught to bring the Ten Commandments and their religious beliefs into the business world. Many Evangelicals who have problems making decisions at work will call up any one of the leaders of these religious offices groups to ask for advice. One woman says that the best advice she got was just to 'pray on it'. 'This is about self-improvement,' the woman explained, 'good behavior, good conscience and networking. It's very American.'

Logically, how can anyone fault people who want to bring morality and ethics back into the workplace? Taken to extremes, however, how can anyone logically argue, debate or negotiate with people who claim to have God firmly on their side? For the American people, led by born-again Christian George W. Bush, invading Iraq in 2003 to liberate the Iraqi people was a mission set down by God Himself. The reaction throughout the Arab world was swift. Those who had used terror to cripple America escalated their attacks. Others who used the media maintained that America and the American people had changed under a religious climate that had pervaded the country. According to Abdul Rahman al-Rashed, a Saudi columnist and former editor of the London English-language Arab daily newspaper *Al-Sharq Al-Awsat*, '[Bush's stance *vis-à-vis* the Arab world] changed the status quo in the region for the first time since the 1979 Islamic revolution in Iran. But besides changing the status quo in the Middle East, Bush's style has changed the mentality of the American people.'[23]

PART TWO

THE EVANGELICALS AND ISRAEL

CHAPTER FOURTEEN

The Petri Dish of Terror

*How beautiful are your tents, O Jacob, and your dwelling places.
O Israel! May those who bless you be blessed and those who curse
you be cursed!*

(Numbers 24:5,9)

Not since the establishment of Israel in 1948 – which
Evangelicals described as the 'most significant of the End-
Time signs, even the super-sign' – and the gain of biblical
territories in 1967, has Messianic fervour among Fundamentalist Christians, especially as it concerns Israel, reached such
intensity as it has today. Because suicide bombings have
become regular occurrences in Israel since the beginning of
the second Intifada or uprising by the Palestinian population
in September 2000, and because the war against terror is now
being fought in the United States itself, the Jewish American
community has not only put aside their domestic agenda but
has moved politically to the right. The majority of the Jewish
community, which supports Israel unquestioningly, needs all
the allies they can get. Israelis, whether they are Orthodox
Jews, members of the right-wing Likud party, or concerned
citizens who are suffering under a failing economy, are
grateful for the financial support of the born-again community – more than $1 billion a year. They also welcome the

187

political support of the Evangelicals, especially since the Christian Right is opposed to any peace accord that would grant the Palestinians their own state. As for the ultimate fate of the Jewish people, most seem to follow what Ariel Sharon, the Israeli Prime Minister, recently said in an interview with me in Jerusalem: 'When the Messiah appears, we can ask him if this is His first time or His second time on earth. Until then, we should be thankful for the support of our Christian friends.'[1]

As terrorist attacks continued throughout the world against American soldiers and other American targets, even the mainstream population in the United States began to see similarities between the Israeli fight against Palestinian suicide bombers and America's fight against Al Qaeda. During a televised news conference in February 2002, then Attorney General John Ashcroft said, 'I grieve more for the world than Israel because Israel will arise and the nations will be plunged into darkness.' His statement was obviously a reference to the Bible and to God's special Covenant with the Jewish people, but taken in a wider context it could have been interpreted to mean that Israel was clearly more aware of the extent of this terror threat and how to protect itself than many other nations, including the United States, who should follow Israel's lead.

Other Evangelicals agreed. Reverend Jerry Falwell said, 'Jerusalem for the Evangelicals is the keyhole in the door to the future, while Israel serves as the Petri dish of terror, the testing ground for methods that will eventually be exported throughout the world.'[2] Clarence Wagner who heads Bridges for Peace in Jerusalem perhaps put it more poetically when he said, 'Israel is the canary in the cage and when the canary stops singing, there's poison in the air. Israel is the front line of our war on terror.'[3]

The men and women who lead the Evangelical movement in the United States are neither impractical dreamers nor unrealistic planners. Without exception, those who follow the word of Christ are pragmatic and have created an ideology that provides them with a plan of action, under the guidance of charismatic leaders. Currently, the American Congress has significant members who are certain that the trappings of modern life, especially scientific progress, have only served to negate a fundamental belief in God and religion. Since the threat of terrorism from abroad comes primarily from radical Islamic groups, they believe that any conciliation, even with moderate Arab leaders, countries or governments, signals an automatic death warrant for democracy. Identifying the Evangelicals who wield power in the United States Senate and House contributes to an understanding of who exactly the 'players' are in this game of biblical politics.

Annette Lantos, a small seventy-five-year-old woman, is immaculately groomed, every hair of her blonde wig meticulously in place, her designer clothes in bright primary colours. The fact that she is able to balance on impossibly high spiked heels is a testament to her determination not to give in to advancing age. Her first cousins were the Gabor sisters – Zsa Zsa, Eva and Magda – Hungary's most famous exports to Hollywood in the 1950s. Not only does Annette resemble them physically, from her fine bones and delicate features to her charmingly convoluted logic, but she also speaks English as they did, with a seductive Hungarian accent. When she describes her born-again experience, her dramatic expressions, theatrical pauses and inflections are almost more fascinating than her amazing story.

Annette Lantos is Jewish, a survivor of the Holocaust, who

189

believed for most of her adult life that God had abandoned the Jewish people. She and her husband Tom have two beautiful daughters, both married to non-Jewish men, who have given them seventeen grandchildren, all of whom are spiritual and have accepted Jesus into their lives. In 1958, Annette had an experience that made her realize for the first time the extent to which she was living a life without faith, religion, or God. Driving with her husband and elder daughter, six-year-old Annette, Mrs Lantos found herself admiring her beautiful, blonde, 'affectionate and loving child', who was especially close to her doting father. The little girl turned to her father and said, 'I love you so much, Daddy, but there's one person I love more than you.' Annette recalls the moment: 'I was puzzled since I knew she couldn't have meant me. When she explained, my husband looked at me in shock, as if to say: what have you been teaching this child?'[4]

The little girl told her father that the only person she loved more than him was God, which seemed unbelievable to the couple. 'We had always totally denied our Jewishness,' Annette explains, 'especially when our children were born, because we were afraid of another Holocaust. We never made religion or God a part of our lives. When I finally told my daughters that we were Jewish, all mention of faith stopped there, although apparently it didn't stop the spirituality that developed in both my children. While both daughters married non-Jewish men they decided, without our prompting, to have as many children as God would give them, to make-up for our families who died in concentration camps. I should have suspected that this spirituality existed in them when they were growing up. But to talk about God in such a matter-of-fact way was startling, especially for a little girl of six.

But that was what little Annette said, which is how my faith restarted for me.'

Several months later, Annette and her husband went to Jerusalem, and she remembers that during the entire trip she felt weak, ill and unable to move out of her hotel room. 'Now as I look back,' Annette explains, 'it was my soul that was sick, not my body.'

On their way back to California, the couple stopped in Monte Carlo. Sitting in a café, Annette Lantos suddenly saw her father walking towards her. 'It was unbelievable, because he had been killed by the Nazis in 1945. I grabbed my husband's arm and told him, "Look, there's my father," but by the time he turned around, my father had disappeared.' She smiles slightly. 'Of course, my husband, who is a realist, insisted that I had been mistaken. We were in Europe, and I had been thinking about my late father so strongly, so it was natural that I should imagine I saw him. But I knew I had seen my father that day, as clearly as I saw my husband sitting there at that café in Monte Carlo.' Two nights later, at home in California, Annette had a dream that explained with absolute certainty how it was that her father appeared before her that day. 'Jesus came to me in the dream,' Annette says quietly, 'and it was then that I knew I had been touched by God, which was why I had seen my dear, departed father. Jesus also told me in that dream that Raoul Wallenberg, the man who had gotten me and my mother forged Swedish passports, which had saved us from the Nazis, was alive in a Soviet gulag.' For Annette, the dream was a revelation, an epiphany, during which she accepted Jesus as 'the rabbi of all rabbis'.

'I knew then,' she continues, 'that He is in the heart of all Jews, who must be inclined towards Jesus. What happened to me was an awakening when my heart suddenly accepted

Him, and since then I have come to separate revelation from intuition. When revelation happens, as it did for me, time stops and the person is transported, for just an instant, into the eternal realm that opens. For me, my eternal self that God created us to be and feel and which all of us have forgotten from time to time, simply opened up.' Annette Lantos claims that from the moment she accepted Jesus, she also knew that she had been present when He was crucified. 'I saw myself standing there during His crucifixion, and I cried. When I had accepted Him, it was as if the floodgates opened, because in came this unbelievable love for everyone, for my children, my husband, for the whole world. I wanted to shout from the rooftops – that is exactly the feelings as I experienced them, and they only lasted a day, but after that I became so strong! I simply lost all fear.'

That Christmas, in 1956, during the Hungarian uprising, Annette Lantos received a package from Budapest. 'In those days nothing got in and nothing got out, but I got this big package and when I opened it, I almost fainted. It was a Haggadah Prayer Book from Passover, 1938, with a silver plaque with my name inscribed on it, which was even more unbelievable, because everything we possessed had been confiscated by the Nazis when they marched into Hungary.'

Annette's father had been one of the most prominent members of the Jewish community in Budapest, a successful jeweller, and the one person in her entire family whom she respected and loved more than anyone else. 'My mother and I went into hiding when the Nazis came, but my father was deported to Auschwitz,' she says. 'When I opened that Haggadah, there was a letter in between the pages, written by my father long before he was deported. He wrote that everyone in the world wanted to annihilate the Jewish people, but despite that, he asked me to promise him just one thing. Even then, he knew that he wouldn't survive. He asked me to remain faithful to the God of our fathers, the God who has brought us through pain and suffering, but who has kept us as a people.' Annette pauses once again. 'But what made his letter even more painful for me was that I had accepted Jesus only days before, and it was in His name that the Jews had been slaughtered.'

In 1964, Annette Lantos went back to Hungary for the first time since the war ended, and discovered that it had been her aunt, one of her father's sisters, who had sent her the Haggadah. The story of how she had found it remained a mystery and, in fact, mystical. 'My aunt told me that someone had come up to her in the street and simply put the book in her hands. And she just knew that she had to move heaven and earth to get it to me in America.'

In 1983, twenty-five years after Annette Lantos found Jesus, she had another dream in which the Lord came to her again. On that occasion, He told her that Raoul Wallenberg had finally died in the Soviet gulag. Years later, in 2001, in another twist of fate, Wallenberg's great-nephew worked at her husband's office as an intern. 'He came to us because he knew about our relationship with his great-uncle. My husband and I were among five Hungarian Jews featured in Steven Spielberg's Oscar-winning documentary about those years during the Nazi occupation. But the most amazing thing is that this young man has the spirit of his great-uncle, and he has helped us raise millions of dollars throughout Scandinavia to bolster Israel and protect the Jewish people from their terrorist neighbors.'

Annette Lantos's special relationship with Jesus Christ, and her unconditional support for Israel and for all the other issues that the Evangelical community hold dear, would not be particularly complicated were it not for the fact that her husband happens to be Tom Lantos, a Democratic congress-man from San Francisco, and the only Holocaust survivor ever to serve in Congress. What sets Tom Lantos apart from his colleagues in the House of Representatives is that he is also the only congressman whose wife is intricately involved with so many political issues that touch the Evangelical agenda. Annette Lantos has an office next to her husband's in the House of Representatives Building, and she and Tom are part of a group of men and women on Capitol Hill who have forged strong bonds with the born-again community.

Elected as a liberal Democrat by an overwhelmingly gay constituency in San Francisco, Tom Lantos frequently comes under heavy criticism in his district for defending domestic issues the Evangelical community supports, including mak-ing sodomy between two male adults in the privacy of their own home a criminal offence, and their fierce opposition to legalizing gay marriage: topics with a direct impact on Lantos's mostly homosexual constituency.

An avowed atheist, Tom is resistant to the point of hostility to his wife's special relationship with Jesus Christ. According to Annette, when she told him that she had found Jesus and 'wanted to shout her love for all humanity from the rooftops', he almost threw her out of the house. Half jokingly, Annette claims that one of her missions in life is to 'save Tom's soul', since she and her Evangelical friends are convinced that despite his resistance and denial, he is a profoundly spiritual and religious man. What unites the couple is their shared unconditional love for Israel and their unequivocal belief that it is the land of the Jewish people, even if their reasons for that belief vary from a total rejection of divine intervention on the part of Tom Lantos to a profound belief in the literal interpretation of the Bible by Annette.

From the beginning, Annette and Tom were very different because of their backgrounds. When they met in Budapest more than fifty years ago, he was dashing, brilliant and penniless, while she was the pampered only daughter of the most prosperous businessman in the Budapest Jewish ghetto. Annette was able to survive the war in Switzerland because of her family's wealth and position, while Tom's family, along with Annette's father, were all deported to Auschwitz. Also saved by Raoul Wallenberg who gave him false papers, Tom Lantos became a member of the Hungarian underground. After the war ended and they were finally married, he and Annette moved to the United States, where Tom taught at Stanford University before going into politics. For the past twenty-four years, Tom Lantos has served in that same district and is currently a ranking member of the Foreign Affairs Committee where, in his words, 'I am able to do what I can for the Jewish people, and for Israel, since in our lifetime we were almost wiped out.'[5]

Through his wife, Tom Lantos is a valued contact between the Evangelical community and the United States Congress. Although Lantos does not share the Evangelical belief in the Abrahamic Covenant from a biblical perspective, he does believe that Israel is the unconditional and irrevocable homeland of the Jewish people. Rather than rely on predictions found in the Bible, Lantos maintains that a strong military is the best weapon to save all democracies, including Israel, from radical Islam.

Tom Lantos is only one example of an American politician who has found a common basis of agreement across party lines with the mostly Republican Evangelical Christians. Despite diverse religious or non-religious convictions, viewing Islam as the enemy of democracy accounts for one element in this brew of biblical politics that unites the religious and the secular within the United States government. Some of his critics – and there are many – accuse Lantos of disloyalty to the Democratic party, especially since he was one of the first and few Democrats who voted to impeach President Clinton. Unlike his Evangelical colleagues, Lantos based his disapproval of Clinton on his push for an Israeli–Palestinian peace accord rather than on the former President's sexual turpitude. Other critics accuse Lantos of voting to impeach Clinton for his own personal political gain, to distance himself from the squalor of the sexual and financial scandals that tainted the Clinton administration.

Today, Tom and Annette Lantos work closely with the American Israel Public Affairs Committee (AIPAC), the Jewish lobby in Washington. The political alliance between the Jewish-American community and the State of Israel was formalized under the aegis of AIPAC, an organization headed and largely directed by American Jews. Rightfully considered to be one of the most powerful organizations in Washington, D.C., AIPAC has 130 employees, including seven fulltime lobbyists. Both Democrat and Republican members are reputed to donate millions of dollars in political contributions to various members of the Senate and the House. Congressman Lantos also works with CIPAC, its Christian Evangelical counterpart, headed by born-again Christian Richard Hellman.

Congressman Lantos is one of the chief proponents of a formal coalition between the two lobbies, and it would seem that, as a Jew, he is prepared to put his personal domestic agenda aside when it comes to the survival of the State of Israel. One prominent Evangelical has said, 'If Mr Lantos is not re-nominated on the Democratic ticket because of his close relationship with the Christian community who oppose gay rights, which is a major issue in his district in San Francisco, we will support him on the Republican ticket.'

Tom Lantos is equally certain about why he thinks those who work for the United States Department of State are 'against any conciliation towards the State of Israel'. According to Lantos, whom I interviewed in his office in Congress, while State Department officials start their careers in a neutral position concerning the Middle East, they soon realize that there are thirty Arab countries to which they will inevitably be assigned and where they can hope to reach ambassadorial status. 'In order to advance their position within the State Department,' Lantos explains, 'it would not serve them well to take a pro-Israeli position. In fact, it would basically serve to eliminate them from holding a diplomatic post in any one of those Arab countries.'

Lantos further affirms that if State Department employees do not get an ambassadorial post within four years of reaching the level of deputy chief within the system, they are forced to retire. 'There is only a four-year window to be appointed Ambassador,' Lantos says, 'so they are fighting for their careers, and few will jeopardize their futures to fight for Israel.'

CHAPTER FIFTEEN

Peace Through Strength

Politics is in largest part a function of culture; at the heart of culture is morality; and at the heart of morality are the ultimate truths we call religion.

(Richard Johr, editor-in-chief of *First Things*)

Jesus was killed by a moral majority.

(Source unknown)

A close friend and colleague of Congressman Tom Lantos is Senator Sam Brownback, a conservative Republican from Kansas and an Evangelical Christian. A staunch supporter of a Greater Israel which would prohibit a Palestinian state, Brownback convened the first congressional summit on sex and violence in entertainment. He also sponsored legislation authorizing the Federal Trade Commission Report which uncovered the widespread marketing of violent and adult-rated entertainment to children. Since the issue of inappropriate content in television and film is something that has gained wide support across party lines, Brownback works closely with Tipper Gore, wife of former Vice-President Al Gore, on censoring videos, film and television, to omit sexually explicit or violent content for adolescents, and, in many cases, even for adults.

During an interview in Washington in 2003, to discuss the Evangelical position regarding President Bush's Road Map for peace, Senator Brownback said, 'I hope you are praying for this President every day, to give him the courage to stand firmly with the Bible when it comes to Israel and the Jewish people.'[1] The senator from Kansas is in prestigious political company. In a speech at Harvard University Bill Moyers, on the occasion of his retirement from PBS (Public Broadcast Service) Television, cited recent Gallup poll figures. 'We are not talking about a handful of lawmakers who hold or are beholden to these beliefs [those who are backed by the Religious Right] but nearly half of the United States Congress.'[2] In fact, according to the Gallup poll conducted just prior to the 2004 presidential election, 45 senators and 186 members of the 108th Congress earned 80 to 100 per cent approval ratings from the three most influential Christian Right advocacy groups. Those elected officials include: Senate Majority Leader Bill Frist, also a major supporter of Israel, who is in favour of the forced transfer of the Palestinians to a newly constructed Palestinian state in the Sinai Desert; Assistant Majority Leader Mitch McConnell; Conference Chair Rick Santorum of Pennsylvania, who once likened homosexuality to incest and polygamy, and naturally voted against abortion; Policy Chair Jon Kyl of Arizona; House Speaker Dennis Hastert; and Majority Whip Roy Blunt. All are naturally Republican although the only Democrat to score 100 per cent with the Christian coalition is Senator Zell Miller of Georgia, who recently quoted from the Old Testament Book of Amos on the Senate floor during a debate on world hunger: 'these days will come, sayeth the Lord God, that I will send a famine in the land.'

Of all the names cited above, and among all the elected officials who believe in the literal interpretation of Scripture,

Sam Brownback is probably more concerned and involved with the question of Israeli security than any other. He is one of the few who has no political reason to support Israel, only his deep belief in Scripture and the word of the Lord. In his home state of Kansas, there are only 14,500 Jews, representing a potential voting block of 0.5 per cent, most of whom are not even aware of his close connection to Israel. In fact, Brownback has never garnered any significant proportion of votes from that community. His support transcends his political ambitions, as he works closely with a woman from his home town who has contributed a great deal to this Evangelical–Jewish alliance.

Esther Levens is a widow who lives in a large modern house in an upscale suburb of Kansas City. She is rich, Republican, and a staunch supporter of Israel and a 'one-state solution' of the Israeli–Palestinian conflict. Levens, who is in her late seventies, was left a large estate by her husband, a successful businessman and an active Republican in their community. He was unofficial campaign manager for Robert Dole, the Republican senator from Kansas who challenged Bill Clinton in the 1992 presidential election, and the official principal fund-raiser for Dole's campaign. Esther Levens remains close to Robert and Elizabeth Dole. After the death of her husband, Levens had what she describes as a 'sudden epiphany' that led her to found the National Unity Coalition for Israel.

During an interview in the spring of 2003 at her home, Levens explained how the idea of a Christian-Jewish coalition first came to her: 'I once saw a poll that said 70 per cent of Americans supported Israel and I knew that only 2 per cent of all Americans were Jewish,' she says. 'I thought, who are these other people? So, I made it my mission to find the other 68 per cent.'[3] Levens learned that those people in the United States who supported Israel were Evangelical Christians. So she set about to form an alliance that could capture the voting power of the two groups, Jews and the Christian Right, to influence the minds of politicians, and foreign policy. With the money her husband left her, and the political connections she had forged during his lifetime, Levens' group has grown into a major entity with a budget of more than $10 million a year. She continues to dedicate her life to financing those candidates, and to funding projects which correspond with her philosophy about Israel and the Jewish people. Today, the National Unity Coalition for Israel represents more than two hundred Jewish and Christian organizations representing millions of Americans dedicated to a 'secure Israel', and is headquartered at Levens' spacious house in a suburb of Kansas City.

One of the most measured Evangelical ministers in that area of the country is Paul Brooks, a man whose congregation numbers about seven to eight thousand, one of the largest in Kansas, and whose weekly television sermon draws thousands and thousands more. During my visit with Mrs Levens, I met with Pastor Brooks and his wife Becky, as we shared a Friday-night Sabbath meal at the home of a prominent Jewish family in the area. A thoughtful man who is a graduate of the New Orleans Baptist Theological Seminary, Paul Brooks is an example of a born-again Christian who has embraced the Abrahamic Covenant in a sincere and pragmatic manner. Brooks believes that when it comes to supporting Israel and the Jewish people, it is 'the responsibility of all Americans not to be silent on the subject'.[4]

'The rise of anti-Semitism in Europe is tremendous,' he says, 'and the reason is the influx of Muslims, which has made Islam second only to Christianity in Europe. The fact is that mainline Christian history does not deal with the issue of anti-Semitism, and it's for that reason that Becky and I

believe prayer helps. We are praying for Powell and Condoleezza Rice and President Bush, and all of them in
Washington who have to make such important decisions,
to do the right thing when it comes to Israel. Scripture is very
clear: in Romans, Paul talks about the unique relationship
that the Jews have with the God of Israel, and that Covenant
remains in place and I believe that the Jews are the chosen
people. The promises of the prophets related to the Messiah,
however, have not been fulfilled, but I believe that what was
written in Scripture was for both our sakes – Christians' and
Jews' – because we are brothers worshipping the same God.
If there is disagreement about whether the Messiah has come
already, or has not appeared yet [it] is no reason for us not to
be brothers. After all, Christianity is just a sect of Judaism,
everything about Christianity is Jewish; we [Christians]
learned to worship God and what we learned about God,
and [what] I preach on Sundays, [is] on the attributes of God
from Nehemiah, Chapter Nine.'

According to Pastor Brooks, the Baptist Theological
Seminary changed when the Southern Baptist denomination
expelled the liberals – those who embraced the mainline
Protestant liberation theology – and replaced them with
leaders who were conservatives, or Evangelical Christians. As
it stands in his congregation, approximately 99 per cent of his
parishioners agree with his position on Israel. 'I am outspoken, and you will not last in my church very long if you
don't agree with my position on Israel, because you will be so
offended that you will leave.'

Brooks, along with a group of prominent Evangelical
ministers, was invited to the White House in 2004 for a
series of briefings by John Ashcroft. 'Every time we are
invited, a different member of the President's administration
briefs us, and Mr Ashcroft is very pro-Israel. It is a big change,

because in the past, the Democrats had a bigger platform for the Jewish people, although curiously the ones who helped the Jewish people more were always the conservatives, except for Harry Truman who was a Democrat and a Southern Baptist.'

Pastor Brooks believes that though the solution to the problem is inevitably political, he is convinced that only through 'divine intervention' will the correct political solution be reached. He believes that the conflict in the Middle East is a cultural war between the Arabs and the rest of the world. 'I do not believe that Allah is the God of the Bible,' Brooks says.

If Allah exists, he is the devil. Mohammedanism was a demonic replacement for Judaism that Satan invented to get hold of people's minds, to sway people away from the truth. One of the great things about Satan is this whole concept of counterfeit. He can become or appears to be what he isn't. Just look at the basis of the religion: when Mohammed first started having his revelations, he thought they were from the devil and he told his wife, 'I think Satan is speaking to me,' and she said, 'No, it's not Satan, it's God.' But even he thought it was Satan, and when he came to Medina and built an army and took Mecca, it was there where his black box was and in that box were 365 gods, one for each day of the year, and he destroyed all but one. The God he chose was the symbol of the moon and the sword, and that is the god of war, that is not the God of the Bible. It is a false religion, a religion built on violence, because the man was a violent man. The Muslim religion is not a genuine religion. I don't hate the Arab people. I feel sorry for them because they have been so badly manipulated.

Pastor Brooks believes that everyone in the world, but most specifically in the United States, must use whatever sphere of influence he has to influence politicians when it comes to the Israeli–Palestinian conflict. Despite the Evangelical Christians who support the Jewish people and Israel in the government, he believes it is 'an uphill battle'.

'When I was visiting the American Consul in Jerusalem a while ago, I told him I felt sorry for the Palestinians, because they have been so badly led. His response shocked me. He said that the problem is not the Palestinians, the problem is the Jews. And when I responded that the Palestinian Authority is incredibly corrupt, he told me that the Palestinians are honest people who have been corrupted by the Jews. At the time, I was visiting with one of my closest friends and parishioners, who donates a great deal of money to the Evangelical and Jewish cause, Richard Hastings, and we both got furious. I asked him what he was talking about when the whole world knew how corrupt Arafat was and still, the Consul insisted that all that Arafat is, he learned from the Jews.'[5]

In November 2003, I was invited to attend an executive committee meeting of Esther Levens' National Unity Coalition in Washington, D.C. Paul Weyrich, seated in his electric wheelchair near the head of the long conference table, hosted the meeting under the auspices of the Heritage Foundation, a right-wing think tank which he heads. Weyrich is probably one of the most committed and combative right-wing conservatives in America today, vehemently against gay rights, drug use and any other supposed 'deviations' from family values. Weyrich, who is obviously bitter as a result of his crippling accident – a fall on black ice – was just as determined to cleanse the world of deviates and Communists long before he lost the use of his legs. When he

204

established the Heritage Foundation in 1973, he was already developing the ideas that would become Ronald Reagan's 'Star Wars' policies and, when Reagan became President, Weyrich provided the blueprints for many of his other policies. Under the precise guidance of Weyrich, the Heritage Foundation, unlike other think tanks, devotes the major portion of its budget to propaganda, fundraising, marketing and public relations.

In 1973, Weyrich, along with Jesse Helms, Jack Kemp, Henry Hyde and other right-wing Republicans, established the American Legislative Exchange Council (ALEC). According to information in *Banana Republicans* by Sheldon Rampton and John Stauber, Sam Brunelli, executive director of ALEC, stated that the goal of the organization is 'to ensure that state legislators are so well informed, so well armed, that they can set the terms of the public policy debate, that they can change the agenda, that they can lead. This is the infrastructure that will reclaim the States for our movement.'[6] The annual budget for ALEC is more than $5 million a year, primarily given by industries ranging from the American Nuclear Energy Council, to the R.J. Reynolds and Philip Morris tobacco companies.

In a brief conversation with Weyrich before the NUC meeting began, I asked him why he sponsored a Christian Zionist conference. 'That should be obvious. Islam is the scourge of the world, and the Jewish people and Israel are the front line against that scourge.'

The atmosphere that day, despite glowering glances from Weyrich, was a friendly mixture of devout born-again Christians and several polite but seemingly disinterested foreign service types from the Israeli Embassy, as well as representatives of the Republican coalition within the House and the Senate. Shari Dollinger, a young woman of barely thirty who has since resigned from Esther Levens' organization, and who is well connected politically, extremely articulate and experienced, ran the meeting. She once served as Senator Brownback's staff assistant and, prior to that, as the liaison at the Israeli Embassy in Washington between the Jewish and Evangelical communities, and has become expert at mobilizing the Evangelical community to new heights of generosity. Two of the main groups that financially support the National Unity Coalition are Bridges for Peace, led by Pastor Clarence Wagner and headquartered in Jerusalem, and the International Christian Embassy in Jerusalem which also has an office in Washington, D.C.

On the day that I visited the group, Dollinger ran the executive committee meeting with confidence and ease. Present that day from the Christian community were the Reverend James M. Hutches, a retired Brigadier General and chaplain from the United States Army and currently President of Christians for Israel, JoAnn Magnuson, director of Bridges for Peace, based in Minnesota, Peter Hébert, another born-again Christian with ties to the banking world, Susan Michaels who runs the International Christian Embassy's Washington offices, and William Murray, a pastor and founder of the Religious Freedom Coalition, another Evangelical organization that lobbies for political support for Israel in Washington.

One of the more illustrious participants was Frank J. Gaffney. A former Assistant Secretary of Defense under Ronald Reagan, he is currently the President of the Center for Security Policy. During a conversation we had, Gaffney said, 'Those who are fervent in their support of Israel are now welcome in the Bush White House . . . What you're seeing today is that the policy of the United States government is being influenced by a group of people on the outside who are influencing those on the inside, when it comes to the American position on the Israeli–Palestinian conflict.'[7]

The guest speaker at the event was Sam Brownback, who talks with a mixture of political knowledge, pragmatism and basic born-again rhetoric. His message was clear: 'The only way to achieve peace in the Middle East,' he said to the admiring crowd, 'is through strength.' According to Brownback, that strength can be achieved only by 'driving American policy in the Middle East to the right', which means courting the conservatives in Congress, the majority of whom are Evangelical Christians.

One of those Evangelicals in Congress is Mike Pence, another close associate of Sam Brownback and a John Ashcroft ally, who has worked tirelessly to advance the domestic and foreign agenda of the Christian Right. Indiana's Republican congressman, Pence considers himself 'a Christian, a conservative and a Republican in that order'. Pence is an ardent supporter of President Bush's war on terrorism, and was one of the architects of the Patriot Act, which allows suspected terrorists to be arrested and held, without being charged and without benefit of legal counsel, for an indefinite period of time. Congressman Pence was also one of the creators of the Department of Homeland Security which has an annual budget of more than $36 billion to be used to improve perceived weaknesses in America's protection from terror attacks. In Pence's own words, he is 'preoccupied with the defense and promotion of the interests of the State and the people of Israel'.[8]

'I sought a seat on the International Committee of this Congress to support Israel,' Pence says. 'In order to change our foreign policy concerning Israel, I involved myself in a number of floor debates and every time Israel is debated, I am down there slugging away with many of my colleagues who are Jewish, mostly Democrats from the Northeast. I have been able to persuade them that we are sincerely committed to protecting and defending Israel.'

During that same interview in his office on Capitol Hill, Congressman Pence stated firmly that he is against the creation of a separate Palestinian state. 'The United States must practice self-control in allowing the people of Israel to prosper according to America's beneficence and God's good grace.' He has had a 'passionate' interest in Israel since the late 1980s, and believes it is partially because his brother married a Jewish woman, which gave him the opportunity to learn more about the Jewish people.

'I stand behind Israel,' Pence told me, 'because I believe in the dream that is Israel, and I believe in the special relationship that exists between the United States and Israel. But I ultimately believe that Israel was forged equally out of the hearts of American Jews for the horror of the Holocaust, as much as it is the dream of American Christians for the promises of God to reappear on earth as the Messiah and King.'

Mike Pence's first term in office coincided with the 107th Congress, which was the first one after the attacks on 11 September 2001. Pence prefaced his remarks concerning Islamic terror and the connection between the United States and Israel thus: 'I simply said that I am an Evangelical Christian from the Mid-West who understands that Israel is the little guy in a tough neighborhood. And the Middle West understands the Middle East better than those guys in Foggy Bottom.'

Pence and his colleagues in the Congress are aiming for a force of 7 million citizens to write to their respective representatives and press for United States action to support Israel. 'We are a tremendous source of political power in this country,' Pence says, 'and my Jewish friends and my demo-cratic co-workers here in the Congress are prepared to put aside their differences for the security and continued existence of the Jewish State.'

Battling it out on Capitol Hill along with Congressman Pence and his colleagues is Richard Hellman, founder and director of CIPAC, which is the Evangelical equivalent of the powerful Jewish lobbying group AIPAC. Having worked most of his life as an environmental lawyer, writing laws and regulations for the Environmental Protection Agency, Hellman was eventually invited to Israel as an environmental consultant when Menachem Begin was Prime Minister. 'It was the most meaningful seven years of my life,' Hellman said in my interview with him in Washington in 2003. 'Not only did I help create Israel's Environmental Ministry, but I reinforced my spirit and my belief in the Lord and in the Jewish people as God's chosen ones.'[9]

Richard Hellman, like Annette Lantos and other born-again Christians, is eager to recount the exact moment when Jesus Christ entered his life to help him realize his true faith. During our meeting, he described the born-again experience that propelled him to devote his professional life to garnering political support for the Israeli State.

'It was spring break,' Hellman begins, 'and my wife was on a trip to Israel. I was alone at home and I fell and immediately knew that I had injured myself severely, because I was unable to move. As it turned out, I dislocated my shoulder and broke my collarbone. But I managed to call my neighbor who happened to be a born-again Christian. She began praying for me and when I was told by the doctors that I would need complicated surgery, my neighbor continued to pray for me. She asked the Lord to heal me so I wouldn't need the operation, and in fact, the Lord heard her prayers. My shoulder and collarbone healed on their own. That was when I knew, and I knelt down and asked the Lord to come into my life, and when He did, He changed my heart. The Lord changed my life as well. I thought I was well situated in my job and with my family, but until I accepted Him, I never realized how much He had healed within me. My marriage was better, my family life was great, and I don't think I would have accepted a consulting job in Israel if the Bible and the Jewish people weren't so important to me.'

CIPAC is the only registered Christian lobby group in Washington which can advocate or oppose legislation. 'When I came back from Israel,' Hellman explains, 'it was with a very specific purpose. I felt that the United States, particularly the Christian communities and those people on Capitol Hill, didn't understand Israel or the threats to Israel. It was all because of the scourge of anti-Semitism under the guise of anti-Zionism, which was when I knew that Christians had to mobilize to change public opinion within the American government.'

Today, Hellman has more than seven million faithful followers who are either members of his lobbying group or who contribute financially to maintain its significance and power. 'Someone once referred to us as AIPAC's little echo,' Hellman says with a laugh. 'Maybe we'll turn out to be the echo that roared.'

In April 2003, Secretary of State Colin Powell met privately with Senate and House conservatives and Richard Hellman, to ask them to withdraw resolutions in support of Israel's incursion into the West Bank, claiming that the resolutions would complicate efforts to broker peace talks. The vote was postponed for a week, and the resolutions were approved despite Powell's efforts at achieving an American-brokered peace accord. Evangelicals are determined not to separate the Israeli–Palestinian conflict from the global war on terror led by the United States against Islamic terror groups. Evangelicals believe that terrorists operate under a divine directive from another God, Allah, who blesses and guides them to die in the course of fulfilling their obligation to achieve global Islam. Evangelicals believe that in addition to the aid and support of Jesus Christ, no war can be won without heavy firepower, intelligence, and able-bodied men and women, to defeat their enemy and bring Christianity to all the citizens of this world.

Hellman believes that a major part of his 'mission' is to educate Congress concerning 'the nature of the terrain in Israel and the importance of maintaining the high ground overlooking the coastal plain . . . Israel's rights under international law,' he says, 'or the mandate covering them has never been finished. The areas of Judea and Samaria and Gaza are still unallocated portions of the mandate. We all know that the Jordanians tried to annexe those areas, but they were refused by everyone except Great Britain and Pakistan. Now, there is the need to solve the demographic problem, and we have recently been pressing on the concept of transfer, since we know that the demographic problem will not change depending on the sovereignty of Judea and Samaria. It is still a serious problem, and three million people cannot be supported in a non-productive territory where there is no agriculture, no industry and, of course, the biggest issue, how to provide water? How do you support the Palestinian people?'

Hellman and those politicians on the Hill who embrace his faith and political opinions have talked about a 'mini' Marshall plan that would begin with a re-settlement process of approximately 100,000 Palestinian families a year into Jordan. 'In seven years,' Hellman says, you can put 700,000 Palestinians into Jordan, although nobody is suggesting that things will happen immediately and that the Palestinians and their children will have better lives instantly. Most people who think the way we do are afraid to say that Jordan is the solution, or if not Jordan, then establishing a new community in the Sinai [Egypt], or in the southern portion of Iraq. If you create an attractive community for many of these people, they will begin the process of moving and begin to deal with the problem. The reality is that they will not survive as a political entity even if they are given sovereignty tomorrow, given their population problem. They don't have water or even a sewage system, so you have to give them an inducement to move and this is the message we try to deliver to guys like Brownback and Jim Saxon from New Jersey who's a Republican but not an Evangelical. Saxon's motive is that he just understands the right thing to do. He understands that Israel is the only democratic state in a region where every Moslem country is totalitarian. Senator Inhoff, Brownback, Pence, Todd Tiart, and also Tom Lantos are in our corner, as are Tom DeLay and Dick Armery when he was in Congress, as well as the famous runner Jim Ryan, who also gives us his heartfelt biblical support.

The interesting thing is that most congressmen and senators support Israel, but the difficulty is the way the bar has been set. Not a lot has been demanded of them. They vote for foreign aid for Israel and they write the President when they don't like the way he is handling the conflict, and they get an A on their paper for that; but what I'm pressing for is that Congress take over as the main branch as was written in the Constitution, and we have some interesting debates on that score. In other words, let Congress take over, not in the execution of foreign policies but in the formulation of policy just as Congress clearly formulated policy on Cuba and the Soviet Union and now on Iraq, which means they could be a strong force for giving fairness and equality to Israel.[10]

Richard Hellman drafted the bill of the Jerusalem Embassy Act of 1995, and still presses the President every six months to move the American Embassy in Israel from Tel Aviv to Jerusalem.

President Clinton took ten passes on the issue and Bush took four. What we also want is for Israel to have full membership and not temporary membership of the Security Council. Now, Israel has a provisory seat on the Western Europe section which was the only regional group that accepted them in a convoluted way which means they won't sit on the Security Council and they won't sit on any decision-making bodies, purely because the United Nations is a strange place. The fact that Israel is the only country treated that way is an example of anti-Israel sentiment. And, the reasons the other countries give is that Israel doesn't fit into the Middle East, that the Arabs don't accept the Jewish people so they have to fit into this Western European section. What was absolutely unconscionable was that Syria, the terrorist state, was president of the Security Council for a month. Absurd! Israeli troops pulled out of southern Lebanon and they respected the United Nations' delineated borders and yet Syria continues to occupy Lebanon. We at CIPAC are pushing for Syria to be sanctioned. And another thing, Israel is the only nation whose Prisoners of War (POW) and Missing In Action (MIA) are not being actively pursued in the Middle East. We are here to combat discrimination against Israel.[11]

CHAPTER SIXTEEN

Connecting with the Land

For God will save Zion and rebuild the cities of Judah. Then people will settle there and possess it.

(Psalm 69:35)

The settlement of Tekoa is one of fifteen ultra-religious Jewish communities in an area known as Gush Etzion. The settlement is located approximately twenty-five miles from Hebron, a Palestinian city in the middle of the West Bank dominated by the militant groups Hamas and Islamic Jihad. Only ten minutes from Jerusalem, Tekoa is steeped in biblical history. Abraham and Isaac are said to have passed through Tekoa on their journey from Hebron to Mount Moriah. Tekoa is where Ruth gathered the sheaves from the fields, where David shepherded his father's sheep and proclaimed his kingdom, and where the Maccabees and other Jewish fighters under Bar Kochba sought shelter in its deep caves. Today, Tekoa is one of the most politically contested settlements in Israel. In 2003, more than 16 residents were shot, 4 fatally, on the main road that passes through dozens of Arab villages en route for Hebron. Incursions by terrorists resulted in the murder of three sleeping children and their parents. Journalists and other visitors who venture to Tekoa are advised to take a bulletproof car.

214

The Israelis who have chosen to live in Tekoa are ultra-religious, ideologues, or both. The residents are determined, as an elder of the community says, 'to live out the prophecy of the Jewish people as described in the Bible regardless of any political decision to dismantle settlements throughout the Occupied Territories'. If Tekoa is referred to as a 'settlement', residents will indignantly say that the word is a misnomer suggesting they 'live in fly-by-night trailer parks and can be easily uprooted'. There are more than 10,000 people living in the Gush Etzion region in houses that were clearly not built as temporary installations.

Rebecca W., a pretty American woman with dark eyes and hair, made *aliyah* – the Hebrew expression for immigration to Israel. She decided to move to Israel after seeking legal and religious guidance to help extricate herself from an abusive marriage. The decision to live in Tekoa came after what Becca, as she is known to her friends and family, defines as a 'spiritual awakening'. She realized that the only way to change her life and make a difference in the world was to commit herself to a political and religious quest. She lives in a pleasant apartment overlooking a pastoral landscape, runs a day care centre, observes the Sabbath and other Jewish holidays along with her Orthodox neighbours, and speaks English with a smattering of Yiddish expressions. She also contributes more than $5,000 a month to subsidize new arrivals from Russia to Tekoa, and she gives to funds for emergency medical and road equipment to extricate terror victims from their cars and buses. Last year, she donated an armoured van to transport handicapped children to a special school in Tel Aviv. As Becca said during a recent interview, 'Money is useless unless it can do some good and the Jewish people are God's chosen ones.'[1]

If she were a Jewish American woman who had made

aliyah to return to her homeland, there would be nothing unusual about her. But Becca is an Evangelical Christian who found Jesus as a small child and started speaking in tongues during her high-school years. She defines herself as 'Baptist by birth, an Evangelical by vision, with strong charismatic leanings, and a staunch Republican'. In Israel, she is also a fervent supporter of the right wing to which she donates her time and money during election years, because she is opposed to the Bush administration's Road Map, and is in favour of the forced transfer of Palestinians out of the West Bank and Gaza.

One of her closest friends is the Evangelical Christian and Republican strategist Ralph Reed, who is also the head of Century Strategies, a consulting firm that devised a plan to mobilize Christian grass roots support for Israel. When he asked Becca to help, she worked tirelessly to organize more than one million Christians in the United States to e-mail the White House in protest against the Road Map. Despite doing this, Becca does not believe that the e-mails will influence or determine the final outcome of any peace process. 'President Bush is a good Christian,' she says. 'He knows very well that it doesn't matter what he does. It is all written in the Bible. It is all up to God and He gave the Jewish people all the land of Israel forever.'

To those who are not aware of the deep commitment that the American Evangelical community has for the State of Israel, a woman like Becca, who chooses to put her life at risk every day by living in an area fraught with violence, is hard to comprehend if not unfathomable. The key, as with all else about Evangelicals, lies with the Bible – all Evangelicals take the Bible literally and consider Scripture infallible. Evangelical Christians from all over the world are the largest group that still visits the embattled Jewish State every year when tourism is at its lowest point in Israeli history. Becca is only one of more than 25,000 Evangelicals who live in Israel on a semi-permanent basis. Bringing Evangelicals to Israel was a strategy originally created by such Christian leaders as Billy Graham, his son Franklin Graham, Ed McAteer, Jerry Falwell, Ralph Reed and Pat Robertson. During an interview Ed McAteer said, 'In order to bring the issue of Israel to the top of their list, we finance and encourage Christians to actually walk the land of Israel and see the Bible come alive. This does more to create support for Israel and the Jewish people politically here in the United States than anything else.'[2]

Other Evangelical Christians do far more than just live in Israel on a part-time basis. They contribute millions of dollars in order that Israelis can live more comfortably, as well as financing the arrival of new immigrants to the Jewish State. A recent law in Israel forbids that any money goes to finance new arrivals in contested areas. The result is that many settlements are in financial trouble because of this new law. The people who subsidize those settlements and the integration of new immigrants to areas in the West Bank and Gaza are mostly American Evangelical Christians. One example is the effort and money poured into the new town of Ariel by one Evangelical congregation on the outskirts of Denver, Colorado.

Ron Nachman, a former member of the Knesset (the Israeli Parliament), from the right-wing Likud Party, is a lawyer with political expertise in finance, constitutional law and the Israeli judicial system. He is a staunch believer in the need to establish permanent settlements throughout the Occupied Territories for security measures and to stake claim to disputed land. Described as a visionary by his friends and colleagues, Nachman had a dream in 1978 of creating a major city in the heart of the West Bank. Along with thirty-nine other Israeli families, Nachman and his family settled in the hills in the West Bank, approximately twenty-five miles east of Jerusalem.

During those first few years, temporary housing was rolled into place and the forty families began to build the community of Ariel. Travelling to the United States during the 1980s, Nachman raised money from the private sector of the affluent American Jewish community, who embraced his vision and gave millions of dollars to construct houses, sidewalks, schools, and eventually several factories and hospitals. At the same time, the United Jewish Appeal in the United States and other Jewish organizations refused to allocate funds for housing projects across the 'Green Line' into those areas of the West Bank that Israel captured after the 1967 Six Day War. In contrast, funds raised in the United States by Christians were sent primarily to West Bank settlements where, Ron Nachman estimates, approximately two thirds of all Jewish settlements still receive aid from Christian Zionists.

During an interview with Ron Nachman at Ariel in spring 2003, he recalled how he travelled the United States during the 1980s, visiting Evangelical churches and talking with religious and business leaders, all in an effort to raise money for Ariel. 'I made a speech for 600 pastors in Los Angeles,' Nachman began. 'I also met Steve Forbes who was a candidate for President of the United States, and I met Jerry Falwell. As a member of the Knesset, I had substituted for Benjamin Netanyahu who was unable to make the trip to America, and it was during that trip that I made the Evangelical community an offer. I told them that it wasn't enough to believe in the Old Testament or simply pray for us. They had to have a real connection with the land. They asked me: how do you do that? And I told them: you plant a tree. This is your tree. So you come and the tree will give fruit. The fruit is yours. It's like a baby you raise. Next time you come, you'll see the vineyards giving fruit. You give these Christians a piece of land, and they come, they plant a vineyard on the mountains of Samaria. It's very spiritual for them. That's the idea we brought to the Evangelical community.'[3]

During part of the trip, Nachman went to Colorado Springs to meet Dr Dobson, one of the most powerful Evangelical preachers, who heads Focus on the Family. 'I remember waiting for him outside his office,' Nachman told me, 'when three United States generals came out. They had been sent to persuade him to come out against women being accepted in the United States Army. Can you imagine, the government sending three generals to talk to an Evangelical Christian? That's how much power they had even back then.'

When Nachman asked for money to fund housing for the West Bank, he made it very clear to his Evangelical friends that he did not want to get involved in such domestic issues as abortion. 'It's not my country,' Nachman explained. 'For me it was enough to see that in France there was a tremendous influx of North African Muslims, or when I was in London to see the mosque in Regent's Park, and know that Winston Churchill was turning over in his grave.'

Nachman profoundly believes that as long as the Evangelicals take the Bible literally and see their religious connection to the Jewish people, it is a 'gift from God'. 'Every Christian group that comes here to Ariel,' Nachman said, 'I meet them personally and I tell them that they are our ambassadors. When they go back to their countries, I ask them to tell their fellow Christians that in the Bible there is no mention of Occupied Territories or the West Bank or Gaza. There is only promised land for Israel in the Bible.'

Today, Ron Nachman is the Mayor of Ariel, an established city with a population of more than 70,000. Ariel has a university and industry, and serves as the capital of the region on which satellite cities depend for work, medical care and education. What makes Ariel exceptional in the context of the present political situation is that, since 1995, its main support no longer comes from the American Jews to whom Nachman first reached out. Support now comes from the Faith Bible Church of Denver, Colorado, led by Pastor George Morrison and his wife Cheryl.

The Morrisons are Evangelical Christians who have 'adopted' the city of Ariel as part of a movement to promote positive relationships between Christian Zionists and those Israelis who are determined to live in permanent settlements in the West Bank. George and Cheryl Morrison lead one of the largest Evangelical churches in the United States with more than 125,000 members who raise more than $10 million a year to support Ariel. During that same interview when I visited Ariel, Ron Nachman maintained that the religious agenda of his Evangelical benefactors is not at all disturbing, since they have enabled him to absorb more than five thousand Russian immigrants a year for the past three years, which dramatically changes the demographic reality in that troubled region. 'It is easy to criticize,' he said, 'when you don't actually live here and realize the religious and political importance of creating cities like Ariel throughout Judea and Samaria [the biblical names for the Occupied Territories].'

A visionary perhaps, but Nachman is also a pragmatist. When George and Cheryl Morrison make their once-a-year pilgrimage to Ariel, the Colorado pastor and his wife are treated like visiting royalty. 'These people have blessed us with their generosity,' Nachman said, 'and we can never repay them except to let them know how much we love them and appreciate their efforts and the efforts of their parishioners.' As a token of appreciation, Nachman travels several times a year to the Morrisons' church in Denver where he participates in religious services, offering prayers for the Evangelical community that they may continue 'to find it in their hearts to support Ariel and to see the return of the Messiah'. According to Nachman, wishing for his Christian friends and benefactors that the Messiah should return 'costs nothing and makes them [the Evangelicals] feel as if we [the Jews] are not fearful of their biblical beliefs'.

An even more important aspect of this unusual alliance concerns the political clout that George and Cheryl Morrison wield in the United States. Influential figures with close ties to the power structure of the Republican Party, they are credited with organizing the one million Christians who marched on Washington in 2002 in support of moving the American Embassy from Tel Aviv to Jerusalem. In my interview with her when she visited Ariel last spring, Cheryl Morrison made it clear that because of President Bush's close association and deep friendship with a well-known Evangelical singer who is a member of their congregation, and other Evangelicals who are in the public eye, the President was aware that if he pushed the Road Map to its planned completion, or denounced the construction of the wall, the Christian Right would not vote for him in 2004. 'It is not that we'll vote Democratic,' Mrs Morrison explained at the time. 'We just won't vote at all.'[4] Or, as her husband suggests, 'We just won't make our Christian youth available to answer phones and stuff envelopes at various campaign headquarters. Or, maybe we'll put up our own Christian candidate to send out a strong message that what he [the President] is doing is just not acceptable to us.' In fact, that is exactly what the Evangelical community did in 1988 when Pat Robertson challenged George Bush for the Republican nomination for President of the United States, and again in 2000, when Gary Bauer challenged George W. Bush.

On the evening that I visited Ariel, Cheryl Morrison had organized a musical event for all the residents of the Jewish community, a programme that is held once a year. Her church choir sang Hebrew songs which pledged their love and support for Israel. Usually, when the group tours settlements in Israel, they are attired in Israeli military uniforms which makes the spectacle even more moving for Israeli citizens. On that particular evening, all the group's luggage had been lost, so they were forced to perform in simple jeans and t-shirts. Still, their performance brought thunderous applause and tears from everyone in the audience. Afterwards, Ron Nachman, with tears in his own eyes, asked rhetorically, 'What does this kind of human contact and emotion and profound feeling have to do with any politician who wants to give away this land?'

CHAPTER SEVENTEEN

The Evangelical Vote

Therefore say: 'This is what the Sovereign Lord says: I will gather you from the nations and bring you back from the countries where you have been scattered, and I will give you back the land of Israel again.'

(Ezekiel 11:17)

THE specific political and religious agenda the Evangelicals uphold, and the fierce desire that pervades the Jewish community in the United States to protect Israel, have spurred the imagination of many to come up with original ideas for supporting the Jewish State.

Today there are Evangelicals with unlimited funds to finance billboards in cities across the country that send pointed political messages to entire communities about the way to vote on specific foreign or domestic policy issues. These same groups of affluent Christians also finance trips to the Holy Land for Evangelical Christians to see for themselves the biblical importance of the State of Israel.

Herbert Zweibon is one of the founders and the current head of an organization based in New York called Americans For A Safe Israel. A small round man who wears pink-rimmed spectacles, Zweibon is a fierce and dedicated Zionist and Jew who believes that under no condition should there ever be a Palestinian state. In order to realize his objective, Zweibon works closely with the hierarchy of the Evangelical movement in the United States, from whom he receives a good portion of his funding, as well as from that part of the Jewish community that believes in a one-state solution to the Israeli–Palestinian conflict.

Richard Land, President of the Ethics and Religious Liberty Commission of the Southern Baptist Convention, and Ed McAteer joined Zweibon in 1992 to arrange and finance trips for born-again Christians, mostly from America's heartland, to the Holy Land for the experience, first-hand, of God's word from the Bible. More than just giving these Christians 'the opportunity to walk where Jesus walked', the trips underscored the importance of the group's agenda of not relinquishing one inch of land to the Palestinians. 'It was a very emotional journey,' Zweibon explains, 'since for most of our visitors to Israel, it was their first introduction to the communities in Judea and Samaria, like Shiloh, Tekoa and Bet El, Israeli settlements deep in contested territories. I remember one West Indian minister standing in the middle of this new synagogue in Shilo and counting the windows to see if they fit the description in the Bible. Don't forget, these people take the Bible absolutely literally, and there is no room for error.'[1]

Herbert Zweibon and Richard Land are involved – as was Ed McAteer – in a billboard campaign all over the United States, calling for an end to the Road Map. 'We have them in Colorado, Arkansas, Missouri, Tennessee, West Virginia, Texas, New Mexico, Georgia and even in Baltimore, because it is near to Washington, D.C., where billboards are forbidden since it is the seat of the government,' Zweibon explains. 'For those people who are not aware of the

Abrahamic Covenant, the billboards instruct them to pray that President Bush honors God's covenant with Israel. We tell them to pray to kill the Road Map, to vote the way it's necessary so that we don't give one centimeter of land to the Palestinian people.'

Herb Zweibon also finances bumper stickers which basically send out the same message about Israel and opposition to any Palestinian state. 'We are not confrontational,' Zweibon insists, 'and we are not critical of the President. We are just asking people to pray, and I'm very comfortable doing that because no one can persuade me that there's a better way to reach millions of people every year who just happen to drive by one of our billboards or find themselves behind a car that has one of our bumper stickers on it.'

Zweibon claims that God clearly helped him and his colleagues realize this plan, since the usual price to advertise on a billboard is approximately $800 a month. 'Multiply that by ten or twelve states, and the cost is nearly $30,000 for three months alone.' According to Zweibon, whose God may be different from the Evangelical God, but one and the same when it comes to the Abrahamic Covenant,

It was God's blessing that I met a black minister from Tennessee, who also happened to be one of the executives at Clear Channel, an Evangelical broadcasting network, who decided that the billboards were not a commercial venture, but rather a public service. The original fee of $800 a month for one billboard suddenly became $200 a month. So with our budget, instead of having only twelve billboards, we suddenly had fifty and since every area is separate and run by a separate individual who makes his own decisions, in some of our geographic areas, our billboards only cost $50 a month. As of now, there are

225

more than three hundred billboards in more than twenty states.

Other Evangelicals are equally vigilant concerning the policy of the White House when it comes to the Israeli–Palestinian conflict. As proof of his own commitment to Israel, each day Gary Bauer sends 100,000 e-mails to Evangelicals all over the United States, asking them to put pressure on the White House concerning their support of Israel. During a particularly tense moment in 2003, Bauer sent e-mails to his Christian friends specifically asking them to let the President know that his comments about the way Israel defends itself against terror were inconsistent with his own doctrine on terrorism, and asking that each recipient send him a copy of the e-mail they sent to the White House in response to his request. 'I was sure I was going to lose a lot of my supporters, because they love the President and see him as one of their own,' Bauer says. 'But the next day, I had more than 75,000 copies of messages sent by Evangelicals all over the United States. And, each one began, "Dear Mr President, we worked for you, and my family and I pray for you every day, but it breaks my heart to tell you, if you keep putting this kind of pressure on Israel, we will not be there for you in 2004." '[2]

The following day, after receiving those thousands of e-mails, Bauer attended a press conference at the White House where the Israeli Prime Minister Ariel Sharon was a guest. By way of introduction, President Bush referred to Prime Minister Ariel Sharon as 'a man of peace'.

In addition, Bauer recognizes that after Carter's defeat for a second term as President of the United States, it would be unthinkable for any American President to imagine he could dismiss the Christian Right when it came to their position on the Israeli–Palestinian conflict.

Gary Bauer also believes that there is a 'common meeting place and a bloc [lobby]' that will vote for a President on the basis of his commitment to Israel. 'What I've said to some American Jews who are socially liberal on value-type issues,' Bauer explained to me during an interview at his office in Washington, 'is that we are just going to have to agree to disagree, because neither of us is likely to change our position. But that said, our differences should not be a *road block* to us working together on the issue of Israel's security.'

Bauer was invited by a rabbi to speak at a synagogue in Great Neck, Long Island, a wealthy, predominantly Jewish suburb of New York City. Bauer admits that the invitation became a controversial issue when he appeared on the podium that evening. 'One rabbi in the audience stood up and yelled that I was against gay marriage and abortion,' Bauer says. 'But the majority of people jumped to my defense. They all asked each other if those issues were more important than protecting Israel's survival. That ended the conversation. It's very simple. A commitment to Israel ultimately means a bond against Islam.'[3]

Gary Bauer, along with the majority of his fellow Evangelicals, views Israel as the only democratic nation in the Middle East. 'Israel is in a neighborhood surrounded by dictators, thugs and self-appointed kings,' he says, 'and in the case of Saudi Arabia, a nation ruled by 16,000 cousins. So I don't know why it's so hard for some Americans to see where our national interests should be.' As well as Bauer, there are many others who are actively involved in influencing the White House and who maintain close relationships with some of the most powerful figures in Washington.

On Capitol Hill, within the House and Senate, every effort is made by congressmen to separate the fight against global terrorism from the Israeli–Palestinian conflict. Generally the Hill refuses to equate Palestinian terrorism against Israelis with international terror attacks committed by radical Islamists against the United States or other democratic Western targets.

Countering this position, Annette Lantos, Congressman Tom Lantos' wife and a born-again Christian, shares her husband's belief that the American fight in Afghanistan or in Iraq, and the terror attacks in Madrid, are related to Palestinian group-sponsored terrorism against Israel. She thinks Palestinian actions should be viewed as such, even by those who do not believe in any biblical prediction concerning the Jewish people or Israel. Annette Lantos is confident that President Bush and Israeli Prime Minister Ariel Sharon need not worry about the Middle East Road Map, because the Palestinians themselves will not uphold their side of the bargain. 'This is God's will,' Annette Lantos maintains, 'and it is not surprising that Jesus protects the Jewish people and the State of Israel. He is the one who sees to it that the Palestinians refuse to renounce terror so the Road Map can work, even if they can't understand that their acts of terror against the Jews work against them in the final analysis.' She shrugs. 'After all, it's all written in the Bible.'[4]

Tom DeLay, a Republican congressman from Texas and fervent born-again Christian, has built his House constituency for his ardent support of Israel, one lawmaker at a time. He mobilizes their support either by threatening their re-election, or by providing late-night snacks of pizza and spare ribs during lengthy congressional vote sessions. DeLay initially gained national recognition as one of the architects of the ill-fated 'Contract with America' that shut down the United States government for several weeks. DeLay is one of Israel's staunchest advocates on Capitol Hill, despite the fact that his constituency is in Texas where Jews represent less than 1 per cent of the population. DeLay agrees with the right-wing Israeli leaders in their mandate to hold onto the West Bank, Gaza and the Golan Heights, and travels frequently to Jerusalem. DeLay has come out in favour of the forced dispersal of Palestinians throughout the Arab world. Now, with Ariel Sharon's new plan to withdraw from Gaza, the Christian Right and the Orthodox community in Israel are shocked and disappointed. They have taken to sending e-mails throughout the world, asking people to make their voices heard as they consider Sharon to be 'a traitor' to their cause.

On 13 April 2004, President George W. Bush stood in the Rose Garden of the White House with Israeli Prime Minister Ariel Sharon at his side and addressed the international media with several bits of news that reflected a change in American policy. President Bush approved Prime Minister Sharon's plan for withdrawing from the Gaza Strip, and he also maintained that unilateral withdrawal in no way harmed his Road Map to peace, but that there were certain realities that had to be accepted before any Israeli–Palestinian peace accord could be signed. Any 'right of return' of Palestinians to Palestine, he said, must be within the confines of a future Palestinian state rather than within Israel itself. His statement surpassed realism, but it was courageous since those involved in trying to achieve a peace accord understood from the inception that no right of return to what is currently Israel could ever be a point of negotiation. One phrase President Bush used, that was a coded assurance to his Evangelical supporters, was when he referred to Israeli settlements as 'Israeli population centers'. With those three words, he validated the Christian Right and the right-wing religious Jewish idea of Judea and Samaria – the biblical name for the Occupied Territories or the West Bank – as part of the biblical land of Israel. After all, the words 'settlement' and

'Occupied Territory', Evangelicals argue, are not found in the Bible. Despite Sharon's plan, which has been sanctioned by the United States, the issue of deporting Palestinians out of the West Bank and Gaza is a subject that comes up at every joint American–Israeli conference.

When I visited Gary Bauer in his office in Washington, he told me he was expecting a conference call from Esther Levens and Senator Brownback to discuss a jointly written letter they intended to send to President George W. Bush about the forced transfer of Palestinians from the Occupied Territories. Earlier, in Kansas City, Esther Levens had told me about the plans for this letter. I asked Levens how she, as a Jew, could sanction the forced transfer of Palestinians, given the history of the Jewish people? She thought for a minute before she replied. 'I suppose you're right. We have to put it in such a way that it doesn't offend people.'[5]

I asked Bauer the same question. 'It is a question of wording,' he told me. 'Obviously it is a sensitive issue and we have to present it in a way that is not incendiary.'[6]

The other question I asked countless Evangelical leaders in America when they were bombarding the White House with e-mails stating their opposition to the Road Map was: 'Is this the moment of truth, when you will know if President Bush is really a born-again Christian who believes in the infallibility of Scripture, or if he is merely a politician who has used you and your religion to garner votes?' Their responses varied according to their intractability on the subject, but almost all claimed that they believed that Bush was a committed Christian, who nonetheless did not really understand or delve deeply enough into Scripture to understand the place that the Jewish people and Israel played in God's plan for mankind.

Given the influence of Evangelical Christians in the

current American administration, the Israeli Embassy has an Office of Inter-Religious Affairs that hosts monthly briefings for Evangelicals, welcomes church bus tours, and organizes breakfasts.

One morning, in May 2002, at the Israeli Embassy in Washington, D.C., church leaders from across America arrived in the nation's capital to listen to a speech given by Ed McAteer. As people arrived, they were given two lapel pins – an American and an Israeli flag – which were promptly pinned to jackets. Each was given a short video, in which a group of Israeli soldiers chatted pleasantly with monks during the siege of the Church of the Nativity in Bethlehem last year. The conference opened with the group singing both *The Star Spangled Banner* and the Israeli national anthem *Hatikva*, which was followed by a song composed by popular American singer Pat Boone, also a devout Evangelical, called 'Israel, O Blessed Israel'. Moshe Fox, then Minister of Public Affairs for the Israeli Embassy, was the first to speak. 'It is no coincidence that our prayers for Christians and Jews complement each other,' he said, before quoting extensively from the Old Testament concerning how God promised the Jews a land flowing with milk and honey. 'I call on you to carry this prayer and help turn this divine promise into a reality,' Fox concluded.[7]

One of the guests that day was Janet Parshall, a popular Evangelical radio host whose daily programme is syndicated to 3.5 million Christian listeners nationwide. 'I've read the end of the book,' Parshall said, referring to the predictions of Armageddon in the Bible. 'I know what happens.'[8]

The day after that prayer breakfast at the Israeli Embassy in Washington, Ed McAteer flew back to Memphis to host a pro-Israel rally organized by the Memphis Jewish Federation, a local charity that provides social services to the Jewish community there. Jewish leaders in Tennessee, unlike their counterparts in New York and Boston, have always mobilized support from the city's Christian coalition. Before the conference began in the huge auditorium, people were holding up signs which read, 'Bless Israel, Bless Sharon, Arafat is the Enemy'. A video played during the speeches, on a large screen behind the podium, showing horrific scenes of the aftermath of several suicide bombings. Ehud Olmert, then Israeli Deputy Prime Minister, appeared via satellite to assure the crowd that Jerusalem would never be divided.

One of the participants was Thomas Lindberg, pastor of the Memphis, who described to the audience a tour he had arranged for American Evangelical Christians to Israel. 'We felt that special nature that God has put upon that land,' Lindberg said, 'and given to His people, the Jewish people of the world. And let me say today that we – and when I say we, I represent the Assemblies of God here in America, three and a half million of us, forty-two million Assemblies of God people around the globe – and all of us love Israel.'[9]

One of those who attended the rally was Greta Simber, a born-again Christian who prides herself on donating money to Israel as well as spreading 'the word of the Lord' to everyone she meets in order to encourage them to support the Jewish State. During an interview, she explained her feelings: 'As far as I'm concerned, this is God's work. We have been charged by the Bible to love Israel, to love the Jews, and await the return of their Savior. It's not that we think we have all the answers, God knows, even George Bush doesn't have the answers, nor does Ariel Sharon, or Yasser Arafat. The only person who has the answers is Jesus.'[10] Mrs Simber also believes in signs and 'divine intervention' during certain pivotal moments on the evening news. She explains: 'When I see that the President of Saudi

Arabia has come to Washington with an idea for a peace plan, and suddenly has to rush back home because his brother had a stroke, I wonder if that isn't the hand of God acting to protect the Jewish people.'

After the rally, Ed McAteer talked about how he and all the Evangelical Christians who share his stand on Israel do not consider themselves instruments of peace but rather staunch supporters of a one-state solution which eliminates any chance of the creation of a Palestinian state. McAteer believes that none of the land now occupied by Israel should ever be returned to the Palestinians. 'There is no doubt that their leadership made bad choices in 1948,' he explained, 'and as a result the Palestinian people have paid a heavy price, but that doesn't change the fact that the land never belonged to them in the first place, and they have absolutely to right or claim on it.'[11]

Gary Bauer not only shares McAteer's opinion but goes even further when he maintains that the born-again End Times scenario is not disparaging of the Jewish people nor does it threaten their existence. In fact, he believes that because of his efforts and those of millions of other Evangelical Christians throughout the United States, Israel and the Jewish people enjoy a more solid financial and political security than ever before in their tumultuous history. 'I have been asked over and over again why we, Evangelical Christians, stand with Israel,' Bauer told me, his short stature belied by a powerful delivery honed during his 2000 presidential campaign. 'Well, my goodness, why would we not stand with Israel? Why would we not stand with the nation about which God says, "If you bless the Jewish people, I will bless you, and if you curse them, I will curse you"? That's good enough for me. I don't need anything else.'[12]

One of Ed McAteer's good friends and colleagues is James

Woolsey, the former director of the Central Intelligence Agency and currently an advisor to the Jewish Institute for National Security Affairs. 'The Evangelicals are important,' Woolsey says, 'but less in a political sense than as a reflection of the widespread support that Israel has in this country. That said, there is no doubt that when [George W.] Bush was elected President the Evangelical community had an un-precedented influence among some of his top administration officials. And while one can say that no one has a monopoly on the ear of this President, there is no doubt that he is more receptive to the pro-Israel message than his father was, or any of his predecessors with the exception of Ronald Reagan. And there is also no doubt that every man or woman today who hopes to be elected to national office knows that they need the Evangelical vote, which means they better make sure their position on Israel and the Middle East is in sync with the Christian Right.'[13]

Of all the American Jews who work with the Evangelical community, there is no one who has had as much success in promoting the message of the Christian Right as well as of the Orthodox Jewish community in Israel as Yechiel Eckstein.

An Orthodox rabbi and the founder of the International Fellowship of Christians and Jews based in Jerusalem and Chicago, Rabbi Eckstein is a controversial figure in the Jewish community because of his willingness to accept his Christian friends' End Times scenario. In an interview in his office in Jerusalem, Rabbi Eckstein justified his refusal to condemn the Evangelical community for their beliefs con-cerning the eventual fate of the Jewish people.

'For an Evangelical Christian, Evangelism is the core of their faith. In other words, if they agree to work with us, they would never dream of asking us to give up the core idea of Shabbat. For them, evangelizing is the core of their faith so we don't have a right to ask them to give up the core of their faith. Instead, I try to find ways that they can fulfill their goals as they see them written in the Bible without it harming our [Jewish] sensibilities. What my Christian friends believe is that by blessing Israel, they are not just being nice, but they are fulfilling their great commission of witnessing the Jewish people, and we're talking more than eighty million adults who are Evangelicals and that is a very powerful number of people who are friends and allies of Israel.'[14]

Some of his peers and colleagues believe that the info-mercials Rabbi Eckstein makes with such Evangelical luminaries as Ralph Reed, Franklin Graham and Jerry Falwell are detrimental to Jewish identity. In fact, the message that Eckstein admittedly sends when he appears on Pat Robertson's Christian Broadcast Network on Sunday mornings is that if an Orthodox rabbi has no problem with the role the Jewish people play when the Messiah returns, then all Jewish people should accept that fate as written in Scripture. During that same interview with Rabbi Eckstein, he admitted that his organization is 'not discouraging End Times interpretations in its televised solicitations for financial support throughout the Evangelical community', despite the fact they are replete with references to New Testament prophecy predicting the death of all who do not embrace Jesus.

Rabbi Eckstein works closely with Ralph Reed to manage the annual budget of the International Fellowship of Christians and Jews (IFCJ), which is around $100 million a year – approximately one tenth of all the money that pours into Israel every year from Evangelical Christian groups throughout the world, predominantly from the United States. That money comes from a base of more than 300,000 donors but only 1,000 of those are Jews. In other words, the American Evangelical Christian community funds all but a minute fraction of the IFCJ's contributions. Ralph Reed maintains that the financial contribution from the Christian community really began when Eckstein called for help in liberating Jews from the then Soviet Union. 'Yechiel Eckstein touched a nerve,' he says. 'In the 1980s, the Soviet Union for the Evangelicals was the Antichrist, which meant we could kill two birds with one stone, if you will. Rabbi Eckstein is the first and only person who discovered the way to translate abstract Christian love for Israel into hard dollars. He realized that even if there were 80 million Christians out there who were unwilling or unable to spend one thousand dollars on tickets to actually come to Israel, they were able and willing to each give one dollar to support Israel.'[15]

Rabbi Eckstein is not at all reticent in affirming that his organization raises funds in the United States predominantly from the Christian community and distributes them in Israel. He also admits that though he works closely with the Israeli Prime Minister, the 'key to his success' is that he does not take a political stand when it comes to the Israeli government's 'Settlement Policy', nor on the American Evangelical position on abortion, school prayer, or any other sensitive issue. 'Even when we had our Washington office,' Eckstein says, 'we focused on the areas of commonality. For instance, last year we gave $20 million here and in the former Soviet Union, under the aegis of one of our organizations called Wings of Eagles that brings Russians to Israel.'

The emigration of Soviet Jewry in the early 1990s was seen as a fulfilment of dispensationalist hopes, rivalling the events of 1948 and 1967. 'Another aspect of our charity comes under an organization called Isaiah 58,' Eckstein continues, 'which helps elderly Jews in Russia who can't move to Israel but who need financial support, medicine and clothing. Here in Israel, we have Guardians of Israel that supports projects [to counter] domestic violence, several rape crisis centers, and generally all the poor people here across the board. Last year we supported 116 different projects which ranged from helping battered women to training about 3,000 Ethiopian immigrants so they could work here. What we do is give the Christians tangible and meaningful ways to bless Israel and the Jewish people.'[16]

If there is ambiguity in any of Rabbi Eckstein's projects and his determination to stay apolitical, it is in his 'Stand For Israel' organization, designed to raise political support in the United States for Israel. The 'Stand for Israel' solidarity campaign was conceived by Rabbi Eckstein and Ralph Reed, an Evangelical Christian and former Christian Coalition leader, and a current advisor to President George W. Bush. For the annual meeting in 2003, the keynote speaker at the affair was the then Attorney General John Ashcroft, who closed his remarks by saying, 'Your ability to generate grass-roots solidarity for the war against terrorism here, in Israel and elsewhere, helps the cause of freedom.'[17]

Also present that day were Jerry Falwell and Richard Land, an Evangelical Christian and the Chief Operating Officer of the Ethics and Religious Liberty Commission, the Southern Baptist Convention's agency for 'applied Christianity', which concerns itself with moral and social issues, and the head of the Southern Baptist Convention, the largest group of Charismatic Christians in America. These men all work together, and with others who share their beliefs in opposing any Israeli–Palestinian peace accord. 'Our support for Israel has been going on for years,' Land continues, 'because we believe that God gave the land of Israel to the Jews forever. They are God's chosen people.'[18]

'And here is where we have a slight issue,' Eckstein explains, 'because Ralph Reed works with the Bush administration as an advisor to the President and also is the head of the Republican Party in Georgia. Obviously he can't go against the Road Map, and because he works with the Prime Minister here in Israel as I do, I can't do that either, even if I wanted to. So, in some ways, while we are not ideological, we are not completely independent.'[19]

CHAPTER EIGHTEEN

Shifting the Centre of Gravity

As Evangelical Christians, we consider ourselves the best friends of the Jewish people. Because of our belief in Scripture and our view that the Jews are God's chosen people, we believe in fighting anti-Semitism when we see it. Still, many times without thinking, Christians make remarks that put Jewish people in a bad light. Remember, what you say might be the only impression your Jewish friends have about how Christians view the Jews. Are your words those that Jesus would want said about His people?
(*Chosen People Magazine*, March 1985)

AVI Granot, an advisor to the Israeli President, has for the past twenty years accompanied Rabbi Eckstein to various fund-raising events in the United States. Granot, who also has the distinction of having been appointed the first head of the Department of Christian Affairs at the Israeli Embassy in Washington, notes: 'In the 1980s the Evangelicals prayed for Israel. In the 1990s they continued to pray for Israel but also began giving money for the new arrivals from Russia. Now, in the 2000s, we have prayer, money, *aliyah* from Russia and all over the world, and our Christian friends are also supporting a failing economy because of terrorism, as well as helping the victims of terrorism to get on with their lives. The response from our Christian friends was that they finally had something concrete to give, because, after all, that's what's written in the Bible.'[1]

Through their organization, Rabbi Eckstein and Ralph Reed contribute to the campaign coffers of right-wing Israeli politicians and are invited regularly to briefing sessions in the White House. According to Avi Granot, when questioned about the political involvement of the International Fellowship of Christians and Jews (IFCJ), Reed justified his position in the following way: 'While the Christian Coalition believes in a Christian nation and a Christian world,' he said, 'we have perhaps been insensitive of the horrors the Jewish people have experienced. The money that we raise for Israel every year is also used to support political candidates who will insure that the land of Israel will never be relinquished under the auspices of a peace accord with the Palestinians. We will do all in our power to ensure that Jews are never again the target of hatred and discrimination.'[2]

In July 2003, Eckstein, Jerry Falwell, Pat Robertson and Benny Hinn, one of the most successful and charismatic televangelists from California, were invited to the White House for a meeting with Colin Powell and Condoleezza Rice. It is well known in Washington that of all President Bush's advisors, Powell and Rice are the main supporters of the Road Map for peace in the Middle East. The meeting was arranged at the suggestion of Ralph Reed and Karl Rove, who believed it was crucial that those invited plead their case to Powell and Rice in an effort to change their minds about conciliation with the Palestinians. When asked by Granot how the meeting went, Hinn, a Pentecostal Christian, repeated what he says at the beginning and end of each of his televised sermons, which reach more than twenty-five million people every week: 'Those who love Israel, politically speaking, are the ones who have influence over this administration. And the Jews who love Jesus are the ones who have influence over their own destiny.'[3] Rabbi Eckstein was more specific. According to him, the potential for the lobby to be the most powerful in American history is possible, if the Jewish people put aside their differences with the Christian community and if the Christians decide to make Israel a priority before their domestic agendas. 'It's a compromise,' he explains. 'The Christians have made an important financial investment in Israel, which means that the threat of Islamic terrorism is more important to our collective survival than their internal agenda.'[4]

To achieve their goals, Ralph Reed's consulting firm Century Strategies has devised a plan to mobilize the Christian grass-roots support. Through American church groups more than one million Christians were organized to e-mail the White House to protest against George W. Bush's Road Map. The consulting group runs newspaper advertisements and commercials on conservative radio talk shows urging Jews and Christians to see past their historical differences and come together at a time of crisis for Israel. 'Christians have the potential to be the most effective constituency influencing a foreign policy since the end of the Cold War,' Reed said during an interview. 'They are shifting the center of gravity in the pro-Israel community to become a more conservative and Republican phenomenon.'[5]

Perhaps Gary Bauer put it best when he said, 'Although Bush is President of all races and religions in America, and makes all the necessary political moves, he wants to try and satisfy all constituents; in the end, it doesn't matter because everything has already been pre-ordained by God.'[6]

Despite the Biblical references and deep belief that Evangelicals hold in their hearts for Israel, and the patriotic concern about Islamic terror threatening the safety of

Americans all over the world, there is a hint of something less noble in their position concerning the Arab world. During an interview, a close advisor to President Bush, who is an Evangelical Christian, insisted upon telling me a medieval Persian tale about the origin of the hashish-crazed 'assassins', in the fortress of Alamut. According to him, the point of the story would be 'self-evident', although he wanted me to know that what it actually proves to him was that the instinct to kill by dying has been 'programmed into the DNA of all Arab people since the beginning of time'.[7]

In the same vein, while the American Jewish community exhibits tolerance in regard to the role of Jews in the End Times scenario, and gratitude for the Christian Right's unconditional support of Israel, some painful differences remain. Beneath the surface, Evangelicals have always seen Jews as targets for conversion rather than friendship. Jews are minor players on a Christian stage that calls for their acceptance of Jesus in order to fulfill the Evangelical prophecy that He will return as the Messiah and Saviour of all mankind. Even with the edict of the Catholic Church from the Second Vatican Conference in 1963, when Pope John XXIII announced that the Jews should no longer be held culpable for killing Jesus Christ, remnants of anti-Semitism still surface from time to time in the Christian world.

The Reverend Jerry Falwell, who considers himself the 'most outspoken [Christian] supporter of Israel and the Jewish people the world over', once told his biographer Merrill Simon, author of *Jerry Falwell and the Jews*, that the Jewish people are 'spiritually blind and desperately in need of their Messiah and Savior'.[8]

Another incident that did not help the Jewish-Evangelical relationship was the revelation that the Reverend Billy Graham had joined with former President Richard M.

Nixon in making private anti-Semitic remarks in 1972. Weeks after the latest round of Richard Nixon's Oval Office recordings were released in 2003, resulting in a storm of reprimand, Billy Graham took full responsibility for his anti-Semitic comments. Even so, his son and successor, Franklin Graham, soon rescinded his father's *mea culpa* by asserting that the taped quotes had been taken out of context and meant to refer to 'liberalism' and not 'Jews'.

The most recent example of friction between the Fundamentalists and Jewish communities involved Mel Gibson's film *The Passion of the Christ*. The film portrays a flawed version of the crucifixion of Jesus, and an egregious depiction of the Jewish people as bearing responsibility for His death, thus stirring up old resentments and prejudice that had, at least on the surface, disappeared. Given its enormous publicity and sensational content, the movie would have opened up old wounds of anti-Semitism that had, in the past forty years, been somewhat healed. The debate concerning *The Passion of the Christ* is filled with ambiguities, catchphrases and innuendos that only fuel the fury.

At the height of the polemic concerning the film, in the Bible Belt (the south-west, south-east and middle of the country), neon signs were posted on motel, business and church marquees that said, 'Jews Killed The Lord Jesus'. The Lovingway United Pentecostal Church in Denver posted just such an announcement. When members of the congregation were interviewed[9] about the hateful message, one man explained, 'We've been debating this for a long time. I think it's safe to say that it took Mel Gibson's historic film to make us realize that the Jews should finally own up to the fact that they killed Christ.' Another member of the church, a woman, added, 'This isn't against the Jewish people. This is an opportunity for them to repent and accept Jesus into their hearts so He can finally come back to earth to guide us towards the End Times.'

Recently, Jerry Falwell called the film an 'unambiguous account of the final hours of Jesus Christ' and maintained that Gibson was only trying 'to arouse people to understand the price paid for their salvation'.[10] Dr Ergun Caner, who teaches at Falwell's Evangelical Liberty University, went on the offensive to refute charges of anti-Semitism, implying that the charge of anti-Semitism was a slur, a persecution: 'The church has been shoved into the closet from which the gays came.' Dr Caner elaborated, saying that it is socially acceptable to intentionally mock and malign conservative Christians, just as homosexuals were treated before their uprising. Jerry Falwell has said repeatedly that, 'We are, in fact, the only group in America that is habitually slandered by Hollywood, the mainstream media and radical politicians, who experience no hint of repercussion.' Popular culture, according to Caner, has an 'aggressive abhorrence of Judeo-Christian values; the notion has taken root in real America. That is why Ten Commandments replicas across the nation are in the crosshairs of the American Civil Liberties Union . . . Just think about this library worker in Bowling Green, Kentucky, who had to go to court to win her right to wear a small cross around her neck to work. Think about why a woman in Taylor, Michigan, had to go to court to win the right to display a small sign in her housing project that reads, "24 hour prayer station". Just think about why the steel cross from the rubble of the World Trade Center has been targeted for removal by "offended" atheists. Think about why high school students in Windsor, Virginia were prohibited from singing a secular song simply because of its title, "The Prayer". Christians feel persecuted throughout America and bullied solely because they choose to walk with the Living God.'[11]

Ted Haggard, a politically well-connected Evangelical Christian who heads the National Association of Evangelicals, bases his support of Israel on his belief in Scripture. And yet he is one of those born-again Christians who came out in favour of Mel Gibson's film, and also issued a warning to the Jewish community: 'There is a lot of pressure on Israel right now,' Haggard said, 'and Evangelicals are Israel's only good friends. Criticism of Gibson's film is short-sighted on the part of Jewish leaders, who risk alienating about two billion Christians over a movie.'[12] When I asked him if his statement should be construed as a threat, Haggard was quick to respond. 'My comments are not meant as a threat but as a word of caution that Jewish complaints may come across to some average Christians as if [the Jews] are against any movie about Jesus.'[13]

Abraham Foxman, the director of the Jewish Anti-Defamation League, is often accused of being 'too vigilant' in charging a group or individual with anti-Semitic sentiment. During an interview recently at his New York office, he explained his reasons for being tolerant of the Evangelical agenda. 'This is their faith and belief,' Foxman explained, 'and my job is not to change their minds about heaven and hell, or whether the Messiah has been here before, or if all the people who don't believe in Jesus Christ will be slaughtered at the end of history or if a movie rewrites history. I have more pressing concerns, and my main concern is on earth in the here and now. The majority of the Christian community are our friends and allies in their support for Israel. That's my only concern, not whether or not Jews can get into heaven.'[14]

Under ordinary circumstances, it might be perplexing that the Jewish people have decided not only to ignore the domestic policies of the Evangelicals, but have also chosen to disregard the Evangelical belief concerning their fate in the End Times scenario or their responsibility in killing Christ.

Events in today's world, however, are far from ordinary. And yet, despite this love affair between Evangelicals and the Jewish people, there are voices within the Christian community who take exception to the expectations of the Evangelicals at the expense of the Jews.

The Reverend Welton C. Gaddy, a Baptist minister and the president of the Interfaith Alliance, a group dedicated to promoting religious tolerance and separation of church and state, says: 'The religious right's literalistic interpretation of prophecy calls for a cataclysmic resolution of the conflict in the Middle East in order for Christ to return. This is not a point of view supportive of Israel. It is a point of view supportive of the conversion of Jews who live in Israel. The religious right envisions a situation in which Jerusalem is not the international capital of Judaism, but the center for realizing the sovereignty of Christ.'[15]

In addition to Gaddy, there are prominent Jewish leaders who do not agree with the Fundamentalist-tolerant position taken by Abraham Foxman or Ariel Sharon. Rabbi David Rosen, a British subject and a modern Orthodox rabbi, served as army chaplain to the Israeli Army in the West Sinai during the 1973 war, before he became Chief Rabbi of South Africa, and then Ireland. In 1985 he returned to Israel, where he serves as the official representative from Israel to the Vatican, and directs all interfaith operations of the American Jewish Committee in Jerusalem. As international president of the organization, which incorporates fifteen religions in sixty different countries, Rosen organizes conferences on religious peace and harmony – especially Jewish–Christian cooperation – throughout the world. While Rabbi Rosen encourages close relations between Evangelical Christians and Jews, he is wary of the Fundamentalist agenda. 'The relationship that Evangelicals have with the Jewish people is paradoxical,' Rosen says. 'On one hand, because Evangelicals are so deeply rooted in the Bible, in the words, land, and people, it enables them to feel a close personal connection to the Jewish people and to the land of Israel. In that sense, it is very positive for us because it lends itself to a positive affirmation. On the other hand, to believe that only the righteous will go to heaven and meet Jesus, while here on earth, there will be Armageddon and the slaughter of all the Jews who don't recognize Jesus, is a scenario that is hardly one which could be a source of music and comfort to Jewish ears.'[16]

David Rosen is also pragmatic when it comes to the attitudes of Jewish-American organizations which have an alliance with the Evangelicals. 'The point is: they can't dance at two different weddings,' Rosen says. 'They might make a coalition with the Evangelicals based on the issues but they can never make a marriage.' According to Rosen, the main motivation for financial contributions from the American-Jewish community to Jewish organizations in America and to Israel is to counter anti-Semitism. 'As far as the controversy is concerned about Mel Gibson's film,' he continues, 'in one way, it fuels anti-Semitism but it also fuels fear within the Jewish community, which translates into money. Therefore, if Jewish leaders claim anti-Semitism in order to garner contributions, they cannot, on the other hand, claim that the Evangelical community is their best friend and most loyal supporter. As I said, they cannot dance at two weddings.'[17]

As for the tacit nod of agreement from Israel concerning the Evangelical–Jewish relationship, Rosen believes that it is not a knowledgeable perception on the part of either Israelis or American Jews, but is encouraged by certain right-wing

Israeli leaders who think they can achieve the geographic goal of holding onto the West Bank, with support from those with different beliefs. 'The reason that Jewish organizations have embraced the Evangelicals,' Rosen claims, 'is because of Israel's attitude of acceptance. It has encouraged that perception of friendship and support. The interesting thing about Mel Gibson's film is that it doesn't promote anti-Semitism any more than any of the Christian websites or other films that circulate throughout the world that tell the story of Jesus and how he was betrayed and crucified. The only reaction of anti-Semitism from the Gibson film comes from within the Jewish community itself, accusing the Christians of anti-Semitism which, in turn, guarantees an increase in donations to Jewish agencies.'[18]

There are Evangelical Christians who, while adherent to their faith, religious dogma and to the Bible, are nonetheless altruistic in their generosity to the Jewish State. Evangelical minister Clarence Wagner heads Bridges for Peace, an organization that opened its doors in Jerusalem in 1976 to live out the message in St Paul's Epistle to the Romans 15:27: 'For if the Gentiles have shared in the Jews' spiritual blessings, they owe it to the Jews to share with them their material blessings.' With an annual budget of $80 million and a nationwide membership throughout the United States, the organization subsidizes the Israeli economy, and supports both right-wing leaders in Israel and the Christian Right in America. The buildings housing the organization, built around a small courtyard and garden, belong to the Ethiopian Church, which still uses the large cathedral behind the complex. According to Reverend Wagner, Bridges for Peace wishes to buy the buildings – not a small investment in the centre of Jerusalem – but the Ethiopian Church has refused to sell the property.

248

Approximately sixty people, mostly Americans, work there, devoting their time to 'do good in the land where Jesus walked'. The American woman switchboard operator, a widow in her seventies, is friendly and eager to explain why she decided to make the move from the mid-western United States to the Middle East. Discovering after she lost her husband that one of her great-grandparents had been Jewish, she interpreted her new freedom and the revelation about her heritage as signs from the Lord to change her life and do something charitable to help the Jewish people. She works at Bridges for Peace as a volunteer, and pays all her own expenses, including travel between Indiana to Jerusalem.

Bridges for Peace has direct contact with Israeli society, sending out field workers to discover what is needed in under-privileged neighbourhoods. Some three hundred and fifty houses are refurbished every year by volunteers who supply the materials and build whatever is needed.

When explaining the charitable commitment that Bridges for Peace has made to Israel and the Jewish people, Wagner talks about what he believes is a new kind of battle raging throughout the world today, unlike any war in the past. 'In the beginning,' he says,

Christians and Jews searched to see if they had acted in some way to justify these Islamic terror attacks. But when Evangelical Christians look to the Bible and realize that it is not their sin that has unleashed this new plight on humanity, but rather a prediction written in the Bible by God Himself, they gather strength to combat this Evil. The Jews were meant to be the caretakers and custodians in the Right Way, affirming the minority, being a society to affirm and be a positive place for people to live. As a Christian, I don't feel subjugated but rather I feel respected

249

in the Holy Land. President Bush should not be afraid of stating his position clearly against Islamic terror, and not try to prove that his campaign is not against the Arab people but rather against a handful of criminals who are operating under the banner of Islam. There is time for that later. Now, Christians and Jews are the only two Bible-based religious and they need to find ways to stand together against this threat.[19]

Wagner, who travels all year to North American cities to bolster support for the Bush administration and raise financial and political support of Israel, believes that there is more enthusiasm among Christian and Jewish audiences for his message today than there has been since the Iranian hostage taking in 1979.

On my last trip, there was a quantum change. In Cincinnati, Sacramento, Portland, Seattle, and also across Canada, in Vancouver, Toronto and Winnipeg, I noticed a distinct change in the attitude of even the more liberal Christians and Jews. These were the people who actually voiced their fear that Americans had forgotten about the threat of Islam after the hostages were released in Iran in 1980. But since September 11th, they woke up again to realize that those same forces of Evil which had been dormant for about twenty years, are back in action, bent on destroying all that we hold dear. Between then and now, people tended to live in this fantasy land where they believed if only Israel just behaved herself, the whole world would become better. Now they realize that Israel has been victimized by the same forces as terrorized us in America or in Spain. Perhaps they're even afraid of what the future might hold, for themselves, since America and

250

the rest of the world is going to be faced with episodes of terrorism on the same level as Israel, although not the same degree because there isn't that proximity to a terror state. I can tell you that any country that doesn't put its foot down against Islamic terror is going to continue to be threatened and it's not because of Israel. It's because Israel has always said, 'I'm sorry, we're here and we're not going to disappear to make you happy.' What that means is that Israel is going to be threatened until Israel disappears and while those Islamic terrorists will never be able to make America disappear they believe – wrongly – that Americans will become fearful of sending troops overseas or doing anything to stop the spread of Islamic Fundamentalism. There's a lot at stake and recent events certainly proved that we, Americans and Israelis, are not about to retreat the way the Spanish did.[20]

During my first meeting with him at his office in Jerusalem in October 2003, Wagner described how he had been raised an Episcopalian but found himself lacking the 'special council of the Lord'. Before he 'found Jesus', he was 'a good person who went to church regularly and did all the things that were required of him'. And yet, he reached a stage in his life where the mainline Episcopalian faith did not offer him enough fulfilment. 'I knew that I was a sinner,' Wagner explains, 'and that was what intrigued me because that was exactly what separates the Evangelicals from other Christians. Jesus died for our sins and until I accepted that, I couldn't be free.'

When Wagner was sixteen, his parents sent him to an Anglican boarding school in Palm Beach, Florida where, according to him, all the students were required to attend chapel every morning. One day, a Baptist teacher asked if he would like to join a Bible study class on Sunday evenings.

Wagner accepted instantly. When the preacher asked if anyone wanted to come up to 'commit his or her life to Christ', Wagner stepped forward. 'It was like drawing a line in the sand. I knew then that Jesus had called me, and there was no doubt that I wanted to be a member of this community. I was baptized and because the Bible says there is only one baptism, when the individual accepts Jesus into his life, that was the moment when I became a Christian. Today, I read the Bible every day and while I'm not perfect, I try to incorporate into my life all of the Lord's teachings. It's not that I make a separate set of rules, because being a born-again Christian is really not that much different than being Jewish, since the Bible was written by the Jews anyway.'

In his life now as the head of an Evangelical organization with a very specific position on the Bible, and consequently on American foreign policy towards Israel, Wagner admits that he chooses his friends from among the people who 'believe' as he does. 'I am not here in Israel to proselytize,' he says, 'but I hope I can be a light to the world and influence the Jewish people and all people to see the light of Jesus Christ . . . Why?' He shrugs. 'Because the Jewish people were chosen by God, and the land of Israel was willed to the Jewish people by the Lord, and in the end, they will accept Jesus when he returns to Israel.'

Surprisingly, Clarence Wagner is one of the more enlightened and intellectual members of his faith. A student of comparative religion, Wagner reads voraciously, including books by Evangelical Christians who have been spurned by their leaders because of their various styles and choices of life. Despite his pragmatism when it comes to the human condition, Wagner is unyielding insofar as it concerns the security and sanctity of the Jewish State.

Jimmy Carter and George W. Bush, both in office during

the two major attacks against the United States by radical Muslims, represented the two distinct and diverse beliefs held by the mainstream Protestant community and the Evangelical Christians. If President Jimmy Carter was determined not to show any partisan feelings towards those who shared his religious beliefs, he was also naïve about the potential political influence his fellow Christians were gaining. Despite the fact that Carter was a born-again Christian, he leant towards the mainline Protestant rhetoric of liberation theology – the religious duty to liberate oppressed people throughout the world. Since mainstream Protestants do not believe that a 'reborn' Jewish State is a pre-requisite for the second coming of Jesus to earth, they have no religious incentive to preserve the Jewish State. Carter, moreover, was perceived as rejecting Evangelical doctrine. The mainstream Protestant community aligned itself with the viewpoint put forth by the Palestinian Christian community, specifically that of the Palestinian intellectual and writer, the late Edward Said. In his writings and lectures, Said referred to the constant 'crucifixion of the Palestinian people', and believed the Arab Christians who lived throughout Israel and the West Bank were the 'true believers, and their Church the true Christian Church'.[21]

'The fact that the Evangelicals are so pro-Israel,' Said wrote, 'and so linked to the Jewish people, only proves why the Palestinian Christians are suffering at the hands of their occupiers.'[22]

On the other hand, the Evangelical response as voiced by George W. Bush is that such Palestinian leaders as Yasser Arafat consistently used the plight of the Christian Arabs as a 'propaganda tool' against Israeli occupation, when the truth is that Christian Palestinians suffer more at the hands of their Muslim brothers than because of Israeli occupation. As a result of the split in the Protestant Church, the mainstream American Jewish community found itself sharing a common goal with the Evangelicals in their continued, unswerving support of the State of Israel. And yet, the Christian Right was, and remains, opposed to almost all other issues that the historically liberal American Jewish community holds dear: separation of church and state, women's rights, sexual freedom and tolerance, and abortion. Had they followed their cultural and social instincts, they would have rejected the offer of friendship from the Evangelical community; but the Jewish community would then have found itself having to accept the mainstream Protestant community's concern about the rights, and entitlement to statehood, of the Palestinians.

PART THREE

THE JESUS FACTOR

CHAPTER NINETEEN

Playing the God Game

Anyone who knows history, particularly the history of Europe, will, I think, recognize that the domination of education or of government by any one particular religious faith is never a good arrangement for the people.

(Eleanor Roosevelt)

BY the turn of the twenty-first century, while the Evangelical community throughout America was becoming more and more politically sophisticated, and bent on transforming their ideology into a potentially powerful political movement that could ultimately influence a presidential election, so were the terrorists. Given the global threat of terror today, there is no doubt that radical Islam has organized terror groups bent on rooting out Western secular influence in Islamic lands. The bombings in Madrid on 11 March 2004 were an example of the success and determination of the terror network. And as a consequence, Al Qaeda has entered in America's lexicon as a generic term for all radical Islamic terror groups.

Since 11 September 2001, Evangelical churches and seminaries across America are not only giving lectures and selling books criticizing Islam but are also promoting strategies to convert Muslims to Christianity. Evangelicals continue to proclaim that the ultimate sin is to send a message to future generations that patriotism can exist without deep religious convictions. In February 2003, when President Bush appeared in Nashville to address the National Religious Broadcasters, there was a backdrop behind him which read: 'Advancing Christian Communications'. His first words to the group were '. . . America's enemies hate the thought that we can worship the Almighty God the way we see fit . . .'

For Evangelical Christians, worshipping God the way they see fit means adhering to the moral values set down in Scripture. Members of the Christian Right like Jerry Falwell believe that since long before the attacks, and certainly since they happened, the civilized world has been in moral collapse, a state of affairs where the devil is getting the upper hand, because of 'situational ethics, cultural seduction, cultural accommodation and an absence of inclusive salvation'. In a speech before the National Religious Broadcasters in March 2004, Falwell pointed to events that added fuel to the devil's war against God. 'The federal courts have legalized sodomy and declared the Ten Commandments to be illegal when they were displayed in a federal court of law.' He also maintained that the Boy Scouts had been disparaged because they upheld 'time-honored moral traditions', the Pledge of Allegiance had been declared unconstitutional, and that the Episcopalian Church had fallen into the depths of immorality when it promoted an openly gay priest to the position of bishop. 'This man should have been defrocked when he abandoned his wife and children to live with his male lover,' Falwell said. 'In the West, the God of Christianity has been superseded by the gods of modernity, money, sex, fame, power. These gods give a good life but they cannot sustain life. If Christianity dies in any Western nation, that means that any Western nation who rejects Christianity is dying.'

Karl Rove, the guiding force behind George W. Bush's 2000 and 2004 march to the White House and his major political advisor, believed that nothing was more crucial to winning the 2004 election than the Evangelical Christian vote. 'I think what is happening within the Christian world,' Rove said, 'is that people realize that being a Christian means [choosing to be] Evangelical or . . . secular. We know the importance of the Evangelical Christian vote because the bottom line is if you're not going to be Evangelical, why play the God game at all?'[1]

Shortly before Ed McAteer died, he told me that he had often called President Bush to task because of his desire to cement an Israeli–Palestinian peace accord. 'I make no secret about the expectations of the Evangelical community when it comes to domestic issues and even more important, when it comes to Israel,' McAteer told me.[2] 'Frankly, George Junior's stand on abortion and all the other issues that are important to us is not bad. It's the way he handles Islamic terrorism in Israel that makes me and millions of other Christians very upset.' When I asked if that would affect the way the Christian Right would vote in the next election, McAteer was pragmatic. 'It's not realistic to hope we can get one of us as candidate on the Republican ticket, so frankly, there is no one better on the Republican side and a lot worse on the Democratic side; which means we will obviously in the end vote for George W. Bush in the next election.'

Pragmatism aside, McAteer was not at all convinced about President Bush's faith or, more specifically, his knowledge of Scripture when it came to the Abrahamic Covenant and God's feelings about the Jewish people. 'I understand that there are people in the State Department and certain of Bush's advisors like Colin Powell, the Secretary of State, who are pushing him towards an Israeli–Palestinian peace accord.

259

But I have to say that it just won't happen, first off because God is against it, and secondly because Mr Bush is not more powerful than what the Lord said thousands of years ago.'

Doug Wead, who is still involved with President Bush when it comes to courting the Christian Right, was also pragmatic about the problems that the President faced in the 2004 elections. 'I'm aware that some people are suspicious of the President's open declarations of faith,' Wead says. 'But the President knows the numbers, and he knows how important faith is to millions of people in the United States. Ninety per cent, in fact, of all Americans believe in a personal God, and that's a very high number. So I wouldn't put any bets on any Middle East peace accord just now.'[3]

The reality, as it turned out, was that it made no difference if President George W. Bush was a true believer or merely an opportunist who had learned the language and the slogans of those on the Religious Right who had the power to vote him into office for a second term. In fact, it made little difference at all if any presidential hopeful was truly deep down a man of faith. 'Regardless of religious convictions and born-again credentials, there isn't one politician in America who is about to do anything controversial when it comes to his foreign policy that will upset the Christian community,' Ed McAteer said during our last conversation. 'As for young Bush's position on domestic issues and his plan for Iraq and other troubled areas in the Middle East, he is making all the correct decisions to please the Christian Right.' He paused. 'And mark my words, any Democrat who's elected President will do the same. We will not let up and we are not going away. We are just getting bigger and more powerful.'[4]

The 'God game' in the 2004 presidential election was just as crucial to the Democrats, since Republicans claimed that the only real Christian is a 'born-again' Christian. During the time when contenders in the Democratic primaries were campaigning, there wasn't one politician vying for the nomination who did not include God and religion in his rhetoric. On 18 January 2004, only twenty-four hours before the Democratic primary in Iowa, Howard Dean, a candidate for the nomination for President of the United States, visited former President Jimmy Carter in Plains, Georgia. Carter refused to endorse any one of the Democratic hopefuls, but it was clear that his relationship with Dean was long-standing and warm. As Carter stood next to Dean at a press conference, he reminisced about how Dean had 'stuffed envelopes' as a volunteer during his own presidential campaign in 1976. He talked about how he and Dean both stood for the same American values, how both had opposed the war in Iraq and, finally, how Dean had not only attended church with Jimmy Carter and his wife that very morning, but how he had also sat in while the former President taught a Sunday school class. In conclusion, Carter put an arm around Howard Dean's shoulder and said to the crowd of supporters in the former President's home town, 'Howard Dean is a Christian like us.' One woman, sitting at a counter in a diner not far from the peanut stand where Jimmy Carter and Howard Dean appeared, did not seem convinced. She said that she was 'certain that President Bush was a better kind of Christian than Howard Dean'.[5]

In the 2004 presidential elections, well-known Evangelical Christians such as Jerry Falwell, Pat Robertson and Richard Land who heads the largest group of Charismatic Christians in America, the Southern Baptist Convention, were, with scores of others, mobilized for Bush. While the political platforms of George W. Bush and John Kerry were vastly different, their campaign strategies about religion similarly focused on courting the Christian Right, especially in the

Southern States' Bible Belt. An ABC/*Washington Post* poll released in January 2004 showed that 46 per cent of Southerners said a president should rely on his religious beliefs in making policy decisions, compared with 40 per cent nationwide and 28 per cent in the East. In an article in *Newsweek* magazine Michael Lind explained the popularity of Bush's doctrine in the South: '[It] melds three Old Dixie traditions, militarism and Protestant fundamentalism and racism.' According to Lind, white Southerners are the most 'martial subculture in the United States, and military academies in the South are as commonplace as liberal arts colleges in New England. Beginning with the Vietnam War, from the first Gulf War to the current occupation of Iraq, the South has strongly supported every American military operation, regardless what it was about or who it was against.'[6] In a Gallup poll in August 2003, Southerners favoured an invasion of Iraq by 95 per cent as compared to a similar Gallup poll taken of the rest of the country where 45 per cent were in favour of war with Iraq. That in itself was good reason for John Kerry to have chosen John Edwards, a North Carolina senator, as his vice-presidential running mate.

In this last election, both Mr Bush and Mr Kerry made God their most crucial running mate, given the needs and demands of a majority of the American people. John Kerry, the Democratic nominee for President of the United States, is a Catholic, the first Catholic to be nominated by either party for President since John F. Kennedy won in 1960. At that time, the American people were apprehensive that the power of the Catholic Church would cloud the constitutional separation between church and state.

According to press reports, John Kerry recently discovered that his paternal grandparents were Jewish. Kerry's grandfather, born Fritz Kohn in Austria in 1873, chose the name

Kerry (from a map of Ireland, supposedly) when he converted to Catholicism in 1902. A year later, he settled in Boston and married a woman who had also converted from Judaism to Catholicism. The fact that Kerry has Jewish antecedents did not change the Evangelicals' perception of him. They focused on his opposition to the war in Iraq, which to them represented the war against Islamic terrorism. Religious Catholics who might have been the most likely to claim Kerry as their own, proud of the fact that he was only the second man of their faith to reach the pinnacle of American politics, were also critical of him.

American Roman Catholic bishops were continuously pressed by Pope John Paul II to make Catholic politicians follow the doctrines of the Catholic Church concerning abortion, euthanasia and gay marriage, all important issues in the 2004 campaign, and all issues where the Catholic Church's positions coincide with those of the right wing. George W. Bush was solidly against abortion, euthanasia and same-sex unions, while the liberal John Kerry had to please the left wing to have any hope at all of winning the election. By admitting his liberal beliefs, however, he found himself in direct opposition to the Catholic Church, which saw a 'grave and clear obligation to oppose any law that attacks human life'. Early in the 2004 campaign, Archbishop Burke of St Louis said, 'I would have to admonish him [Kerry] not to present himself for Communion. I might give him a blessing or something, but not Communion.'[7] At the time of Kennedy's 1959 candidacy, such a statement would have been the kiss of death; Americans were terrified of the church invading domestic politics. But times were different in 1959.

When John F. Kennedy was in the White House, abortion was illegal in all fifty states, and same-sex marriages were not even on the political horizon. Given the advances in scientific technology and medicine since 1960, Kerry had to deal with the abortion problem, and the issues of partial-birth abortion and stem-cell research. All along, Kerry repeatedly voted against restrictions on partial-birth abortions in Massachusetts, and had always stated that he would *not* nominate a pro-life candidate to the Supreme Court.

The reaction from both religious groups, however, did not stop Kerry evoking God and religion during his campaign. In an interview in *Vogue* magazine in March 2003, John Kerry said, 'We [Democrats] have to prove we're as God-fearing and churchgoing as everybody else.'

In the end, what cost John Kerry the election was one crucial error that he made only weeks before the Republican Convention in New York, at the end of August 2004.

On 31 July 2004, an article had appeared in the *New York Times* that announced the appointment of Martin Indyk as John Kerry's Mid-East advisor. Indyk, formerly American Ambassador to Israel for two terms during Clinton's presidency, and currently the head of the Saban Center at the Brookings Institute, has been working to convince the American government to send in troops to intervene in the Israeli-Palestinian conflict. He has even suggested that those troops should create a protectorate over the West Bank and Gaza. That decision, taken by the Democratic candidate, illustrated the difference between the political defeat of Bush One and the eventual victory of Bush Two.

According to sources close to John Kerry, he chose Indyk because he felt that he was the best man to get the Israeli government to pay more attention to him. In fact, Kerry was reportedly insulted that the Israelis had not sent a high-ranking official to meet with him. The feeling within the Kerry camp was that Israel was too closely involved with George W. Bush to pay attention to an opposition candidate they were sure would lose the election. But the history of antipathy between Indyk and the Israeli government goes back a long time. On 14 April 1996, shortly before President Clinton presided over the ceremony in the Rose Garden in which Prime Minister Rabin and Chairman Arafat shook hands, the Palestinian Liberation Organization (PLO) convened a special session of its Palestine National Council (PNC) to consider one of the conditions that Bill Clinton had set down in order that Arafat would be welcome at the signing ceremony and treated with the respect accorded any head of state: that the PLO would renounce forever the covenant that called for the destruction of the Jewish State. In the end, the participants agreed that Arafat would create a committee to 'further discuss' the subject.

At the time, Martin Indyk was one of President Clinton's top advisors on the Middle East, and widely considered to have been influential in planning the Oslo process that eventually gave Arafat control over the Palestinians in the West Bank and Gaza. After attending the PNC conference in April, Indyk reported to the President that the PLO had, in fact, ratified their constitution so that the covenant was cancelled. As a result, on 1 May 1996 Arafat was welcomed, as promised, at the White House to participate in the historic ceremony. Indyk's report, however, was a lie. The PLO had never renounced their intentions towards Israel.

In December 1998, Martin Indyk accompanied Bill and Hillary Clinton on a visit to Gaza. During a special meeting with the members of the Palestine National Council, Mr Clinton asked for a show of hands as to whether they had cancelled the covenant and intended to make peace with Israel. Clinton learned the truth when Yassir Abed Abbo, Arafat's spokesman, told the American President that the PNC had never cancelled the covenant. Throughout the years following the ill-fated Oslo accord, and as recently as 2001, Martin Indyk continued to lecture on his position to dispatch American troops to the West Bank and Gaza as well as urging Israel to work with Arafat to rid the area of the Hamas and Islamic Jihad terrorists responsible for the violence. Indyk has never acknowledged that Arafat's own military groups, the Tanzim and the Al-Aqsa Martyrs' Brigade, are also responsible for suicide bombings. Because of these two positions, in geopolitical circles Indyk had been rendered obsolete until John Kerry appointed him as his chief advisor for Middle East policy. Needless to say, if any Evangelical had the slightest doubts about John Kerry, they evaporated with the inclusion of Martin Indyk in Kerry's inner circle of advisors.

CHAPTER TWENTY

Safeguarding the Future

This would be the best of all possible worlds if there were no religion in it.

(John Adams, second President
of the United States)

What have been the fruits of Christianity? Superstition, bigotry and persecution.

(James Madison, fourth President
of the United States)

AFTER the victory of George W. Bush in November 2004, Jerry Falwell claimed he was 'invigorated' by what he called the 'greatest victory' in the history of the Religious Right. In fact, buoyed by the re-election of Bush, he voiced his intention to 'resurrect the Moral Majority', the movement he started in the 1970s that was the inspiration for the 'march on Washington by Christian soldiers'. After the 2004 election, Falwell was both exuberant and cautious. While he maintained that the Religious Right had won the 'greatest conservative victory in history', he also warned that it was 'the most dangerous time for our movement ever'. The movement, he said, 'must now fight complacency in the face of looming battles over gay marriage and possible vacancies on the Supreme Court'.

'We therefore will be pounding, pounding doors through the media and the pulpits of our churches,' Falwell announced, 'for the next forty-eight months to make sure we don't get into trouble.' There is no doubt that Falwell and a number of evangelical networks are responsible for helping place constitutional amendments barring gay marriage on eleven states' ballots. And all of them passed, which is a tribute to his efforts to drive conservatives to the polls to vote. It is a strategy that Falwell will use again. 'Between now and '08,' Falwell said, 'we are going to be putting on state ballots family initiatives and controversial initiatives to awaken our people out to the polls – all in an effort to elect another social conservative to succeed Bush in 2008.'[1]

The politician and Evangelical Christian who is considered to be the 'new face' of the Republican Party is William Harrison Frist, a Republican senator from Tennessee who was a heart and lung transplant surgeon before he entered politics. Currently serving as the Senate Majority Leader, having replaced Senator Trent Lott who was removed after making racially charged remarks against blacks, Frist is known among his friends as a man with a 'healing touch'. In fact, Frist has claimed that not only has he the ability and skill to heal people by his medical knowledge but he can also heal them just by touching them. In fact, when Frist was given the second most important job in the Senate, his response was that he accepted it with a 'profound sense of humility very similar to placing that heart into a dying woman or a child or a man'.[2] Many of his colleagues and supporters refer to him as the 'messiah' of the Republican Party, the man who would carry the torch after George W. Bush had served out his second and last term. Or, if Bush were to fail to be re-elected,

Frist is considered the most likely Republican candidate for 2008. Clearly Senator Frist considers that he is 'touched by God', as he wrote in his autobiography *Good People Beget Good People*,[3] and has admitted that it is indeed not difficult to cross the line between healer and doctor in the most mundane sense of the word, since doctors are considered near God, blessed and revered by the families of those they save. 'We make God-like decisions over those lives that hover on the edge of death and those who we save consider their near-death experience something akin to being born-again,' Frist has said. A colleague once asked him, 'How can you play God like that?' Frist replied, 'Because I understand a born-again experience only too well.'[4]

Tall, slim, dapper and generally unsmiling, Frist is always dressed meticulously and groomed so that every shellacked hair is in place and unmoving on his head. He is elegant, articulate and has made his mark in the Senate and throughout the Republican Party with a style that is a combination of his wealthy upbringing and the sort of ego that is present in almost all transplant surgeons. The myth of Bill Frist, however, actually began long before he was born when his grandfather Jacob Frist ran in front of an oncoming train to save a woman and child who had wandered onto the tracks. Grandfather Frist was hailed as a local hero in newspapers throughout Tennessee. In response, people from all over the country besieged him with mail, most of which said something along the lines of 'Your brave act was such as our Savior would have us do.' The Frist family wealth comes from Jacob Frist's son Thomas, Bill's father, a doctor who founded the Hospital Corporation of America, making a small fortune and transforming the family into one of the richest in America. Shortly after that, he began to preach the power of his calling, especially to his children. Of all the Frist

269

children, Bill was the most like his father with his charm, missionary spirit and ambition. And yet there were disturbing contradictions in his character. The man who would become a senator and healer claimed to love animals, yet he systematically went to animal shelters to retrieve abandoned cats for his own surgical experimentation.

'By day, I was the boy who decided to become a doctor because of his father,' Senator Frist explained, 'and by night, I was not going to let a few sentiments about cute furry little creatures stand in the way of my career.' As for his personal life, he had been engaged but, according to him, came to face to face in the hospital with a nurse whom, he claimed he felt immediately, he had 'known in another life'. Flying back to Tennessee, he broke his engagement that night and went on to marry the nurse with whom he claimed to have had a 'soulful and cosmic connection'.

In 1994, after deciding to enter politics, Frist chose Bush's mentor Karl Rove as his own advisor and guide. Whether because of Karl Rove's influence, or because his religious beliefs dominated his life, Frist voted against gay employment rights and against the Endangered Species Act. He also voted in favour of President Bill Clinton's impeachment and against campaign finance reform. Despite the fact that Frist had come to power promising to be a 'healer', repairing the rifts between the Right and the Left, he voted for reducing Medicare growth and minimizing the role of government in health care.

On 10 November 2004, only days after President Bush won a second term, John Ashcroft formally handed in his letter of resignation as Attorney General, a letter which suggested that Mr Bush would have a prosperous second term but that he [Ashcroft] was 'too tired' to continue on in the administration. 'The objective of securing the safety of

Americans from crime and terror has been achieved,' Ashcroft wrote. 'The rule of law has been strengthened and upheld in the courts. Yet, I believe that the Department of Justice would be well served by new leadership and fresh inspiration.' Ashcroft's resignation did not come as a surprise to the President, since he had been talking for months about his desire to leave government service. Rumours spread that Mr Ashcroft was ill, although his closest colleagues at the Department of Justice maintained that the Attorney General was anxious to leave once he had 'accomplished everything he had set out to do'. One aide said, 'Ashcroft recognized that if he is going to leave, it would be best to leave while on top . . .'

Within days, George W. Bush nominated a close friend and political ally to the post. If confirmed by the Senate, Alberto Gonzalez, a Mexican immigrant, would be the first Hispanic Attorney General in the country's history. On the surface, Alberto Gonzalez is vastly different from John Ashcroft who had been the poster boy for the Evangelical Christian Right. Gonzalez, a Roman Catholic who was raised, along with his seven siblings, in a house without running water or other amenities, is known less for his ideology than for his loyalty to George W. Bush. Conservatives have always been wary of Gonzalez and have often joked that his name in Spanish means Souter in English, a reference to the liberal Supreme Court Justice David Souter, whom George Bush appointed to the bench during his 1988–92 presidency. One of the incidents that caused Gonzalez to incur the suspicion of the Christian Right was a decision that he made when he was on the Texas Supreme Court in 2000, joining a majority of the judges in upholding a pregnant teenager's right to seek an abortion without notifying her parents. Mr Gonzalez also was at odds with

271

conservatives within the Bush administration over affirmative action. When the use of race in admissions at the University of Michigan came before the Supreme Court in 2003, Gonzalez argued that the administration should not take a 'hard-line position in favor of the white students who were claiming that the school had made them victims of reverse discrimination'.

The controversy concerning Alberto Gonzalez is not limited to the Christian Right, but is also heard on the liberal side, as well as among certain members of the Bush administration. Curiously, while Gonzalez has been perceived as more liberal than Ashcroft on internal moral issues, his most public controversy was his role in administration memos regarding the treatment of prisoners taken in the war on terror. In fact, he has been one of the architects of White House policy on detaining terror suspects for extended periods without access to lawyers or courts. In February 2002, he wrote a memo which allowed Bush to claim the right to waive international treaties and anti-torture rules when it came to prisoners of war who did not 'officially' serve other countries. In response, human rights groups criticized the memo, which they claimed allowed for abuses like those which occurred in Abu Ghraib. The most interesting aspect of the polemic concerning Alberto Gonzalez is that while he is perceived as being as tough or tougher on terror as was his predecessor, John Ashcroft, he is reputed to be far more liberal on such issues as abortion and assisted suicide. The fear among Conservatives is that Chief Justice William H. Rehnquist, who is undergoing treatment for thyroid cancer, will eventually step down to be replaced by Alberto Gonzalez. In other words, to be conservative from a global perspective when it comes to America's war against terror is quite different from conservatism on a domestic level when it comes to all the moral issues that the Christian Right hold dear. The philosophical divide about Alberto Gonzalez is typical of the polarization of the various camps on the Right and the Left.

This time around, the enemy is not limited to a country or a leader but includes any person who happens to share the same religious beliefs as the specific target of America's military might, whether he be an Al Qaeda operative, Saddam Hussein, or an Arab-American who owns a grocery store in Detroit. Given the events that currently dominate the international scene, President George W. Bush believes that this war in Iraq will not only give the United States positive geo-political results, but will further cement the support of the nearly eighty million Evangelicals – his most ardent supporters – who consider that any war against Islam is nothing less than a crusade to rid the world of Islam's threat. As a secondary gain in Iraq, Evangelicals are certain that the American defeat of a major Muslim nation will undoubtedly open it up for Christian missionaries to convert new souls.

Concerning all moral issues, the compassion or conservatism in Mr Bush's programme involved a radical departure from precedents established in the United States since Roosevelt's New Deal, and often ignored the Constitution's structure of government. The policies of a great majority of the Republican Party sought to re-establish the starkest form of Early Protestant ethic and eventually to replace all government social programmes and agencies with privately funded religious organizations. Almost every group connected with the Religious Right has benefited from President Bush's moral approach to politics. Since he was elected in 2000, he has pushed bills through Congress or used his veto power to proscribe laws, including those which concern gun control or compensation for victims of criminal use of arms. 'We ought not to worry about faith in our society,' Mr Bush has said. 'We ought to welcome it into our programs. We ought to welcome it into our welfare system. We ought to recognize the healing power of faith in our society.'[5]

CHAPTER TWENTY–ONE

A Precarious Balance

Believe nothing, no matter where you read it, or who said it, no matter if I have said it, unless it agrees with your own reason and your own common sense.

(Buddha)

GIVEN the on-going tumultuous situation in the Middle East and the spread of Islamic terror throughout the world, the sincerity of Evangelical belief in the Bible is not in itself a danger. The danger is if the Christian Right is using that unwavering Evangelical belief in Scripture to further their own political goals regarding the State of Israel. Thus the Evangelical community has added another dimension to the conflict, one whose ultra-religious rhetoric is as potentially volatile as that of other extreme religious groups in the region.

Throughout history, it has taken little to create anti-Semitic sentiment. Immediately following the attacks in Madrid on 11 March 2004, voices from Europe and the Far East proclaimed that there was no political justification for terrorism, no liberation or revolutionary movement that can validate the murder of innocent civilians. If the civilized world really believes that no political problem justifies clandestine terror groups' use of fear and blackmail to win

275

their fight, or to destroy countries that embrace philosophies, politics, or religion differing from theirs, then terror attacks committed by Palestinians against Israelis would be viewed in the same way. But they are not and never have been.

For anyone who believes that Israel must exist, it is difficult and problematic to criticize the Christian Right for supporting the Jewish State financially, politically and morally. For anyone who believes that Israel is forced to adhere to a different standard of international law than other countries who are victims of on-going terror, it is unimaginable to condemn the Christian Right for their determination to stand united with the Jewish State against world opinion. And yet, to understand the motivations of the Christian Right when it comes to Israel is to realize that their love and support will do more harm than good in the end. For those who know that Israel indeed stands alone in the global community, dependent only on the United States for financial and military aid as well as for the power to veto any condemnation of it by the United Nations, to express disapproval of the Christian Right is an unbearable decision. To hate unequivocally defines prejudice. To love unconditionally is also a form of prejudice. Defining an entire race of people as the devil is as dangerous as defining an entire other race of people as God's chosen ones. Generalities based on biblical rhetoric allow for no margin of human error. When the French President Jacques Chirac took a stand against American intervention in Iraq, he made one statement that merits quoting: 'A true friend,' he said, 'is someone who could criticize or disagree or point out the error of a decision without harming the friendship.'[1] His motives for not joining in the liberation of Iraq are irrelevant. The statement he made was pure in its phrasing even if it didn't tell the whole story of why France refused to join the American coalition.

Fears engendered first by the take-over of the American Embassy in Tehran and its hostage crisis, then by the terrorist attacks on New York and Washington in September 2001, along with the on-going suicide bombings of the second Intifada in Israel, and attacks against the American military in Iraq, have spawned a climate of Islamophobia in the United States.

As Evangelicals embark on this last crusade to bring democracy and Christian values to the entire world, while considering Islam the enemy of Christianity, their beliefs, inspired by Scripture, about Israel and the Jewish people have waxed even more passionate. That passion, based on their belief that the Jewish people hold the key to the return of Jesus as the Messiah, forces the so-called 'chosen people' to pay an extraordinary price. As Jan Morrison, whom I met during the Feast of Tabernacles in Jerusalem, told me: 'While I believe that the Jews are God's chosen people, in our theology all but a remnant will be wiped out. This isn't me talking, that's God talking. I'm not responsible for the fate of the Jewish people. It's not that I don't care what happens to the Jewish people, it's just that it is God's plan that those who don't accept Jesus will be slaughtered.'[2]

Throughout all my years travelling throughout the Middle East and writing about the Israeli–Palestinian conflict, I have always believed that Israel must endure at all costs. My feeling remains, even after witnessing the tragedy of the Palestinian people at the hands of their own leaders and the Arab world, along with their suffering under Israeli occupation. I have always believed profoundly that the biggest obstacle to peace is the self-serving interests of leadership on both sides of the struggle. I have spent enough time with ordinary people throughout the West Bank and Gaza, as well as in Israel, to know that families grieve with the same intense pain whether their loved ones have been wearing explosive belts, or have been passers-by killed in the explosion. The hopes, dreams and desires of both peoples grew out of normal human instincts for education, decent living standards, work and an absence of fear in their daily lives, whether in Ramallah or Tel Aviv. There was never an either/or, and as far as I was concerned it was only a matter of time before the people would put enough pressure on their leaders to force a solution.

Realistically, I also believed that the first step to any enduring two-state solution was a divorce between two peoples trapped for decades in a loveless marriage. Only after scission could reconciliation with respect and trust be built gradually, with time. My hope was that, freed from that loveless marriage, Israelis and Palestinians could evolve mutual affection and friendship. They are all Semites, after all, with genetic, linguistic and cultural commonalities. Islam respects Abraham as a prophet. Before Zionism, Jews were tolerated, even respected, and exempted from warfare, as People of the Book, from the time of Mohammed through the Ottoman Empire.

When the Palestinian people began rebelling against the dishonest financial dealings of Yasser Arafat and the Palestinian Authority in 2004, I was heartened. Those of us who had spent time in the West Bank and Gaza before the Israeli government allowed Mr Arafat to take up residence in Ramallah knew that the area was fraught with deprivation and misery. But after ten years of Mr Arafat, the situation had only worsened, until the Palestinian leader was marginalized and forced to remain in his headquarters. After his death in November 2004, while there was the requisite mourning throughout the West Bank and Gaza, there was also a very definite sense of relief within the Palestinian leadership, and a feeling of hope among the people. Prime Minister Ariel Sharon's announced intention to withdraw unilaterally from Gaza was a crucial first step to divorce. His successful formation of a National Unity Government, with Shimon Peres from the left-wing Labour party taking over as Deputy Prime Minister, made an eventual total withdrawal not impossible. Admittedly, my own reaction was selfish. Withdrawal from Gaza meant that the Arab world and the Palestinian leadership would be forced to mobilize, making that unlivable area flourish, building parks, schools, hospitals and creating decent living conditions that include clean water and efficient sewerage systems to avoid disease and pollution. They would no longer be able to blame inhuman conditions on Israeli occupation. Further, the logical outcome of withdrawing from Gaza was that Egypt would then be forced to allow Palestinians to cross freely to work, to visit friends and family, to seek medical treatment, and to benefit from a more flourishing economy. For Israelis, Sharon's plan would mean that the world might stop blaming them for the abysmal living conditions endured by the Palestinian people, starting with the Jordanian control of the West Bank and Egypt's control of Gaza and continuing after 1967 when Israel had power over the area. For the Palestinians, a real autonomy would begin when they could choose leaders who put their people's interests before their own political careers or financial gain.

But since Mr Sharon announced his plan, Orthodox Jewish groups in Israel, including a handful of settlers residing in Gaza, as well as Evangelical Christians throughout America, have been virulent in their criticism of the Israeli Prime Minister who previously could do no wrong. By evoking the Bible as irrefutable proof that Gaza is also part of the Abrahamic Covenant, they are prepared to sacrifice

279

the safety of the Jewish people, including hundreds of young Israeli soldiers forced to perform their military duty guarding settler ideologues, where they are neither welcome nor safe, in support of a biblical text promising the reappearance of Jesus Christ as the Messiah.

As the Arab world becomes richer, more technologically developed, and more politically sophisticated and assertive, as well as more populous, Israel's position becomes more and more unstable. It would only take a shift, such as a revolution in Saudi Arabia threatening to cut off the oil to the United States, for the balance which has maintained Israel to end. By encouraging the Jewish State to be intransigent with the Palestinians, and seducing it into an attempt to take over as much land as possible between the Nile and the Euphrates rivers in the immediate future, Evangelists are signing a death warrant for Israel later on.

Just as guilty of prejudicial love for the Jewish people are those in the American Jewish community who support Evangelical beliefs, albeit for more pragmatic reasons. American Jews who support the Christian Right imply that other American Jews should subordinate their duties to the United States as American citizens in favour of their obligation as Jews to do what is 'good' for Israel: namely, to support it unswervingly. At the same time, Israeli Jews who look to the Christian Right for comfort allow the born-agains to meddle in their internal and external politics, thus altering or deforming the evolution of the State of Israel. For the Christian Right, sacrificing the safety of the Jewish people and compromising the existence of Israel as an independent state, while insuring the on-going miserable plight of the Palestinians, is a small price to pay for the return of Jesus as the Messiah. Clearly, the logic from the Evangelical perspective is valid: they will be rewarded by an eternity with Jesus Christ in heaven. For the Jews, their reaction is baffling, since according to Evangelical beliefs concerning the End Times, the disappearance through death or conversion of those Jews who refuse to embrace Jesus Christ is assured. Perhaps they can't begin to imagine a proclaimed Messiah being announced any time soon, relegating the idea to some distant, foggy, unthinkable future.

Racial profiling in the guise of providing security has become prevalent, as has equating belief in God with patriotism, and regarding love of the Jewish people as a commandment from God. But what is the ultimate price of this kind of biblical patriotism? What do Evangelicals envision for those groups viewed as obstructive of the Second Coming – the Muslims who kill 'heretics' in the name of Allah, certain European countries that refuse to align themselves militarily with America, or the Jews who killed Christ?

Although the Jewish people talk of these envisioned End Days as happening in the far-off future, it might be useful to remember that in the course of history, several people have presented themselves as the Messiah since Christ's time, both to the Jews and to the Gentiles. There have always been some who believed in them. Suppose such a Messiah comes along who is accepted by the Fundamentalist churches, but not by the Jews. Will the Fundamentalists then take it upon themselves to help enact the massacre of non-Christians, a scenario described in lurid detail in *Glorious Appearing*,[3] the latest in the 'Left Behind' series, which has sold more than 55 million copies?

However tragic the circumstances were and however horrific the attacks of 11 September 2001, the Bush administration has overused those events to justify political and social edicts now in place throughout the country. Although on 2 November 2003, President Bush said, referring to

Islamic terrorists, 'We refuse to live in fear,' the reality has been quite different. The American people have been living in fear for four years. Every week since those attacks, the United States government has issued colour-coded warnings on the country's security, sending out pernicious messages: don't trust your neighbour, watch the sky, buy duct tape and gas masks, and be vigilant when you see Middle Eastern 'type' men and women on public transportation. Meanwhile, the war in Iraq and the daily loss of American lives have stimulated latent feelings of anti-Semitism in some who consider that the Jewish people are responsible for what the world is suffering at the hands of Israel's enemies.

The danger to society of any religious Fundamentalist movement is that their charismatic leaders purport to be directly in touch with God, whether they be priests, rabbis, preachers, imams, and even secular politicians, such as Colonel Ghadaffi in Libya, who told of God speaking directly to him in a famous interview in the 1970s with journalist Oriana Fallaci.[4]

Throughout history and all over the world, arrogance fuelled by godliness has wreaked more destruction in human history than the Black Death, AIDS, floods and starvation. No action becomes unthinkable if everything is 'according to God's will'. On a personal level, for the charismatic, there is no desire or impulse, no stray thought, but is Word from God. In their drive to make their beliefs realities, members of a Fundamentalist or charismatic movement are told that the workings and impulses of their minds are all inspiration from the Lord as well. I learned this early in my research, during an interview with a Pentecostal Christian woman.

Julia Pendegrast is a sixty-year-old woman who lives in a split-level house in an upper middle-class suburb in

America's heartland. She is white, college-educated, intelligent, and speaks in staccato phrases, prepared to quell any doubts or questions that might arise from her unusual story. The wife of a prominent attorney whom she met in the course of a trial when she worked as a court stenographer, she is a well-respected member of her community, conscious of her social and moral obligations to those less fortunate. Although not particularly political, she is acutely aware of both domestic and international issues which affect Americans today. She speaks with knowledge and self-confidence about the economy, the stock market, crime, globalization, and the threat of terrorism ever-present throughout the world, especially against American and Jewish targets. In fact, she has recreated history to show the importance to God of Israel, which will fulfill the prophecies of the Apocalypse. She says that Chaim Weizmann, first President of Israel and a chemist, saved the Allied forces from Adolf Hitler. 'England had run out of the chemical needed to make ammunition,' she explains, 'and Weizmann developed an alternative. As a reward for his saving the world from Hitler,' when 'Weizmann said he wanted a land for the Jewish people', Britain gave it to him. The creation of Israel triggered the 'reign of Jesus Christ, the Messiah, which is about to begin.'

'And because God told me I would never die, I will be here to witness His return to earth.'[5]

Born a Baptist, Pendegrast accepted Jesus as her personal saviour when she turned sixteen after her first encounter with Him: 'It was during my Sweet Sixteen birthday party, and Jesus appeared to me in the ladies' room. He told me that I was old enough to make my own choices and . . . I chose to devote my life to Him, the Eternal One.' She explains that, 'Because of this gift the Lord gave me, my prayers go directly to the third level of heaven where Jesus sits at the right hand

283

of God. As you talk to the Almighty, the Eternal One, you will hear from Him, and I have always heard from Him, through Scripture. Later He began to speak out loud to me.' She talks about God's Covenant with Abraham for the land of Israel, and she offers a 'historical' confirmation of that fact: 'Pilgrims were persecuted in England . . . because they believed that God had given Israel to the Jewish people. The Church of England . . . tried to force them to renounce [this idea] . . . which is why the Pilgrims fled to America.' Pendegrast's mission for the Lord began in 1979, during one of her regular visits from Jesus Christ, at the time of the Iranian hostage crisis. 'He told me . . . it was a time to mobilize Christians to fight the evils of Islam' through prayer.

In 1981, both of her parents were diagnosed with terminal cancer. While caring and praying for them, she heard from the Lord about the mission He had in store for her. 'I was in Scripture, and the spirit lit on a particular verse and suddenly, it all made sense, and I heard the Lord's words very clearly, that I should declare a holy convocation on Friday night, 11 September 1982.

'Thanks to the Eternal One, I knew what I had to do to make His project for me work out,' Pendegrast says. 'That night He came to me again in my dreams and told me to call my ministry The Word of the Lord.'

She knew that to 'birth' her ministry, she would need a large sum of money. She recalled the 'mysterious ways' of the Lord who helped her work out the financial details: 'The Lord put everything together, because He knew that my ministry would come forth right after my parents' deaths, which meant that, if I managed things properly, I would have the money to make it work . . .'

Two months after that all-night prayer session, Pende-grast's mother died, and shortly after that, she was able to convince her father to release $500,000, both her and her only brother's inheritance, in order to 'birth' her ministry. 'I told my father . . . I had been . . . discussing [it] with the Lord for the past few years. Daddy asked me if I had discussed this with Mother before she passed, and I told him that she was in favor of my taking the money.' Pendegrast's mother's sister, Thelma, who was also very spiritual and mystical, confirmed that and encouraged her brother-in-law to release the money. 'We both knew that my only brother would understand,' Pendegrast explains, 'because it was God's will.' The truth is that Pendegrast did not discuss her divine mission with her brother, explaining that she was waiting for 'God to tell me it was the right moment to explain things to him'.

Aunt Thelma had a certified public accountant who met with Pendegrast and explained that it was best to get all the money before her father died. In that way, there would be nothing left in the will for her brother to contest. Shortly before her father died, Pendegrast suggested that he spend several weeks with his son and his family. 'Daddy stayed with my brother in Indiana for three weeks; it gave me enough time for the accountant, my Aunt Thelma and a wonderful man from my church to help set everything up, including all the legal issues.' Tears well in her eyes. 'Thank the Lord Daddy signed everything before he left for Indiana. He died two days after he came home, and I could see the Lord's fingerprints . . . My brother is a good Christian, so I felt certain he would understand God's ways and God's plans for me.'

After the funeral, Pendegrast told her brother what God had advised her to do. Her brother was shocked and angry. Today, her Ministries of the Word of the Lord is an Evangelical organization with a membership of more than 75,000 Christian women from all over the United States. As for her brother, Pendegrast admits they have not spoken since.

The significance of Julia's tale is that she would normally be the sort of person who would never dream of stealing money from her brother or anyone else. In more calm and lucid times, the Commandment 'Thou shalt not steal' would clearly have meant what it says. True, Julia's larceny cannot be compared with massacres and other atrocities attributed to divine guidance, such as Jim Jones' Passion Play in Guyana, or the Inquisition, or the Crusades or the Holocaust, but multiply Julia by 80 million people, and you get a terrifying anarchy. No rules count, all laws can be broken, in order for God's wishes to be fulfilled. Anything goes as long as it is based on faith and religion. The Social Contract can be broken with impunity.

The United States is at risk of transforming itself from a democratic country, founded on a constitutional separation of church and state, into a theocratic state where the religious doctrine of one particularly powerful group of people will become law. Those who believe that introducing religion into the political and cultural fibre of a democracy is harmless are naïve. The risk of a dominant religion legislating its beliefs onto a society lies in its potential for fuelling hatred against other religious groups, and intolerance for any behaviour that deviates from its rigid norms.

Using their financial resources, political clout and sheer numbers, Evangelicals have attempted to overturn *de facto* the Constitution, deform the American domestic agenda, and twist foreign policy to accommodate their issues. As a result, the United States as the sole remaining superpower is faced with a difficult moral dilemma. Are Americans the Last Crusaders, bringing Christian values to the non-Western world? Or are they fighting a pragmatic war to protect themselves from a subtle lethal enemy that has no distinctive uniforms or recognizable signs, where the front lines are ever-changing? Has it become necessary to cancel the rights of some to protect the safety of all, in a war which has its foundation in culture and religion?

For those who believe that faith is a private matter that has no place in politics, government, or the military, protecting the world against the evils of terrorist tactics includes upholding the laws of the land, which embody what we stand for. The existence of God should not be a matter for public debate in a democratic or secular society, nor be part of any global campaign to rid the world of people who, whatever their reasons, are bent on instilling fear, causing unbearable pain and suffering, and destroying human life and culture. If the battle today is against Islamic terrorism, it is also a battle within each one of us to react with a morally fair and measured response that will offset the destruction on all sides of this war. In the United States, as in the entire world, from the moment religion becomes a factor in any conflict, automatically religion becomes an impediment to any reliable or durable solution. Even more certainly, when religious extremists are in power, the result guarantees that those who do not adhere to their particular faith will suffer the consequences, and all in the name of God. In a world fraught with violence and hatred, a religious battle has few winners and many, many losers.

Notes

Introduction

1. Alvin Toffler, *Future Shock*, Random House, 1970.
2. Gallup poll, cited in, among other publications, the *Economist*, 4 November 2004.
3. Bill Moyers, *Zmag*, 2 February 2005. Moyers drew on a George Monbiot article in the *Guardian* (20 April 2004) for his analysis of Fundamentalism's irrevocable beliefs.
4. Author source.
5. William Boykin, quoted in *Los Angeles Times*, 16 October 2003.
6. Joseph Lieberman during a campaign stop in Macon, Georgia, during the Democratic primaries in summer 2004.

1 Being Right with God

1. This four-part definition of evangelical Christianity derives from John C. Green's work at the University of Akron in Ohio. Found in his two books which he co-authored: *Religion and the Culture Wars: Dispatches from the Front* , 1996 and *The Bully Pulpit: The Politics of Protestant Clergy*, 1998.
2. Tim Egan, BBC News, 9 November 2004; http://news.bbc.co.uk/ 1/hi/programmes/3992067.stm
3. Sydney Blumenthal, *Guardian*, 11 November 2004; http://www. guardian.co.uk/usa/story/0,12271,1348261,00.html
4. Tim Egan, BBC News, 9 November 2004; http://news.bbc.co.uk/ 1/hi/programmes/3992067.stm
5. Sara Diamond, *Spiritual Warfare*, South End Press, 1989, p. 39; quoted in Sheldon Rampton and John Stauber, *Banana Republicans*, Robinson, 2004, p.52.

6. *The Passion of the Christ* grossed $600 million worldwide in 2004, $370 million in the USA.
7. Quoted in *New York Times*, 11 November 2004.
8. Bush made this statement in his speech to the nation, 19 November 1999 and repeated it in his State of the Union address, 2 February 2003.
9. During a sermon given by Jerry Falwell at his Thomas Road Baptist Church in November 1999 and again in November 2003.

2 God's Chosen Nation

1. L. Nelson Bell, *Christianity Today*, 21 June 1967.
2. Billy Graham quoted in *New York Times*, 17 March 2002, as part of the transcript from the Oval Office conversation with Richard Nixon in 1972.
3. Gary Burge, *Who Are God's People in the Middle East? What Christians Are Not Being Told about Israel and the Palestinians*, Zondervan Press, 2003.
4. Ed McAteer, interviewed by the author in March 2003.
5. Author interview with Ashcroft, Washington, D.C., October 2003.
6. Author interview with Ed McAteer, 6 March 2003.
7. George W. Bush, speech on national American television, December 2001.
8. George W. Bush, speech on national American television, December 2001.
9. Condoleeza Rice, *Meet the Press*, NBC, January 2002.
10. Franklin Graham, cited in *New York Times*, *Newsweek*, *Wall Street Journal*, October–December 2001.
11. Jerry Falwell and Pat Robertson, cited on Christian Broadcast Network from September 2001 and continually 2002–4.
12. Quoted on *Larry King Live*, CNN, December 2002.
13. George W. Bush, speech, Nashville, 11 February 2004.
14. George W. Bush, joint news conference with Jacques Chirac, 6 November 2001.

3 An Engine of Civil Policy

1. Thomas Jefferson, taken from the Jefferson Bible, introduction by Forrest Church, Beacon Press, July 2001.

2. Woodrow Wilson, address to joint session of Congress, 21 April 1917.
3. Francis B. Carpenter, *Six Months at the White House with Abraham Lincoln*, Digital Scanning, 2001, p282.
4. Vinson Synan, *The Century of the Holy Spirit: 100 Years of Pentecostal and Charismatic Renewal 1901–2001*, Nelson Reference, 2001.
5. James Watt made this statement during the first Reagan administration, testifying before the United States Congress, 5 February 1981.
6. Author source.
7. John Ashcroft, author source.
8. John Ashcroft, author source.
9. John Ashcroft, author source.

4 A Vision of a New World Order

1. H. L. Mencken, *The Monkey Trial: A Reporter's Account*, 1925.
2. Mencken, op. cit.
3. George W. Bush, press conference, White House, September 2003.
4. The following information and quotes on the Family are from Jeffrey Sharlet's article, 'Jesus Plus Nothing', first published in *Harpers* magazine, March 2003.
5. Sharlet op. cit.
6. Donald Warren, *Radio Priest: Charles Coughlin, the Father of Hate Radio*, Simon & Schuster, New York, 1996.

5 Spreading the Gospel

1. Michael T. Benson, *Harry S. Truman and the Founding of Israel*, Praeger Publishers, 1997.
2. Wilson Ewin, *The Assimilation of Evangelist Billy Graham into the Roman Catholic Church*, Québec Baptist Missions, 1992.
3. *Catholic Sentinel*, 25 September 1992.
4. Ian R. K. Paisely, *Billy Graham and the Church of Rome*, Bob Jones University Press, 1972, p46.
5. Billy Graham, quoted in a dispatch from the Religious News Service, 27 September 1979, on the eve of the papal visit to the United States.
6. *Philadelphia Evening Bulletin*, January 1978.
7. Pat Robertson, *The New World Order*, W Publishing Group, 1992.
8. Michael Lind, *New York Review of Books*, vol. 42, no. 2, 2 February 1995.

9. Bill Bright, *Have You Heard of the Four Spiritual Laws?*, New Life Publications, 1993.
10. David Riesman (1909–2002) was known for his influential studies on post-Second World War American society.
11. Stephanie Coontz, *The Way We Never Were: American Families and the Nostalgia*, Basic Books, reprinted 2000.
12. Paul Landis, quoted in Stephanie Coontz, op. cit. p33.

6 On the Lord's Side

1. Jerry Falwell biographical material comes from the Thomas Road Baptist Church library; www.trbc.org

7 The Politics of Prayer

1. Jerry Falwell, sermon at Thomas Road Baptist Church, 4 July 1976.
2. Pat Robertson first made this statement during his *700 Club* broadcast on his Christian Broadcast Network in February 1980 and again on CNN, 24 February 2002.
3. Pauline Maier, Merritt Roe Smith, Alexander Keyssar and Daniel Kevles, *Inventing America*, vol. 2, W. W. Norton, 2002.
4. Ed McAteer, interviewed by the author in March 2003.
5. It was an extreme Orthodox rabbi from the Gush movement in Israel, Eleazar Waldman, who first made the statement that 'the redemption is not only the Redemption of Israel but the Redemption of the entire world. But the Redemption of the world depends on the redemption of Israel. From this derives our moral, spiritual and cultural influence over the entire world. The blessing will come to all of humanity from the people of Israel living in the whole of its land.'
6. Author interview with William J. Murray, January 2004.
7. Barbara Bush, *Barbara Bush: A Memoir*, Scribner, 1994.

8 A Covenant-Keeping God

1. *New York Times*, November 1980. Quoted in Jerry Falwell, *Listen America!*, Sword of the Lord Publishing, 1980.
2. The bombing took place on 7 June 1981.

3. Ed McAteer, interviewed by the author in March 2003.
4. Author interview with David Parsons, International Christian Embassy, Jerusalem, October 2003.
5. Author interview with Malcolm Heddings, International Christian Embassy, Jerusalem, October 2003.
6. Author interview with Malcolm Heddings, October 2003.
7. Author interview with Malcolm Heddings, October 2003.
8. Author interview with David Parsons, April 2004.
9. Author interview with David Parsons, April 2004.
10. Author interview with David Parsons, April 2004.
11. Author interview with David Parsons, April 2004.
12. Author interview with Andreas Griffin, Nis Ammim, Galilee, April 2003.

9 To Walk Where Jesus Walked

1. Author interview with Jan Morrison, Jerusalem, October 2003.
2. Author interview with Carlyle Anderson, Jerusalem, October 2003.
3. Author interview with Rita Angela, Jerusalem, October 2003.
4. Author interview with Gina, Jerusalem, October 2003.

10 The Almighty('s) Dollar

1. Pat Robertson, *The 700 Club*, Christian Broadcast Network, 29 October 1982.
2. Ed McAteer, interviewed by the author in March 2003.
3. George Bush, address to the American people, 31 January 1991.
4. Bill Clinton, 11 September 1998.

11 The Resurgence of the Christian Right

1. Jerry Falwell, *Crossfire*, CNN, 22 October 2003.
2. Jerry Falwell, *Crossfire*, CNN, 22 October 2003.
3. Author interview with Benjamin Netanyahu in September 2003.
4. *Dabru Emet* was signed and printed in November 2000.
5. Elaine Kamarck, statement made on US television after the nomination of Al Gore for President in 2000.

6. Reverend James Robison, in an interview with Dick Staub, *Christianity Today*, 10 March 2003.
7. Author interview with George W. Bush for TF-1, November 2000.

12 Fear and Loathing in America

1. Author interview and visit to Louisiana, May 2003.
2. George W. Bush on *Oprah Winfrey Show* as cited in *New York Times*, 19 September 2000.
3. Author source present at signing of bill, 7 November 2003.
4. Author source.
5. Author source.
6. Author source.
7. Nancy Reagan in an interview with MSNBC, quoted by Reuters, 9 May 2004.
8. Gary Bauer, interviewed in his office in Virginia in July 2003.
9. Dwight D. Eisenhower, 14 June 1954.
10. Dwight D. Eisenhower's diaries quoted in his autobiography, *Mandate for Change 1953–1956: The White House Years*, Doubleday, 1963.
11. Author interview with Gary Bauer in New York City during the Republican National Convention, 30 August 2004.

13 With God on the Campaign Trail

1. Author interview with Robert Knight, October 2003.
2. David Huizenga, Tele Care Church Ministry sermon, February 2004.
3. George W. Bush, *Larry King Live*, CNN, 24 February 2004.
4. Tom DeLay, CBSNews.com, 30 September 2004.
5. Ed Gillespie, throughout the US press during Marriage Week, 15–19 October 2003, when the Pew Research Center took its poll.
6. Jerry Falwell, 'Jerry Falwell Forms Anti-Gay Marriage Coalition', Doreen Brandt, 365gay.com news center, Washington Bureau. (See also Falwell's website: www.onemanonewoman.com)
7. Jerry Falwell on the *Travis Smiley Show* on National Public Radio, July 2004.
8. Linda Harvey, purpose statement on same-sex marriage, homosexuality and the education of children, Mission America 2003.
9. Billy Graham, quoted on CNN, October 1964.
10. Author source.

11. Elizabeth Birch, in the *Advocate*, 12 September 2000.
12. Margaret Leber, quoted in *New York Times*, 9 March 2004.
13. Jim McFarland, quoted in *New York Times*, 9 March 2004.
14. Bill McCartney and David L. Diles, *From Ashes to Glory*, Thomas Nelson, 1995.
15. Cardinal Mahoney, *WRS* (*Western Reform Seminar*) *Journal*, 4/1, February 1997, pp.40-8.
16. Taken from a speech made by Hayford to the Promise Keepers during their regional conference in Anaheim, California, 14 May 1994.
17. James Ryle, 'The Sons of Thunder', message preached at Denver Evangelism conference, November 1990.
18. Statement made by Deborah Tyler during a conference she organized in Dallas, Texas, July 1996.
19. Bill McCartney, Promise Keepers' seminar, Van Nuys, California, June 2003.
20. *New York Times* magazine, 25 May 2003.
21. Scott Stewart, *New York Times* magazine, 25 May 2003.
22. Author interview with David Miller in September 2003.
23. Abdul Rahman al-Rashed, June 2003.

14 The Petri Dish of Terror

1. Author interview with Ariel Sharon, Jerusalem, October 2003.
2. Jerry Falwell, *Crossfire*, CNN, 22 October 2003.
3. Author interview with Clarence Wagner, Jerusalem, October 2003.
4. Author interview with Annette Lantos, Washington, D.C., June 2003.
5. Author interview with Tom Lantos, Washington, D.C., June 2003.

15 Peace Through Strength

1. Author interview with Sam Brownback, Washington, D.C., June 2003.
2. Bill Moyers, 21 December 2004.
3. Author interview with Esther Levens, spring 2003.
4. Author interview with Pastor Paul Brooks, spring 2003.
5. Author interview with Pastor Paul Brooks, spring 2003.
6. Sheldon Rampton and John Stauber, *Banana Republicans*, Robinson, 2004.

7. Author interview with Frank J. Gaffney at the time of the National Unity Coalition executive committee meeting in Washington, D.C., November 2003.
8. Author interview with Mike Pence, Washington, D.C., June 2003.
9. Author interview with Richard Hellman, June 2003.
10. Author interview with Richard Hellman, June 2003.
11. Author interview with Richard Hellman, June 2003.

16 Connecting with the Land

1. Author interview with Rebecca W., April 2004.
2. Author interview with Ed McAteer, March 2003.
3. Author interview with Ron Nachman, April 2003.
4. Author interview with Cheryl and George Morrison, April 2004.

17 The Evangelical Vote

1. Author interview with Herbert Zweibon, October 2003.
2. Author interviews with Gary Bauer between June 2003 and August 2004.
3. Author interview with Gary Bauer at his office in Virginia, July 2003.
4. Author interview with Annette Lantos, Washington, D.C., June 2003.
5. Author interview with Esther Levens, spring 2003.
6. Author interview with Gary Bauer at his office in Virginia, July 2003.
7. Moshe Fox, Washington, D.C., May 2003.
8. Janet Parshall, Washington, D.C., May 2003.
9. Thomas Lindberg, Washington, D.C., May 2003.
10. Author interview with Greta Simber, April 2004.
11. Ed McAteer, interviewed by the author in March 2003.
12. Author interview with Gary Bauer in July 2003.
13. Ken Silverstein and Michael Scherer, 'born-again Zionists', www.MotherJones.com, September/October 2002 issue.
14. Author interview with Yechiel Eckstein, August 2003.
15. Author interview with Ralph Reed, Jerusalem, February 2004.
16. Author interview with Yechiel Eckstein, August 2003.
17. John Ashcroft, Chicago, 17 October 2003.
18. Richard Land, interview with Herbert Zweibon, New York, October 2003.
19. Author interview with Yechiel Eckstein, August 2003.

18 Shifting the Centre of Gravity

1. Author interviews with Avi Granot, June 2003 and November 2004.
2. Ralph Reed, as recounted by Avi Granot during June 2003 interview.
3. Benny Hinn, as recounted by Avi Granot during June 2003 interview.
4. Author interview with Yechiel Eckstein, August 2003.
5. Ralph Reed, as recounted by Avi Granot during June 2003 interview.
6. Author interview with Gary Bauer, July 2003.
7. Author source.
8. Merrill Simon, *Jerry Falwell and the Jews*, Jonathan David Publishers, 1984.
9. Author interviews with several members of The Lovingway United Pentecostal Church in Denver.
10. Jerry Falwell, 'The Fashionable Effort to Denigrate the Gospel', *Christian Post*, 28 October 2003; www.christianpost.com/article/editorial/76/section/the.fashionable.effort.to.denigrate.the.gospel./1.htm
11. Ergun Caner, lecture posted on Jerry Falwell's Liberty University website; www.liberty.edu
12. Author interview with Ted Haggard, New York, June 2004.
13. Author interview with Ted Haggard, New York, June 2004.
14. Author interview with Abraham Foxman, November 2004.
15. C. Welton Gaddy, interview with *FrontLine*, WGBH educational foundation, 5 March 2004.
16. Author interview with David Rosen, Jerusalem, June 2003 and November 2003.
17. Author interview with David Rosen, Paris, April 2004.
18. Telephone interview with David Rosen conducted by author, February 2004.
19. Author interviews with Clarence Wagner, Jerusalem, October 2003 and Paris, June 2004.
20. Author interview with Clarence Wagner, Paris, June 2004.
21. Author interview with Edward Said, Jerusalem, January 2002.
22. Edward Said referred to his writings in an interview with the author in Jerusalem in January 2002. See also Sr. Elaine Kelley, 'Following Visit to Gaza, Delay at Erez Checkpoint, Edward Said Recommends "a certain kind of courage" ', *Washington Report on Middle East Affairs*, June 1999; www.Washington-report.org/backissues/0699/9906035.html

19 Playing the God Game

1. Karl Rove, as stated in Bush campaign headquarters in Missouri, 2004.
2. Ed McAteer, interviewed in March 2003 before his death on 5 October 2004.
3. Doug Wead, as stated in Bush campaign headquarters in Missouri, 2004.
4. Author interview with Ed McAteer, March 2003.
5. As reported in *Time* magazine, 18 January 2004.
6. Michael Lind, *Newsweek*, 8 April 2002.
7. Archbishop Burke, *St Louis Post Dispatch*, less than a week after he was installed as archbishop on 26 January 2004.

20 Safeguarding the Future

1. Jerry Falwell, WorldNetDaily exclusive commentary, 13 November 2004.
2. William Harrison Frist to Senator Tom Lantos, 2 January 2003; recounted in author interview with Tom Lantos.
3. William Harrison Frist, *Good People Beget Good People*, Rowman & Littlefield, 2003.
4. Author source.
5. George Bush quote taken from *The Jesus Factor*, on most public broadcasting stations throughout the United States, 29 April 2004.

21 A Precarious Balance

1. Jacques Chirac, address to France on Bastille Day, 14 July 2003.
2. Author interview with Jan Morrison, Jerusalem, October 2003.
3. Tim LaHaye, *Glorious Appearing*, 2004.
4. Oriana Fallaci, *Interview with History*, Houghton Mifflin, 1977.
5. Author interview with Julia Pendegrast, January 2004.

Select Bibliography

Ashcroft, John, *Lessons From a Father to a Son*, Thomas Nelson Inc., 1998

Benson, Michael T., *Harry S. Truman and the Founding of Israel*, Praeger Publishers, 1997

Burge, Gary M., *Who Are God's People in the Middle East? What Christians Are Not Being Told about Israel and the Palestinians*, Zondervan Publishing Company, 1993

Bush, Barbara, *Barbara Bush: A Memoir*, Scribner, 1994

Carpenter, F. B., *Six Months at the White House with Abraham Lincoln: The Story of a Picture*, Digital Scanning, 2001

Coontz, Stephanie. *The Way We Never Were: American Families and the Nostalgia Trap*, reprint, Basic Books, 2000

Diamond, Sara. *Spiritual Warfare: The Politics of the Christian Right*, South End Press, 1989

Eisenhower, Dwight D. *Mandate for Change 1953–1956: The White House Years*, Doubleday, 1963

Ewin, Wilson. *The Assimilation of Evangelist Billy Graham into the Roman Catholic Church*, Québec Baptist Missions, 1992

Fallaci, Oriana. *Interview with History*, Houghton Mifflin, 1977

Falwell, Jerry. *Listen America!*, Sword of the Lord Publishing, 1980

Frist, William H. with Wilson, Shirley. *Good People Beget Good People: A Genealogy of the Frist Family*, Rowman & Littlefield Publishers, 2003

Green, John C., Guth, James L., Smidt, Corwin E., Kellstedt, Lyman A. and Poloma, Margaret M. *The Bully Pulpit: The Politics of Protestant Clergy*, University Press of Kansas, 1998

Green, John C., Guth, James L., Smidt, Corwin E. and Kellstedt, Lyman A. *Religion and the Culture Wars: Dispatches from the Front*, Rowman & Littlefield Publishers, 1996

Herzl, Theodor. *The Jewish State*, Dover Publications, 1989

LaHaye, Tim F. and Jenkins, Jerry B. *Glorious Appearing*, Tyndale House Publishers, 2004

Lindsey, Hal. *The Late Great Planet Earth*, Zondervan Publishing Company, 1970

McCartney, Bill and Diles, David L. *From Ashes to Glory*, revised edition, Nelson Books, 1995

Maier, Pauline, Smith, Merritt Roe, Keyssar, Alexander and Kevles, Daniel J. *Inventing America*, Vol. 2, W. W. Norton & Company, 2002

Olasky, Marvin. *The Tragedy of American Compassion*, Regnery Publishing, 1992

Paisely, Ian R. K. *Billy Graham and the Church of Rome*, Bob Jones University Press, 1972

Rampton, Sheldon and Stauber, John. *Banana Republicans*, Robinson, 2004

Robertson, Pat. *The New World Order*, W. Publishing Group, 1992

Simon, Merrill. *Jerry Falwell and the Jews*, Jonathan David Publishers, 1984

Synan, Vinson. *The Century of the Holy Spirit: 100 Years of Pentecostal and Charismatic Renewal 1901-2001*, Nelson Reference, 2001

Toffler, Alvin. *Future Shock*, Random House, 1970

Walvoord, John F. *Israel in Prophecy*, Zondervan Publishing Company, 1962

Warren, Donald. *Radio Priest: Charles Coughlin, the Father of Hate Radio*, Simon & Schuster, 1996

Index